D0204236

This book is dedicated to
Veronica and Paul, Florence and Solly,
for all they gave me, including this story

The Family*

THE AUTHOR'S PARENTS:

Florence Greenglass (a.k.a. Florence Winters, and,
later, Veronica Dubner), b. 1921
Solomon Dubner (a.k.a. Sol, *Shloime*, and later, Paul),
1916–1973

THEIR CHILDREN:

Joseph Louis Dubner, b. 1947
Mary (Mona) Rose Dubner, b. 1948
Martha Mary Dubner, b. 1950
Ann Stella Maris Dubner, b. 1951
Peter Harry Joseph Dubner, b. 1953
David Gerard Joseph Dubner, b. 1956
Elizabeth Mary Dubner, b. 1959
Stephen Joseph Dubner, b. 1963

FLORENCE'S FAMILY:

Esther Bernstein (mother), 1890–1970
Harry Greenglass (father), 1882–1952
Della Greenglass (sister), 1916–1990
Moishe Bernstein (grandfather), 1844–1934
Sorah-Rukhel Bernstein (grandmother), 1853–1942
Barney Greenglass (uncle), 1878–1949
Tessie (Feit) Greenglass (aunt), 1884–1958
Ethel Greenglass (cousin), 1915–1953
Julius Rosenberg (cousin by marriage), 1919–1953
Michael Rosenberg (cousin), b. 1943
Robert Rosenberg (cousin), b. 1947
David Greenglass (cousin), b. 1922
Ruth (Printz) Greenglass (cousin by marriage), b. 1925

SOL'S FAMILY:

Gittel Dubner (mother), 1880–1931
Shepsel Dubner (father), 1880–1951
David Dubner (grandfather)

Shayna Frayda (Rozenowicz) Dubner (grandmother)
Nat (*Nachman*) Dubner (brother), 1904–1977
Dottie (Lautenschlager) Dubner (sister-in-law), b. 1907
Mickey Dubner (nephew), b. 1933
Harriet Telson (niece by marriage), b. 1936
Vicki Dubner (grand-niece), b. 1956
Matthew Dubner (grand-nephew), b. 1964
Fannie (*Fageh*) Dubner (sister), 1906–1954
Morris (*Moishe*) Dubner (brother), 1911–1976
Bess (*Peshe*) Dubner (sister), 1913–1997
Sam Einbinder (brother-in-law), b. 1914
Gloria Einbinder (niece), b. 1935
Carol Einbinder (niece), b. 1942
Harriet Einbinder (niece), b. 1946
Martin (*Mottel*) Dubner (brother), 1922–1975
Irene (Domber) Dubner (sister-in-law), b. 1923
Kevin Dubner (nephew), b. 1957
Bernard (*Baruch*) Dubner (brother), 1924–1925
Yidis Dubner (aunt), 1885(?)–1949
Chaya Dubner (aunt), 1887(?)–1958(?)
Peshe Dubner (aunt), 1913–1975
Avram Kalb (uncle), 1894(?)–1995
Lou (*Leibl*) Kalb (cousin), b. 1919
Sarah Kalb (cousin), b. 1924
Rose Kalb (cousin), b. 1925
Liba Dubner (aunt), 1897(?)–1942
Shepsel Dubner (uncle), 1900–1942
Reba (Tarkoff) Dubner (cousin by marriage), b. 1915
Martin Dubner (distant cousin), b. 1920
Moishe Zilberman (distant cousin), b. 1910
Moti Cooper (distant cousin), b. 1933
Elana Eden (distant cousin), b. 1940
Odi (Cooper) Dori (distant cousin), b. 1956
Solomon Dibner (distant cousin), b. 1923
Nora Dibner (distant cousin), b. 1955

*These are my relatives named in the book. There are, of course, many, many more Dubners and Greenglasses; to have included them all, I believe, would have taxed not only the reader but the printing press itself.

Prelude

God is the meaning beyond absurdity.

—Abraham Joshua Heschel

THE DAY I remember best was a Sunday, in early summer. As always, my mother and father woke up early, washed their faces, put on their church clothes, and began rousting the kids one by one to do the same. There were eight of us, and I was the youngest. My father stationed himself outside the bathroom door, whistling "Ave Maria" and knocking when your three minutes were up. Then we piled into the car, a pink-and-gray Rambler, Beth and I sitting on laps in the back, Ann's arms locked around me like a seat belt. I had on my suit coat, bright red, which used to be Dave's and, before that, Peter's. As usual, we got to church late. Peter and Dave sprinted around to the back door—they were altar boys—as my parents marched the rest of us all the way up front. We occupied an entire pew, kneeling and rising and sitting with the precision of a military squad. My mother wore a tidy pink dress and, on her head, a lacy white scarf called a mantilla. I turned around to look for Tina Jorgensen, a blond girl from my kindergarten class, but my mother pinched my neck. "Keep your eyes on the altar," she said. "Keep your eyes on Jesus." My father wore his baggy gray suit, a white shirt, and a maroon tie, knotted squarely. With his thick eyeglasses and graying brush cut, he looked as solid and respectable as a regular businessman. But during the first hymn he sang way too loud, his head thrown back, and the skin on his throat trembled like the wattles on a turkey: "Immaculate *Mary*, your praises we *sing*, you reign now in *Heav*en, with *Jesus* our king." I could feel everyone watching; even Father DiPace shot us a look. My family had a way of attracting attention. Still, I was proud to be a part of them. I sensed that we were blessed somehow, that we came to church not simply because it was Sunday but because our lives revolved around God with the same appreciation and dependence as the Earth revolves around the Sun.

After Mass came catechism, and then Mrs. Ferry trotted over and shook my hand, as if I were a grown-up, and inside her handshake was a stick of Doublemint gum. This was a weekly ritual, for which I thought of Mrs. Ferry as the Blessed Angel of the Sugar-Deprived, since my mother didn't allow us to eat refined sugar. I tucked the gum into my pocket for later. We all helped Father DiPace stack the missals, and then climbed into the Rambler, its seats now hot from the sun, for the ride home. We lived in a drafty old farmhouse a hundred and fifty miles north of New York City—which, I knew, was where my parents had come from. But they never talked about that life. The past was past, the present was the present, and our future lay in Heaven. That, they made clear, was all we needed to know.

None of us had eaten since Saturday night, since you had to fast for Communion, so while we changed out of our church clothes, my mother made a batch of whole-wheat waffles with blueberries, and we had a contest to see who could get their tongue the bluest. Dave won. My mother yelled at us not to wolf our food. My father didn't eat the waffles. He went into the pantry for a few pieces of matzo and then got a hunk of gefilte fish from the refrigerator. He offered everyone a bite, but we had all tried it once, and that was enough.

Because Sunday was a day of rest, there were no chores except taking care of the animals: milking the cow, collecting eggs, moving the goat to a fresh stake, feeding the cats and dogs. The afternoon was totally free until it was Rosary time. In the warm weather we recited the Rosary on the lawn, my mother and father perched on wobbly lawn chairs as the rest of us knelt in a circle, Mary's and Martha's towering hairdos glimmering in the sunlight from all the Aqua Net, the stray bits of driveway gravel digging into my hairless knees.

But until Rosary time we could do as we pleased. None of the older kids felt like playing catch with me, so my mother, still wearing her pink dress, grabbed a baseball glove, and we whipped the ball back and forth. She had a good arm. My father sat on the porch with the newspaper, shirtless, the cloth scapular around his neck dancing in the breeze like a giant brown moth. I kept hoping he'd come play with us. As the afternoon wore on, he began sneaking peeks over the top of his paper. Finally he jumped up and strolled across the lawn, right through the middle of everyone, his arms thrown out at his sides, singing in a rich and creamy voice: "My Yiddishe mama, I love her more than ever now. My Yiddishe mama, I used to kiss her wrinkled brow." Then he grabbed my mother by the waist and kissed her forehead, and we all giggled at his outrageous display of affection, and this only spurred him to sing the song again, this time in a funny language I couldn't understand.

Now, of course, I know that the funny language was Yiddish. I also now know that, many years earlier, my mother, Veronica Dubner, was a beautiful young ballerina named Florence Greenglass. My father, Paul, was known then as Solomon, and he was a soldier posted in the South Pacific during World War II. They were both Jews, and they both fell in love with Jesus. Soon afterward they found each other, like a pair of needles in a haystack, and embraced Catholicism with such a fury that by the time I was finally born, we bore all the marks of a large and vigorously devout Catholic family and, outside of a little Yiddish and some gefilte fish, only those marks. Why should it have been otherwise? We, the children, were a separate slice of time, like one prehistoric era laid over the last.

Until not so long ago all I knew, and dimly at that, was that my parents had once been something called Jewish. In our home, "Jewish" was nothing but a word. When it arose, and it rarely did, we were told that it had nothing to do with us. What on earth *was* Jewish anyway? We lived in the back of beyond; ours was an existence circumscribed by Mass and catechism, rusting hay rakes and muddy fishing ponds, the kids you could play with (the churchgoing Catholics) and those you couldn't. For all I knew about Jews, my parents might have just as well been Baptists, or Elks, or carnival workers.

But about ten years ago I wound up living in New York City, my ancestral homeland, the most Jewish city in the Western world. There, a certain disquietude began to take root inside me. I could not name this force but neither could I make it leave me alone. And so I followed the noise inside my soul, and before long it led me back to my parents. I became consumed with a desire to know how a pair of young Jews named Florence Greenglass and Sol Dubner had become my Catholic parents. I wanted to know about their families, the Jewish grandparents and aunts and uncles I'd never met, many of whom had cut off my parents when they converted. I especially wanted to know what it was that had made my parents stop being Jews. And as I tried to unfurl the intricately coded scrolls on which their beliefs were inscribed, I searched all the while for clues to what I might believe.

My father died in 1973, when I was ten years old. So it was my mother to whom I brought my questions, nearly twenty years later. She had sold our farmhouse by now and moved to Florida.

Whenever I visited, we would sit at her kitchen table with a tape recorder, her walls crowded with pictures of my brothers and sisters, nieces and nephews, Jesus and Mary, and assorted saints, popes, and angels. My mother, fifty-odd years after she converted, remains the most devoted Catholic I have ever encountered.

She proved to have a remarkably acute memory for any matter pertaining to her conversion. She could recall, for instance, the inscription on a prayer missal she had been given as a baptism gift when she was twenty-one years old. She could recite the sermon that had first unclouded her soul. At such moments I felt as if I were sitting with an oracle. The surety of her voice, the incandescence of her eyes: She might well have been narrating the very creation of the world. Which, in a sense, she was. With the eyes of an adult, she had watched her own birth.

The details of her life before she became a Catholic, however, were harder to come by. It was as if the force of her conversion had short-circuited that part of her memory. Or perhaps she simply saw no use in reliving that which she had outlived. Still, because I am her son, and because she passed on to me a certain stubbornness, I kept asking questions. Over time she answered all but a few that were simply too uncomfortable. She re-created her childhood and her ballerina years and put me in touch with dozens of friends from the old days—who were so struck by the odd trajectory of her life that they often remembered its details better than she. Interviewing my mother over the years was an exercise in peeling back layers. She would plant the seed of a story, then claim to have forgotten how it had turned out. After a few months she might bring it up again, with a few more details; a year later she would tell the entire story from start to finish, and I would be too excited over what she had remembered to be exasperated at having been strung along. I gradually realized that her story, like any family story, was a palimpsest, one set of myths scribbled over the last, the old writing always bleeding through if you looked hard enough.

And what about my father?

In one of the first interviews with my mother, I posed an impossible question, the plea of a fatherless son. What was he *like,* I asked her; what was the nature of his character?

She responded without pause. "Oh, he had a *sterling* character. An exceptional character, enthusiastic and charismatic, very sincere, and not a manipulative bone in his body. I was more manipulative. Maybe I learned that from my ballet teacher. Dad, though, he was just a wonderful person, with a great belief in the faith."

But that was Paul Dubner she was describing, not Sol. My mother, as it turned out, barely knew Sol, since he had already conyerted by the time they met, and since both of them were so eager to move forward that they rarely spoke about their pasts.

So I would go looking for my father—for Sol, that is, rather than Paul. I would scrutinize his letters and his pocket notebooks. I would track down his relatives, and after navigating the tender issue of why we'd never spoken, I would rummage through their memories. Some of them were reluctant to speak with me, and some were astonishingly warm. Fortunately, this latter batch of relatives also had good memories. Through them I came to know my father—well enough, at least, to write his story—though I would gladly trade all they told me for the chance to sit down with him now for just an hour.

Once, when I was about seven years old, my sister Beth and I were walking home from town. Just past the Greisslers' hayfield, we hit the thickest fog I'd ever seen. I remember trying to grab a handful of it and being surprised that I couldn't. That is how I felt about my father as I searched for him: that he was swirling all about me, just out of reach.

My mother says that I can ask him anything I want in Heaven. I am not so sure how I feel about that. For my mother, there is nothing speculative about Heaven. It is the just reward of those who live as my father lived, and as she has lived. Her faith is unyielding, her passions clear. If my father is fog, my mother is a mountain. There is no mystery as to where she stands or what she is made of; there is no place within our family from which she cannot be seen or her shadow be felt. Writing about her and my father in the same sitting practically gives me vertigo, so dense is the presence of one and so ethereal the other.

And yet long before I was born, they performed nearly identical acts of spiritual bravado. I realize that they are hardly the first Jews to have become Catholics. But I can understand how, say, a Jewish merchant in fifteenth-century Spain, given the options of conversion, expulsion, or death, might have chosen to convert. I can also understand how a man like Madeleine Albright's father yearned to outlive the Nazis and lead the secure, prestigious life of a diplomat. I can even understand how countless Jews of my father's generation whittled down their names and their noses just to get past the country-club gate.

My parents' conversions, though, had nothing to do with survival or prosperity—or with logic. Of this, I must constantly remind myself. Peering into their past, I have often caught myself reaching for some sort of conclusion, as if it were an algebraic equation I was trying to solve, or a murder mystery. But these were mysteries of faith that my parents lived, and such mysteries cannot be solved any more easily than a dead man can rise again.

In the end I came to understand that all religion, like all politics, is local. We believe as we do because of the families we are born into, the teachers we learn with, the dark-of-night fears and candle-bright desires that flit between our minds and hearts. It is impossible to see all these connections as they are being forged, just as it is impossible to grab a handful of fog. Only when a good piece of your life has unspooled can you look back and see how one connection led to the next, how a seemingly random sequence of events conspired to propel you down a certain path— and then you begin to doubt that there was anything random about your journey at all. You begin to ask yourself: Are all these connections truly a product of chance and reason, or do they represent our connection to the Divine, inlaid on our souls like some indelible fingerprint of God?

This book is a story of three people with noisy souls: my mother, my father, and me. For a long time I thought it was only their journey that I was writing about. Later I came to think of the story as mine. Now I realize that there is not so much difference between the two.

BOOK ONE

The Lord said to Abram: "Go forth from your native land and from your father's house to the land that I will show you."

—*Genesis 12:1*

1

MY mother tells me that, even as a little girl in Brooklyn, she had a stubborn streak. She dreamed of running away from home; she thought nothing of talking back to her mother, whose name was Esther.

Every night, Esther would climb the stairs from the candy store, a sharp grunt on each step, and say, It's the *shklofferai* is what it is, the slavery. Your father, he works so hard he must be made from iron.

And Florence, in her singsong voice, always gave the same retort: Well then, he better not go out in the rain or he'll get all rusty.

It was only her mother that Florence made fun of. She loved her father very much. His name was Harry, and on Election Day he would carry her on his shoulders to the voting hall. He would step behind the curtain and say, I'm going to send a hello to Mr. Roosevelt now, sweetie. Shall I give him your regards? Florence looked so much like her father—the same round face and full lips—that some of the customers called her Little Harry, and she didn't mind at all.

Her father liked to laugh, but her mother didn't seem to know how. It's the arthritis, she would say, here and here and here, pointing at her swollen ankles and elbows and knuckles. It's because of the cold in this place, she'd say.

It was true that their apartment was cold. There was heat in the store, but that was a business necessity. The store was what mattered: Harry Greenglass, Candy and Cigars. Finally Harry was not failing at a business. Even now, with the Depression all around them, the pennies rolled in. Harry was lucky to be near Crown Heights, a Catholic neighborhood, with plenty of trolley drivers and policemen and garbagemen whose jobs were safe. The Lower East Side, where his brother, Barney, ran a sewing-machine shop, was choking on its own poverty.

Harry opened up every morning at six and closed whenever it got to be ten minutes between customers, usually near midnight. Esther spelled him for lunch unless it was so busy that the both of them worked. On Saturdays, Florence and Della, her older sister, helped stack the newspapers.

No matter how well the store was doing, Esther let Harry know it wasn't good enough. That was her way. Harry had seen how it would be as soon as they were married and decided he would be best off keeping quiet. It wasn't always easy. Esther would prattle on about her brother, the big fabric man, who just bought a new house, and how his wife always had new hats and how their children were smarter and healthier than their own children, how little Irving could eat a whole head of lettuce and drink a whole quart of milk at one meal. And did you see their bushes, Esther would say after a visit to the new house, how my brother carved the bushes so they look like big parlor chairs? So nice and fency!

Esther still had a lot of Yiddish in her English. Harry had

worked hard to get rid of his. That, he knew, was the way to make it in America. Treat the customer well, a nice smile and a little talk but not too much, and nothing too serious. Harry loved America.

He was the first in the family to come, in 1898. He was eighteen years old, and his name was Herschel. He rode a bicycle all the way from Minsk to Hamburg, sleeping in ditches and barns. In New York, he fixed things and sold things, and on the first day that he was allowed to file for citizenship, he did so.

Last name? the clerk asked.

Greenglass, he said. He pronounced it American, GREEN-glass, not GRIN-glosh.

First name?

Harry.

Birth date?

The Fourth of July, he fibbed.

Do you renounce forever all allegiance and fidelity to every foreign Prince, Potentate, State or Sovereignty whatever, and particularly to the Czar of Russia, of whom you have been heretofore a subject?

You betcha.

Eventually his whole family came, everyone who hadn't starved to death in Russia: Harry's brother, Barney, their three sisters, and their uncle, old Moishe with the dusty beard. Moishe then sent for his wife, Sorah-Rukhel, and the two of their children who were still alive, one of whom was Esther.

Esther's family settled in the Bronx. Old Moishe didn't seem to notice he was living in America. He would halfheartedly sell pencils on the street for half an hour, then spend the rest of the day in synagogue, praying and gabbing. And for what, Harry wondered, so the family could starve here the way they starved in Russia? Harry had no use for starvation and, truthfully, no use for God either. He was thirty-five years old already; his cousin Esther was twenty-seven. He was particularly fond of her—so much so, in fact, that just five months after they were married, in the summer of 1916, Esther had a baby, whom they named Adeline, Della for short.

For several years, Harry fixed sewing machines alongside his brother on the Lower East Side, the streets crowded with Jews and horse manure. When he heard about an empty store in Brooklyn with an apartment on top, he moved quickly. He didn't understand why a Jew and a ghetto had to stick together. In Brooklyn you could plant a few flowers, maybe even a cherry tree in the backyard.

Florence was born five years after Della. She was a pretty little girl, with curly black hair, but frail, with a murmur in her heart. Esther took her regularly to Dr. Zatz, the Arbeiter Ring doctor with the slicked-back hair. The visits were free, and they got what they paid for. She just needs some fresh air, Dr. Zatz would say, checking Florence's pulse, his fingers oily from patting down his hair, what do you expect living in such a city? And Esther would bundle Florence off to Brighton Beach and ply her with cod-liver oil and tomato sandwiches.

From the start, Florence and her sister, Della, didn't get along. Florence's favorite playmate was her grandmother Sorah-Rukhel. When she visited, Esther didn't make bacon and told Florence not to say anything about ever having eaten bacon, because Bubbe believed in God and God did not allow bacon. Bubbe spoke only Yiddish, but Florence could speak Yiddish too, and they would giggle and cuddle like friends. Bubbe's cheeks were soft, like flower petals. At night she sat on the edge of Florence's bed and told stories about beautiful Queen Esther. She taught Florence how to thank God for the good day and ask Him for a good husband when the time came.

Florence always looked forward to the Passover Seder at Bubbe's house. The only bad part was having to kiss old Moishe, her grandfather, because his beard scratched her face like steel wool. The whole family came. Uncle Barney Greenglass was quiet but friendly, like Harry. His wife, Aunt Tessie, was a lot like Esther, always worrying that something terrible was going to happen to her children. They had a daughter, Ethel, who was a year older than Della, and two sons, Bernie and David. Florence's other uncle, the big fabric man, pinched her cheeks too hard and teased her for being scrawny. Florence didn't care so much for her cousin, either, Irving the lettuce-gobbler. Every year Florence would ask her mother to teach her the Four Questions so she could ask them at the Seder. What's the use, her mother would say. Your cousin Irving's the boy, and he's the smart one anyway, so Irving gets to ask the questions.

Sometimes Bubbe came to stay with Florence's family for several weeks. On Saturday morning she left the apartment early, before Florence was awake. Esther and Harry were already downstairs in the store. Florence sat at the kitchen table in the dead quiet, wondering what to do with herself. She began to play with the miniature tea set that her blind Uncle Anschel had carved from peach pits. Finally she heard her mother grunting her way up from the store. Go on down to the shul now and get your Bubbe, she told Florence, carry her Siddur and her eyeglasses. She won't carry on Shabbos.

They walked home along Classon Avenue. Florence reached up and pulled a leaf from a tree. Her grandmother stopped. You shouldn't do that on Shabbos, she said, but God will forgive you because He knows you don't know better.

When her grandmother wasn't around, Florence was lonely. She liked to play stickball out on Lincoln Place, but her mother always shouted her in from the store because stickball was a good way to break a leg. On Saturday afternoon, all of Florence's friends had to go inside to get ready for Confession. Florence knew they were Catholic and that she wasn't. Edna Farrell had a pretty necklace with colorful beads and a cross, and Florence asked why she twisted it around her fingers and didn't wear it on her neck. It's to pray with, Edna told her, not to wear.

One day Florence was playing outside with another friend. They had to go to the bathroom, but the friend had lost her house key, so they waited on the stoop. Well, her friend said, we'll just have to say a prayer. Florence watched her close her eyes and move her lips and in a few minutes a man came home and let the girls inside.

Florence thought about what had happened. She knew it wasn't magic, quite; it was certainly a different way of looking at things. She didn't mention it to anyone. Who would listen? Her parents didn't have time for questions, and her sister wouldn't be interested.

Late in the spring of the year that Florence was eleven years old, she caught a bad cold. Dr. Zatz told Esther to keep her out of school until she was better.

Florence lay in bed all day, too bored even to sleep. Finally, through the open window, she heard her friends coming home from school. She heard doors slamming, feet running by. She heard them choosing up sides for stickball and the first jolly whaps of the Spaldeen on the pavement.

At that moment Florence Greenglass, the little girl who would become my mother, had what might be called the first existential thought of her life. Lying in bed, the cruel taunts of the outside world drifting through her window, she thought, Boy oh boy, life goes on all by itself whether I'm there or not.

2

EARLY one Friday afternoon, during the second October of the Depression, Solly Dubner was walking home from school by way of Pitkin Avenue, the lifeline of Brownsville. He was fifteen years old, and of all the things he loved, he especially loved to whistle.

Whistling was forbidden in his father's house. You might as well invite the Angel of Death for a visit. That, at least, is what his father believed. Every morning before synagogue, Shepsel Dubner stopped downstairs in the family's restaurant to pour some salt in his pocket, as a *kineahora*, a sacred protection, to choke whatever demon might accost him on the short walk from Sutter Avenue to Stone. For longer trips, more salt.

Solly knew all his father's *kineahoras*—canaries, he called them—and was careful to obey them in his presence because, who knew, they might work and because any disobedience, however slight, made his father angry. And when his father was angry for whatever reason, he took it out on Solly's mother, Gittel, rarely shouting but unfailingly choosing the half dozen words that would conjure the bitterest tears. Solly, who loved his mother dearly, would have rather taken the strap any day. But Shepsel would never strike his children, for it was so written.

And if one were to ask him, Where is it written?

It is written, it is written, he would say impatiently. The where is not important.

Shepsel Dubner was a simple man, stern but righteous. Even Solly's uncle Avram, an ardent socialist who considered Shepsel's ideas about God unworthy of comment, would not speak ill of him. For hadn't Shepsel paid Avram's passage from Poland and taken him in? True, Shepsel made Avram go to synagogue every morning and pray with tefillin—Avram a grown man already, introducing those leather straps to his hairy arm!—but no price could be placed on the kindnesses that Shepsel and Gittel had extended him. It was not as though they had three pennies to spare. Their restaurant was small to begin with, and during the Depression, the poor Jews of Brownsville somehow got even poorer. Nevertheless, Gittel always put an extra piece of chicken in Avram's soup, with the understanding that Shepsel did not need to know.

That was Gittel's way. She would slip Solly's baseball gear out of his room when Shepsel wasn't looking and stow it under a kettle in the restaurant. Shepsel would not violate Shabbos by handling money, but Gittel was not so strict, and with the money she quietly collected from the restaurant on Saturdays, she bought a silver wristwatch for Dottie, the sweet young girl who had just married Nat, the oldest of their six children. They were a good pair, Nat and Dottie; he always stood up to Shepsel, and she was the kind of girl that Gittel had once been: pretty to look at and pleasant to be with.

Gittel was now fifty-one, and had been putting on weight even though she rarely felt well enough to eat. Only on Shabbos did she find her appetite. She still looked forward to Shabbos, still believed in it. Nat and Dottie always came home for Shabbos dinner—not because they wanted to but because Nat was a good older brother and why should all the others have to suffer Shepsel alone? Nat was worried especially about Solly. Shepsel seemed to have a particularly hard heart for him. Solly was different; he wanted more out of life, and Nat knew that more was the one thing that could not be found in their father's house.

Solly knew this too, and so he did his whistling on the street. Entire songs, from start to finish, even the string parts when the melody took a break. "My Yiddishe Mama" was his favorite. Someday he'd sing it in a nightclub maybe, with his mother in the audience.

He was slim and, for his family, tall, about five feet seven, with thick black hair, bushy eyebrows, and a square face whose features were ordinary but had arranged themselves in a handsome manner. He walked with a bounce, as though grateful for his very stride. His head jerked from front to side, side to front, like a bird's, always alert for something good to happen. He was, in general, an optimist. He nearly always wore a smile, a strange, quiet smile that, if you didn't know him, might be mistaken for a smirk. Solly was welcome wherever he went but happiest on his own.

As he walked home from school that Friday afternoon, Pitkin Avenue was fragrant with salami and cigar smoke. The corners were jammed with young men a few years older than he was, wearing short plaid coats and snap-brim hats. They barely looked like Jews at all. Some of them, Solly knew, were junior mobsters, trying to break into Murder, Inc. He had no desire to go that route—none of the Dubner boys had the stomach for duplicity, much less murder—but he got a kick out of watching them. So he stuck to Pitkin as long as he could, whistling all the while, no need to hasten the end of the day, no Torah study on Friday evening but no baseball either, for he would be imprisoned all night long at his father's Shabbos table.

Finally, Solly turned off Pitkin onto Stone Avenue and then Sutter. And from a second-floor window, a man in his undershirt shouted down to him: Hey, Solly, what the hell are you whistling for—don't you know your mother's *dead*?

He sprinted home and found a sign in his father's Yiddish scrawl: RESTAURANT CLOSED ON ACCOUNT OF DEATH.

GITTEL'S death ripped a hole in the family. She was the eldest of four sisters who had come to America, and all but one lived in the same building on Sutter, above the restaurant. Three big families, all the cousins mixed up like marbles—Solly and his three brothers and two sisters, plus Tante Chaya's five children and Tante Peshe's three. On Saturday afternoons they all ate their Shabbos lunch together: Gittel's three-day cholent, Chaya's gefilte fish, Peshe's almond cakes. But after Gittel died, the aunts moved a few blocks away. They blamed Shepsel for working their sister to death, since it was Gittel who ran the restaurant while Shepsel spent his days in synagogue. His piety sickened them. Such nerve he had, calling their husbands goyim because they wouldn't daven with him. You could not find a more honest Jew than Shepsel Dubner, but he lived in constant fear that God was peeking into his mind or his dinner bowl, and he wouldn't deign to as much as share a meal with a Jew who was less vigilant.

Even as a little boy Shepsel had been pious. He was born in 1880 in Sedletz, a town in eastern Poland, which was then under Russian rule. He was hardly a scholar, but he never questioned what the Torah or his rabbi told him to do. He became a shoemaker; he worked hard and did not hold an undeservedly high opinion of himself. He was a small man, five feet two, with paper-white skin, brown hair, gray eyes, and a thick red beard. His right eye was lazy and sometimes went dead. If you were confused over which eye to address, Shepsel would shut the dead one for a moment to let you know.

Within a day's trip of Sedletz lived any number of Dubner cousins, all of whom had emigrated from Dubno, near Lvov, when too many Jews there were turning up dead, thanks to the pogroms that rained down ever more frequently. Among these cousins was Gittel Dubner, a sweet-tempered girl the same age as Shepsel. In 1903 they were married, and by 1906 they had been blessed with a son and a daughter, Nachman-Berel and Fageh.

That year, Shepsel received a letter from a cousin in America. It said that Brooklyn was a sliver of promised land, with boatloads of Jews coming every day and a synagogue on every corner. And in Brooklyn the one sound you never heard was the nighttime thunder of Cossacks on horseback, hunting down Jewish babies to crack their skulls.

Shepsel knew what happened to Jews in America. They cut off their beards, said good-bye to G-d. Still, though he was only twenty-six years old, he had seen enough of the terrible things done to Jews in Poland to last ten lifetimes. So, leaving behind Gittel and their two children, he set sail from Hamburg with a bag of cheese sandwiches and seven dollars. It was a small amount but a good amount: Seven was three plus four, gimmel plus dalet, and that, in American, spelled G-d.

In Brownsville—Little Jerusalem, it was called—Shepsel found a synagogue full of landsmen. From his cousin he borrowed just enough money to go even further into debt with his own shoe shop. He tried not to curse America, even to himself, for he knew what lay above him: a Watchful Eye, an Attentive Ear, and the Book of Judgment in which all his deeds were recorded.

It took four years to save enough money to send for his family. When he met the ship, seven-year-old Nachman came clomping down the gangplank with just one boot. Gittel had paid a man to smuggle them across the border, and when Nachman lost a boot in the darkness, the smuggler told him that yes, he could go back for it, but they weren't waiting for him.

Within a year of Gittel's arrival, she bore a son, then a daughter and three more sons, one of whom, Baruch, died as an infant. The other children were called Moishe, Peshe, Shloime, and Mottel, though their friends knew them as Morris, Bess, Solly, and Martin. The oldest girl, Fageh, was now called Fanny, and Nachman became Nat. Even with six children, Shepsel liked a quiet house. As it was written: a word is worth one coin; silence, two. His children learned to eat noiselessly and not to scrape the chair when they got up.

For many years Shepsel ran his poor shoe shop, with Nat working alongside him. Shepsel did not like the man Nat was turning into. He spoke only English, even though he knew Shepsel barely understood. He was more interested in baseball than Torah and had his own opinion about everything. There had been no money to send Nat and the other boys to yeshiva; the shoe shop barely managed to feed the family. Shepsel finally decided to close his shop and start a small kosher restaurant. Fanny was old enough by now to help Gittel with the cooking, and with a restaurant at least they wouldn't go hungry.

Most of the work fell to Gittel. By the time Shepsel was out the door for morning prayers, she was already plucking chickens for the soup; at midnight she was boiling the chicken feathers to stuff a down comforter, for they couldn't afford coal.

As the oldest son, Nat was the first to rebel against his father. Nothing made him angrier than how Shepsel treated his mother. As if her work were easy, and as if Shepsel and his cronies, nattering away in a synagogue that stank of pickle brine and rotting leather, were saving the world.

One morning, at the breakfast table, Shepsel asked Nat if he had put on tefillin to say his morning prayers.

Sure, Pop, I laid tefillin.

Let me see how you laid the tefillin.

Nat rolled up his sleeve to show where the leather straps had cut into his skin. With a smirk he rolled the sleeve down. It was an easy game, fooling his father. When Nat woke up, he would pull the tefillin straps tight as he could, then quickly unwrap them. If you did it right, it looked like you had worn them long enough to say all the mumbo-jumbo prayers that Nat had already forgotten how to say.

WHAT sins had Shepsel committed to make his sons run from the Torah? How had the Evil Eye found him? He held out to his sons a ring of pure gold, and they went running instead to play in the dirt. How could it be, when his father, his grandfather, on and on, all the way back to Abraham, had woken up every day and thanked G-d that they were Jews? They were mocked and chased and killed, and still they thanked G-d—and now, in America, with nobody chasing them, they didn't want to be Jews anymore?

In truth, Shepsel was troubled by only two of his sons, for Morris and Martin were sufficiently obedient. Nat, though, was already a lost cause, and Solly would rather play baseball or read a novel than study Talmud for even an hour. This was especially painful to Shepsel because Solly had such promise. He had a good head for Scripture—even the rabbi said so—and a beautiful voice, good enough to be a cantor. He was honest and he was kind; he never left his head uncovered, never talked back, and he waited on his mother as if she were Queen Esther. But he was simply not devoted to the life of a Torah Jew.

Solly, for his part, didn't mind so much being a Jew as long as he could be a Jew like Hank Greenberg. No Jew had ever hit a baseball like Greenberg. Solly devotedly followed Greenberg's exploits in the *Daily News*. This was not accomplished without a certain amount of stealth, for Shepsel did not allow English newspapers in the house, and at two cents, the *News* was beyond Solly's reach. So he would loiter outside the barber shop and dart in as soon as a customer tossed a copy aside.

His infatuation with the sports pages led Solly to conclude that he should become a sportswriter, ideally covering the Dodgers for the *Daily News*. Then he read *The Great Gatsby* and *The Sun Also Rises* and decided that he would write novels in Paris. And if that didn't work out, he could be a bandleader, like Benny Goodman; already Solly played the saxophone, and not badly.

For a boy of fifteen, he suffered no shortage of dreams. The trick was to sort them out. One dream was all it took, a nice sharp single up the middle. *Just drive in the run. Do the little things right and the big ones take care of themselves. Improve yourself because no one else will.* These were the exhortations he jotted to himself in a notebook he carried in his back pocket, just like a real newspaperman. *Happiness is right around the corner— just find the right corner, fast!* But whatever the dream, his father would slap it down. Solly had recently asked his mother to ask his father if he could take saxophone lessons, and Shepsel agreed. But when it came time to hand over the money, he acted as if he'd never heard of the idea.

Solly was the closest thing to a black sheep in his family. At least that was the way he saw it. His father wouldn't allow a crumb of happiness to land in his lap. If he had wanted to become a rabbi, his father would have moved heaven and earth. Shepsel was in love with his religion, and he was so sure of it all. He could tell you how every single mitzvah, every good deed, generated a spark that floated into the sky and how a million sparks would create such a bright light that the Messiah would come. But if you asked him *how* that mitzvah made a spark or *why* you could eat this food and that food but not the two of them together:

Because you're supposed to, Shepsel would answer. Because the Torah says so and because I say so.

But why are we supposed to?

Because we are Jews.

But why are we Jews?

Because G-d made us Jews, Shloime. You forget, the Torah? G-d gave to the Jew a special mission.

What mission?

To obey G-d.

But why do we have to obey God?

Why do we have to obey G-d! Because we are supposed to!

Concerning their religion, there was no question Solly could ask his father for which he received an answer that was remotely satisfying.

ON that October Friday in 1931, Gittel Dubner died without warning. Shepsel's face was so white that Solly and the others were afraid to speak. From upstairs, Tante Peshe's shrieking fell on their ears.

She had died on a Friday morning, and Shepsel, in accordance with Jewish law, wanted to bury her that afternoon, before Shabbos. But if he did so, Gittel's sister in Philadelphia, Tante Yidis, wouldn't be able to attend the funeral.

Everyone understood this problem, but the only person brave enough to confront Shepsel was Dottie, his young daughter-in-law.

You can't bury her today, Dottie told Shepsel. I don't care what the religion says, you have to wait for Yidis.

So Gittel was laid out in the kitchen of the restaurant, her casket packed with ice. Shepsel gathered his sons to sit with the body until Sunday, when Yidis would arrive. As the ice began to melt, Dottie wondered if she had made a mistake. A metal bucket was placed beneath the leaking casket. The dripping, the rising stench, the stab of his mother's death—it was all too much for Solly, and he stood up to get some fresh air, but his father pressed him back into his seat.

On Sunday the entire family stood beside the grave, Shepsel beating his chest. After reciting Kaddish, they returned home to sit shiva, the seven-day period of mourning. Outside, Stone Avenue was black with mourners from the neighborhood.

Everyone agreed that the only bad thing Gittel Dubner did her whole life was to die.

3

AT thirteen years of age, Florence Greenglass had no passions yet to speak of. Life, for all its ebb and flow, seemed to lie flat. Her brain worked well enough that she earned good grades, but she was a lazy student. What she read, she read for fun. She liked playing the piano but hated to practice. She was, for the moment, wholeheartedly unambitious. Her father was kind, affectionate even, but too busy for counsel; her mother's only advice was that Florence should eventually locate, charm, and marry a Jewish man whose manner was agreeable and whose means were at least sufficient but preferably abundant.

Florence's one fear, however intermittent, was death. In her Catholic neighborhood she had noticed that when someone died, a large bow of purple ribbon would appear on his door. Florence's friends would then debate whether the deceased was going directly to Heaven or would require a stint in Purgatory. It was considered uncouth to speak of a neighbor, even the most wretched neighbor, as Hell-bound.

Among the Jews, though, or at least the Jews she knew—which is to say, her own family—it was different. Death was to be avoided, dreaded, ultimately tolerated but never discussed, especially around the children. Not that death was the only topic to be so forbidden. Florence never heard the adults talk about the botched operation that left her Uncle Anschel blind; nor would she learn, until many years later, that Anschel had had a son who was snatched from the street and taken to the woods in New Jersey, where a man did horrific things and then killed him. Her family was so closemouthed that Florence did not know that her grandfather Moishe was dead until, at the Passover Seder, she saw that his chair was empty.

At least she had had her last encounter with Moishe's scratchy beard. She did wonder, though, what had become of him. Not his corpse—that she understood—but the rest of him. *Was* there more of him? She wasn't sure. She could not forget the realization she'd had lying in bed that day, hearing her friends playing without her. If things didn't change when she wasn't here, what did it matter if she was here or not?

But she *was* here. What for then? To think of herself as merely a random collection of muscle and teeth and curls was unspeakably sad. And yet the other possibility—that there was some sort of purpose to life that she must fathom and follow—made her dizzy. She might try to wrestle with such a thought, but then Della would rush into their room, her face twisted into a knot of sisterly ire: *Who* said you could use my hairbrush? Florence suspected that somewhere there were people who executed their lives on a plane wholly above her own family's, but she was lost as to how to arrive there.

All around her, life went on. Though the Depression had deepened, Harry's candy store was doing well. He didn't have time for friends, but more important, he had no enemies. In time he relocated to a larger store, at the corner of Lincoln Place and Bedford Avenue, next door to the Savoy movie theater. He had the Italian carpenter put in a green marble lunch counter and bright new windows. The lunch trade came quickly: Jewish salesgirls from Loehmann's and black auto mechanics from the Reo showroom. The real rush was on movie nights, Friday and Saturday. When a romantic picture was playing, Harry put in an extra order for vanilla ice cream, the flavor preferred by girls; for westerns, chocolate. He hired a counterman and put Esther to work making salads. On the weekends, Florence or Della would waitress, though not at the same time, for they would snipe at each other, and at the customers.

So Harry was no big fabric man like his brother-in-law, but he was doing all right. He was still a Greenglass, he liked to say, but never again a greenhorn. He could occasionally afford to buy Florence and Della new dresses at S. Klein. Even Esther had grown slightly, though only slightly, less cantankerous. Harry was able to send her and the girls to the Catskill Mountains for the first three weeks of August. They sent postcards twice a day, and he wrote back to say that business was fine, the heat was terrible, the blue larkspur was blooming in the backyard garden, and the corn was nearly up to the clothesline.

Florence recognized that the quality of her life had indeed improved. She too liked going to the mountains and to the spa in Sharon Springs where you sipped the different waters. The copper spring tasted like pennies, the sulfur spring like matches. Esther said the water was good for the intestines, but Florence just drank it for fun.

There were, to be sure, imperfections in Florence's world. In her sixth-grade history lesson, a girl named Ann Ross, with blond hair and very blue eyes, had stood up and declared: My father says that Hitler has the right idea about the Jews.

Florence squirmed in her chair. What was she *saying*? But then Florence reasoned that though her family was Jewish, they weren't in Germany or even Russia anymore, so it was all right.

There was another time: Florence was just about to ring the bell of a friend's building when the door opened and an older boy stepped out. What do you want, little Jew? he said, and spat in her face.

She didn't mention either incident to her parents. What would they say? And when was there the time to talk? With the new store, her father was working even longer hours, and her mother had enough to be frightened about already. She had been quick to refuse when Florence wanted to play the trumpet at school: You'll get cancer in the lip, Esther said, and cancer in the lip in my daughter I am not allowing.

One day a friend of Florence's who took ballet lessons invited her to come along. The teacher was a tall, severe Russian woman named Asta Souvorina. Florence had never seen anyone like her. She was old, like her own mother, but she wasn't beaten down. There was an intensity spilling from her, and it attracted Florence like a magnet.

Esther wouldn't hear of her daughter taking ballet lessons. With your weak heart you'll drop dead, she said, from all the jumping around. But Florence insisted, and she began studying with Madame Souvorina the following week.

Madame, as she demanded the girls call her, had performed with the Russian Imperial Ballet. Her father, an official in the Czar's service, had built a theater just for her, but he was killed during the Revolution and Madame fled to America. That, at least, was the story circulating among her students. One did not address Madame directly about such matters.

After school Florence would take the subway into Manhattan, first once a week, then twice. Within a year she was attending Madame's studio every day. Florence proved to have a good line for ballet, a slim waist and strong thighs and graceful wrists.

Not that it was Madame's style to compliment.

Oh, that looks just like a horse's hoof! she would shout at Florence. Point your toe!

Madame's legs were by this age stiff and scarred. But with one touch of her toe to the floor, she could intimate the correct position of the entire body. She dressed in long, flowing gowns, as if she might be summoned at any moment to an officers' ball. Her face, diamond-shaped, was breathtakingly emotive; she was still remembered in some quarters as the Sarah Bernhardt of dance. When she demonstrated mime, Florence would study her face as if it were the map to paradise, then attempt it herself.

At which point Madame would shriek: Oh, you did that just like a cow!

Madame lived in the basement of a brownstone on West Seventy-fifth Street. She had turned her living room into the ballet studio. Two parlor lamps, their shades discarded, stood at either end of the barre. Off the studio was a cramped kitchen and the small room where Madame slept and did her writing. She was preparing a manuscript about Russia's conversion to Christianity. Madame herself, when she came to America, had converted from Russian Orthodoxy to Roman Catholicism. But she was as temperamental a Catholic as she was an artist and attended Mass only when it suited her; to Madame, the minutiae of religious obligation were less interesting than the glorious and bloody drama that was the life of Jesus Christ.

Madame had long been on the lookout for a young ballerina who might become the star that she herself had been, and Florence Greenglass seemed to be the one. Though she looked fragile, there was something almost unbreakable about her. She was both powerful and graceful. Madame would never praise Florence directly, of course. In fact, she grew sterner with her than the other students, regularly commanding twenty repetitions when ten would have sufficed.

Florence understood and accepted this dynamic. In the rigor she found peace and in the dance itself she found bliss: a single flurry of *Coppélia* could make her forget that she had ever been a mere shopkeeper's daughter from Brooklyn. Her exhaustion was enormous, a welcome departure from the ordinariness of her family.

By her senior year of high school Florence cared about nothing but ballet. She barely saw her family, and this suited her fine. Only occasionally would she attend the parties that her school friends invited her to. One was a dance given by the youth wing of the Communist Party. She didn't know the first thing about Communism but figured that any group with "Party" in its name would at least throw a good dance. Instead it was packed with angry young people shouting about things she didn't understand and wasn't interested in.

She had heard about these activists. Her cousin Ethel Greenglass, Uncle Barney's daughter, was one of them, along with Ethel's boyfriend, Julius Rosenberg. Ethel was six years older than Florence. She had fallen flat out in love with Julie when they met; he was very sweet and, like Ethel, something of an intellectual. Still, Florence had a hard time understanding how they got so worked up about the Communists.

Ethel was a good singer, perhaps good enough to be a professional. But her mother, Aunt Tessie, thought this was a crazy idea, just as Esther thought Florence was crazy for dancing.

Truth be told, Florence and Ethel had much in common. Their mothers clearly favored the boys in the family—in Ethel's case, her brothers, David and Bernie; in Florence's case, her cousin Irving the lettuce-gobbler. Both girls therefore were closer to their fathers. But it was the mothers who ran the house, and Aunt Tessie and Esther insisted that their daughters should be concerned less with the arts and more with finding a suitable Jewish husband. So both girls had sought and found an escape: Ethel in Julius Rosenberg and the Communist Party and Florence in Madame Souvorina and ballet.

By now Florence was practically living at the studio. When Madame was sick, Florence taught her classes; she did Madame's shopping and cooked her meals. Because Madame was a vegetarian, Florence became a vegetarian. She knew that Madame was also a Catholic, but what little Florence had learned about Catholicism from her childhood friends seemed fantastical. How could anyone believe in a virgin birth? And what was one to make of the Resurrection?

Madame was not interested in arguing with Florence, or anyone, the eternal verities of Christendom. If you are so curious, she told Florence, you should read about it yourself.

Read where? Florence asked her.

Don't you know the Gospels, the Epistles?

What are the Epistles?

What are the Epistles?! The letters, from St. Paul.

Who is St. Paul?

Florence was astounded to discover that a living, breathing person—a Jew, no less—had left behind such testimony. Everything she had ever heard about Jesus seemed so far away, like a fairy tale. But Paul had *been* there. No, he hadn't actually met Jesus, but his letters, she felt, had the ring of truth. After all, Paul was an educated Jew who had traveled widely. Why would he write of being struck down blind on the road to Damascus, hearing Jesus calling to him from the clouds, had it not happened just that way?

Florence had never done much thinking about God. She had set foot in a synagogue only a few times, with her grandmother. What did God look like anyway? Perhaps he looked like old Moishe, with a long, dusty beard; perhaps he had the face of a cloud. Or, Florence thought, perhaps the face of God was the face of Jesus, the young, loving, tortured face she had seen on the wall of Madame's bedroom.

*   *   *

FLORENCE was going to be a big star. She and Madame both were determined. Her elevation was extraordinary, her turns hard and true. Above all, she felt the music, and feeling the music was the one thing that Madame could not teach anyone.

Madame invited other ballet masters to appraise her work. Florence was never told what they said and understood that she was not to ask. Madame was Madame; ready was ready.

Now Madame was speaking of arranging an audition for Florence at Radio City Music Hall, as a soloist. But there were intermediate steps to be taken. Florence was eighteen years old, and the moment she graduated from high school, Madame found an agent who began booking her into nightclubs. Yes, Madame conceded, nightclubs were crude—the pianist might be as drunk as the patrons—but that was not Florence's concern.

There was also the matter of her name. In the sleek lettering of the Radio City marquee, "Florence Greenglass" would appear a grotesquerie. After much deliberation, she and Madame decided upon a stage name: Florence Winters.

As eagerly as she anticipated stardom, Florence's mind continued to swirl with nagging questions: Why had she been born and where would she go afterward? And might Jesus have anything to do with the answer? As a young girl she was always bemused when her Catholic friends talked about Heaven, as if they were so sure of it. But St. Paul, in his Epistles, was sure of it too: "Then we who are alive, who are left, shall be caught up together with them in the clouds to meet the Lord in the air."

She was determined to find the truth for herself. On the subway, in the dim light of Madame's studio, in nightclub dressing rooms, Florence read the Bible. First the Gospels, then some of the Old Testament. She was surprised to learn that it was the Scripture of her own Jews that called for a Messiah like Jesus. Why, then, were the Jews so intransigent? Her own mother was not religious at all, yet she wouldn't even pronounce the word

"Jesus"—"That Man," Esther would say, if she had to say anything at all.

Florence found a Catholic library in downtown Manhattan, safely distant from her home, and continued her education. She studied the lives of the saints and was moved by their goodness. But the catechism of the Catholic Church seemed obtuse and left her baffled. Perhaps Jesus really was the Messiah but the Catholic Church was not the True Church? She looked into the Episcopalians and the Christian Scientists, but they struck her as wishy-washy, man-made. How could the True Church have sprung from such a human desire as Henry VIII's lust for Anne Boleyn?

Florence continued to bring her questions to Madame, who finally suggested that she speak with a Catholic priest. Madame directed Florence to the Church of the Blessed Sacrament, on West Seventy-first Street, just down Broadway from the ballet studio.

Blessed Sacrament was a massive limestone building with a glorious rose window. The priest's name was Father Conroy. He was a tall, handsome young Irishman, full of enthusiasm, and he seemed to grasp Florence's predicament. He sat with her for a while, then taught her a prayer that he promised would help. Late at night, as her parents slept in the next room, she would get on her knees, fold her hands together, and whisper: *Give me the grace to know Your truth and the strength to follow it.*

At home Florence kept a low profile. She did not mention that she was performing in nightclubs, and if she brought a Catholic book into the apartment, she was careful to keep it hidden. Too many times she had seen her mother in action. Florence had begun dating a singer, a good-looking Catholic boy named Joe, and he once came to meet her family. Esther spotted a cross in his lapel and, once he left, she lit into Florence: How could you *do* this to me!

Soon after, Joe enlisted in the Army, and when Florence heard on her parents' radio that the Japanese had bombed Pearl Harbor, she turned, as her mother later told her, a pale shade of green.

Florence did her part for the war. In the nightclubs she performed less Petipa, more cancans and Cohan marches. She spent every Wednesday night at a servicemen's canteen on West Forty-third Street, dancing and playing cards with homesick soldiers. She was often joined there by Gertrude Smith, another ballerina from Madame's studio. The two young women shared a quiet confederacy, for Gertrude was also a Jewish girl from Brooklyn and she too had found herself thinking about Jesus.

They were a wholesome pair, Gertrude and Florence, slow to decipher the nuances of show business. Booked for a weekend nightclub performance in Beacon, an hour's train ride up the Hudson, they gladly accepted the free room that came with the job. On Friday night, the performance itself went fine. Afterward, through the walls of their room, came curious sounds: the slamming of doors, the giggling of young women, and, if they weren't mistaken, the grunting of grown men. The two ballerinas slept with one eye on the door and, in the morning, requested new lodging.

Florence continued to pray the prayer that Father Conroy had taught her: *Give me the grace to know Your truth and the strength to follow it.* Over time, her curiosity had become a need. She was already twenty-one years old. She had watched her beloved grandmother, Sorah-Rukhel, grow old and sick. Would Florence simply expire one day, as her grandmother would soon expire, her chest gripping with fear over what lay beyond, her mouth dry with regret?

Madame had said that Florence did not need to be a Catholic to taste the Sacraments of the Church, and so she did. She began attending Mass at Blessed Sacrament and even went to Confession. Entering the chamber, its air a thicket of leather and velvet and candle wax, she was breathless with anticipation. After telling the priest her sins, she hurried to a pew to recite the Hail Marys he prescribed.

Penance, she decided, was a wonderful concept. There was much about the Church that attracted her, especially its discipline. Through Madame she had come to trust discipline and believe in it; now she craved the discipline of belief itself. How gratifying it would be to spend each day basking in the light of pure faith, to face without anguish the character of her own soul and to know the direction it was traveling. If she were meant to embrace this Messiah, surely he would summon her.

And so he did. At Mass one morning before ballet rehearsal, she listened intently to the priest's sermon. He cited the Gospel of John: *God said, This is my beloved son in whom I am well pleased; hear him.*

Hear him—listen to Jesus, and do what he said. The instructions could not have been simpler, or more welcome. Florence, having exposed her heart, was now rewarded with the kiss of God upon her ear. The shadows of her soul were flooded with sunlight; a sublime peace settled over her.

She understood that she had received the gift of faith, and she would be eternally grateful. Now, of course, it was time to act. Hear him and *do what he said.* For the next two months she studied the catechism with Father Conroy at Blessed Sacrament. And on Christmas Eve of 1942, just before the Midnight Mass, Florence laid her head inside the marble baptismal font, Madame Souvorina at her side. Though your sins may be as scarlet, Father Conroy intoned, through this baptism your soul shall be white as the driven snow. Florence could feel the Holy Ghost take up residence in her body.

She knew that her mother would be horrified, but she was not about to tell her. On the wall of her bedroom, Florence mounted a small porcelain font of holy water. Coming home late one night, she found it missing. Now her mother knew. But when, in the morning, Esther confronted her, an incoherent fury of barbs and threats and shrieks, it was no worse than watching a thunderstorm through a plate-glass window. She was protected; its rage could not touch her.

A few days later Harry took Florence aside. He looked seriously into her eyes. I wish I *could* believe, he said tenderly, laying his hand on hers.

Florence was overjoyed by her father's reaction. She had read recently about the three types of baptism: the actual baptism by water; a baptism of fire, by which a martyr gives his life; and a baptism of desire, which was incomplete but genuine. That was what her father had undergone, she told herself, a baptism of desire, for he truly meant what he had said. He truly wanted to believe. Who wouldn't?

4

EVERYONE who knew Solly Dubner in the late 1930s could see that a blanket of despair had befallen him. Though he was only in his early twenties, the courage of his youth had melted away and his optimism had withered.

He tried to keep his various dreams afloat, but he couldn't seem to put any two good things together. He had graduated from high school in 1933, a year ahead of schedule, concentrating on literature and French. But Shepsel wouldn't even consider letting him visit Paris—and besides, there was no money. The family's restaurant had foundered soon after Gittel's death. With the Depression still raging, Shepsel needed Solly to help pay the rent. All his older brothers and sisters, Nat and Fanny and Morris and Bess, were married by now, with their own rents to pay.

He found a job as a file clerk in downtown Brooklyn. It paid thirty-five cents an hour. To keep his mind sharp, he took a night course in bookkeeping. For fun, he and a few friends rented out a cellar clubhouse and called it D.D.I.—the Do Drop Inn or Drop Dead Instantly, depending on who asked. They invited neighborhood girls over to dance and harmonized late into the night, on songs from the radio or the Hebrew prayers they all knew, the Shema and Kiddush.

More and more, though, Solly kept to himself. He had once been in the foreground of the family, everyone's favorite cousin; now he clung to the margins. He couldn't stand up to his father the way Nat did. When Shepsel scolded Nat for not keeping a kosher home, Nat simply turned his back. But for Solly, the very thought of breaking a rule, no matter how minor, hurt his stomach. In his father's house, at least, he did as he was told.

Still, he never complained, never passed an unkind word against Shepsel, even when he visited Nat and Dottie. Solly spent the night with them whenever he couldn't bear to go home, which was often. When their son, Mickey, was born, Solly watched with a particularly fragile joy as Dottie held the baby to her breast. Dottie, nine years older than Solly, was as close to a mother as he had. He still missed Gittel terribly and spoke of her constantly.

Every year he thought about enrolling at City College, but Shepsel had become dependent on Solly's file-clerk paycheck. Shepsel worked just two days a week, inspecting butcher shops to make sure the meat was kosher. He earned a little extra money at the cemetery, flagging down mourners' cars and offering to say a good and proper Kaddish over their loved ones. He did this every Sunday, stowing his paper bag of cheese sandwiches in the rotting hollow of a maple tree at the cemetery gate. It was very important, he told Solly, to say prayers for the Jewish dead, just as important as helping the living.

At the age of fifty-eight, Shepsel remarried, a sixty-two-year-old widow named Olga Chrystal. She was a stout woman with thick eyeglasses who was Shepsel's equal in both stubbornness and righteousness. She wasn't so much a stepmother to Solly as a female version of his own father, and he began to stay with Nat and Dottie even more often.

As the Depression dragged on into 1939, it seemed as if half of Brownsville was on Home Relief. Yet every month Tante Peshe bundled up whatever food and clothing could be spared for the Dubners still living in Poland. Her youngest sister and brother, an aunt and uncle whom Solly had never met, were each married with young children, and they were terribly poor. After a time, Peshe stopped receiving their thank-you letters. The Germans had marched into Poland in September, and as the winter wore on, Peshe tried convince herself that her bundles were getting through but that for some reason her brother and sister couldn't write back.

When the war at last came to America, Solly immediately enlisted in the Army. Finally he could escape his father's house. By May 1942 he was on a troop train bound for San Francisco, where he boarded a transport ship to Hawaii. He was attached to a medical corps, working as a file clerk in an Army hospital on Oahu, plastic sheeting hanging down where there hadn't been time to build walls.

The Army agreed with Solly: All the rules were laid out for him, and unlike those in his own home, these made sense. Still, he missed Brooklyn. He'd spent his entire life there, among Jews like himself. In the Army, everyone and everything were different, and he began to grow disoriented. Some days all he wanted to do was crawl into his bunk and stay. He spent some time in sick bay, but his fatigue wouldn't yield to rest.

In his letters home, though, Solly did not mention his troubles. His brothers Morris and Martin were also in the Army now, both of them stationed Stateside. Their letters to the family were perfunctory, but Solly, who still fancied himself a potential writer, wrote long, voluble dispatches, mostly to Nat and Dottie. His letters told of how strange it felt to be in such a beautiful place during such an ugly time. He asked if the Dubners in Poland had been heard from. He explained that the medics were short-staffed and that he sometimes helped admit patients to the hospital, soldiers wounded in the Pacific theater. To his young niece Gloria, his sister Bess's daughter, he sent home a grass skirt, and promised to show Gloria how to shake her hips—he'd done a bit of research, he confessed—when the war was over.

After two years on Oahu, Solly was transferred to an Army hospital on Christmas Island, a remote island even deeper into the Pacific. The volume of letters home increased. Here, he wrote, he had nothing but time. To Shepsel and Olga, he sent polite updates, written in Yiddish, wishing them good health and assuring them he was safe. The letters that Nat and Dottie received were more forthcoming. He told them that out of perhaps three hundred American servicemen on Christmas Island, he was the only Jew. A group of Catholic nuns called Maryknolls ran an orphanage for the natives, and he helped out whenever he could—which was often, since he mainly sat around waiting for casualties who rarely arrived. He said that he was reading, reading, reading, anything he could get his hands on, anything to keep his mind from turning to mush. Nat and Dottie also received a photograph of Solly in khaki shorts, his overseas cap tucked into his waist, standing against a thatch wall. "Behind a chapel," he had written on the photo.

In his next letter came another picture, which showed the interior of the chapel: rough-hewn wooden benches, a thatched podium with a wooden cross, and, above it, a huge oil painting. It portrayed a fleshy woman with dark hair, cradling an infant to her breast. Both mother and child were bathed in a beatific light. Solly hadn't written anything on the back of this picture, and Nat and Dottie were perplexed as to why he'd sent it.

5

FLORENCE'S audition at Radio City Music Hall was finally set. If all went well, she would become a soloist at one of the most famous venues in the world. With the country still at war, Americans were hungry for heroes, for celebrities, and Florence was eager to satisfy them.

Madame had been pushing hard these last months. Florence was beginning to wonder: Is it my success she is so furious about or her own? She still endured Madame's litany of insults every day, rehearsing for hours before rushing off to a nightclub performance in New Jersey or the Bronx. In rehearsal, Madame made her strap on leg weights to improve her elevation; her calf muscles burned even while she slept.

She attended Mass nearly every morning, often with her friend Gertrude, who had also become a Catholic by now. Even though it was Madame who had primarily influenced Gertrude, her

mother blamed Florence, and hung up whenever Florence telephoned.

Florence soon met a nightclub singer named Peggy Reilly, a
wiry and excitable young woman, a cradle Catholic who was
bursting with faith. Peggy too was known to read the Bible in
dressing rooms; she and Florence instantly fell in like sisters under
the skin.

With Peggy and Gertrude as allies, Florence felt blessed. If their
Saturday night performances ended early enough, they would
meet at the 1:30 A.M. Mass at St. James Cathedral in downtown
Brooklyn. Otherwise, they would attend the 4:30 A.M. Printer's
Mass at St. Malachy's in Manhattan. After a quick Automat meal
they'd ride the subway together back to Brooklyn, getting to bed
before their families were awake. Neither Florence nor Gertrude
dared parade past her parents to go to church on a Sunday morning. Florence had once attended Mass in her own neighborhood,
but a woman in a nearby pew looked so much like Esther that
her heart froze. It would hardly be beyond her mother to follow
Florence into a church and drag her out by the hair. Florence
spent as little time at home as possible and avoided her mother
as best she could.

Harry had recently sold the Savoy Sweet Shop and retired, at
the age of sixty. With eighty-two hundred dollars in cash, he
bought a two-story attached brick house on Crown Street. Esther
had to admit that Harry, with no head for business, had done all
right. Their new house had a large backyard where Harry could
plant all the blue larkspur and corn he desired, and Esther was
smitten with the formal dining room, even though their only
guests were her brother, the big fabric man, and his wife. Esther
still envied them. Irving, their son, was going to become a dentist;
their daughter had married a doctor. Even Della, Florence's older
sister, was settling down; she had found a good state job in Albany and had a steady boyfriend. All this made Florence, the
crazy Catholic ballerina, seem that much more *meshugge*. Esther's

brother had recently spotted Florence on the Coney Island board-walk wearing a crucifix—a crucifix, on her neck!—that she tried to hide when she saw him.

THE stage of Radio City Music Hall seemed to stretch on for miles. The vast auditorium was empty but for the dance mistress and her assistants, sitting just beyond the arc of the stage lights. Florence could barely make them out. Suddenly the pianist began to play her number, and Florence, with eight years of Madame's instruction coursing through her head, began to dance. She did not need to think about her routine any more than a deer would think about running through the woods. When she was through, she exhaled with the satisfaction of a job well done. The dance mistress promised to call Madame within the week.

Two days later, while rehearsing at the studio, Florence landed sideways on her foot. She heard a crack, like a peppermint stick snapped in two. Gertrude helped her get to Bellevue Hospital, where an X ray showed that she had broken a bone. Florence's first thought was that she would have to call the Radio City dance mistress to tell her that she was unavailable; her second thought was that God had somehow intervened.

Why else had He made Florence such a frail creature, she wondered, if not to bring her close to Him? Had she not caught that terrible cold long ago, she might never have challenged the very premise of her life. And had she not broken her foot, she might not have had an opportunity to step back now and see where this life of hers was leading.

She spent the next six weeks recuperating at home, keeping her bedroom door shut. The rest felt good; her entire body needed an overhaul. All she had wanted these past years was to be a famous ballerina, to leave her mark on the world, and to please Madame.

Now she had a chance to reflect, pray, and read. She began

with *The Story of a Soul,* the autobiography of St. Thérèse of
Lisieux. Born in France in 1873, Thérèse was an insecure, sickly
child who was shattered by her mother's early death. Suddenly,
at fourteen, she experienced the blistering love of Jesus and was
cloaked, as was promised in Scripture, by a peace that surpassed
all understanding. She recognized that death would claim everyone—her own health was constantly poor—and that the only solution was to pursue an everlasting life. Thérèse, like Florence,
was fiercely single-minded. When told she was too young to join
a convent, she took her case to the mother superior, then to the
bishop, and finally to Pope Leo XIII himself. As a nun, she gave
her life over to self-denial and prayer. She died, happily, at the
age of twenty-four, believing that life on Earth was only an audition of sorts while waiting for Heaven.

Florence read St. Thérèse's story again and again. She felt a
communion with her. Thérèse was a little saint who had led a
little life. Madame was always encouraging Florence to make herself larger than life, to leave her smallness behind. But that was
easy for Madame. Florence knew, in her gut, that she had a small
soul—no less precious than a large one, she assured herself—and
that it was Thérèse's path she must follow, the path of prayer and
sacrifice, not Madame's.

How could she have imagined otherwise? All at once her ambition felt vulgar, outsized, like a street urchin dressed in a ball
gown. True, ballet was a thing of beauty, but it was not going to
change the world the way prayer could change the world. Besides,
ballet was not the cleanest profession. Florence knew what went
on between dancers, even the married ones, and she'd seen how
they liked their vodka. Florence had never paid attention to her
mother's rantings against ballet, but even Father Conroy had told
her that show business was a bad influence on the soul.

She knew that Madame would storm at her, would call her an
ingrate, a ridiculous girl. Indeed, that is exactly what happened

when Florence informed Madame that she was quitting ballet. Soon after, Florence wrote a long letter to Joe, the Catholic nightclub singer she had been dating. Florence explained that she had fallen even more deeply in love with another man, by the name of Jesus, and anyone interested in her would now have some real competition. Joe was not a serious Catholic, she knew, and her letter would end the relationship.

But what was Florence to do now? As her broken foot healed, she kept St. Thérèse and the Virgin Mary busy with prayers for guidance. She considered becoming a nun, but decided against it when she failed to receive a revelation in her prayers. St. Thérèse's book had convinced her of the power of prayer; when God had something to say to her, He would let her know. She took a few apologetics courses at St. John's University, studied the recent papal encyclical on Christian marriage, and then enrolled in Misericordia, a Catholic nursing school on the Upper East Side of Manhattan. If the war kept on, she could join the Army's nurse corps. Regardless, nursing school would get her out of her parents' house and into a healthy Catholic environment.

Every Monday night, Florence met Gertrude at Blessed Sacrament for a meeting of a group called Catholic Action; these were young Catholics intent on spreading their faith, supervised by Father Conroy. Every Wednesday night, Florence and a few other student nurses, their white capes snapping in the river breeze, attended a novena to St. Joseph, the patron saint of vocations. Florence prayed to St. Joseph, pleading that he reveal her role in life.

One Wednesday night she received a revelation that nearly struck her down. It was as if God were speaking directly to her. She hurried back to her dormitory and phoned Father Conroy.

I've got the most wonderful news, she told him.

I'm all ears, he said.

I'm going to be married.

Who's the lucky man?

Oh, I haven't met him yet, Florence said, but he'll be a Catholic, that much I know, and we'll have as many children as God will allow.

6

THE man who would become my father was still named Solomon at the time, but he no longer thought of himself as a Jew. It was a Saturday night toward the end of 1944. Technical Sergeant Sol Dubner was home on furlough and, having spotted a USO posting about a Catholic church in Manhattan that threw a weekly servicemen's dance, that was where he was heading.

It is impossible to say exactly what he was looking for that night, what measures of zeal and longing and uncertainty were streaming through him. And if I had the chance to ask him now?

Just what was it that happened overseas, I would ask. Did it start in your head and then your heart followed, or was it the other way around?

That Saturday night, as best as I can piece together, transpired like this. Sol found the church, which was the Church of the Blessed Sacrament, and in the gymnasium, where a four-piece band was playing for the soldiers, he found the priest in charge of things, who was Father Conroy. He asked the priest if they could speak in private. Sol had any number of questions, only some of which the priest could answer. At the end of their conversation he said, Have you ever heard of a creature like me, Father, a Jew who wants to become a Catholic?

As a matter of fact, Father Conroy answered, I have. He told Sol about the group of young Catholic activists he met with every Monday night. Two of the women, he explained, were Jewish converts—ballerinas, the both of them—who could probably answer whatever questions Father Conroy couldn't.

On Monday night Sol returned to Blessed Sacrament. The meeting was held in a brownstone next door to the church. About fifteen people, mostly women, including Florence and Gertrude, crowded around a long table. They sipped punch, nibbled on doughnuts, and sneaked glances at the handsome soldier in uniform. For nearly two hours he sat quietly as they discussed the war: Hitler's waning strength and how they, as members of Catholic Action, needed to shout their message now, not whisper it; there was no better time to bring more young people into the Catholic fold. Terrible as the war was, they agreed, it presented a golden opportunity to show the superiority of Catholic teachings, how perhaps the war might even have been avoided if Europe hadn't strayed so far from the Truth.

The meeting was about to break up when Father Conroy asked the visiting soldier if he had anything to say. Sol stood up, folded his hands behind his back, and introduced himself. The room went dead quiet.

I know it's getting late, he said, so I'll try to keep it short. I can't say I quite understand what's happening to me but it sure is wonderful. I guess you could call me Exhibit A in the mystery of faith.

He told them he was a Jew from Brownsville. These last several years, he explained, he felt as if he'd been walking around in the dark, and he had gotten so used to it that he'd forgotten there was another way to live. While he was stationed overseas, though, someone finally turned on a light, and the light was Jesus. Florence listened sharply. She saw that there was a natural kindness about this soldier, an earnestness. He mentioned his father, a traditional Jew named Shepsel, who sounded an awful lot like Florence's grandfather Moishe. He hated what his decision would do to his father, the soldier was saying now, but there seemed no way around it—didn't Jesus say that he had come to set a man against his father?

He explained that he had already been baptized as a Christian, but hadn't yet settled on a denomination. He was nearly ready to become a Catholic, except he was confused about the role of the Virgin Mary. He revered Mary, he said, and understood how powerful she was. But, he asked the group, since she isn't a member of the Holy Trinity, why do you worship her? Why would you pray to the Virgin Mary when you can pray directly to God?

As everyone around the table jumped in, Florence waited impatiently. She saw that the soldier wasn't satisfied with their answers. Finally, she had her chance.

Well, it's like this, she told the soldier. You don't *worship* the Blessed Mother, you ask her to *intercede*. Let's say I want a dress that my sister has, all right? I might go to my mother and say, Mom, would you ask Della if I could wear that dress? It's just better that way sometimes. That is part of the beauty of Catholicism, that you have all these wonderful saints you can pray to. Who better to petition God than His mother, the Queen of Heaven?

As the meeting broke up, Sol thanked Florence. I can tell, he said, that you've thought all of this through for yourself. It sure isn't the simplest thing in the world.

Oh, she said, I don't know about that.

7

NAT and Dottie hadn't seen Solly in nearly three years when he burst in with presents for everyone. They could see there was something different about him; it seemed as if the spark of his youth had returned, as if he once again had something at stake.

They had opened a candy store on Graham Avenue in Williamsburg, with a small apartment in the back. It smelled of chocolate from the store and horse manure from a nearby police stable. Mickey, who was nearly twelve years old, wanted to drag Solly outside for a game of punchball, but Solly was eager to catch up on the family.

After a time, Dottie sat down alone with Solly. She wanted to know if something special had happened to make him seem so alive again.

Well, yes and no, he said.

Tell me the yes part, she said.

He tried to explain: the deep melancholy he'd experienced overseas, some reading he'd done, some conversations with a chaplain.

Are you trying to tell me you're becoming a Catholic? she asked. Why?

Instead of answering, he told her about a girl he'd just met, a beautiful girl who used to be a ballerina.

But why, Dottie asked him, why do you want to become a Catholic?

He would explain later, he said, when his head was straight: after a few years in the Islands, even the New York traffic shook him up. There would come a time, he promised, when he'd tell her everything.

He asked Dottie if they could keep the news between them, and kissed her on the forehead.

WHEN she had received her revelation that she was meant to be a Catholic wife, not a nurse or a nun, Florence quit nursing school and, reluctantly, moved back home. The entire family knew of her conversion by now, and Esther's shame was limitless. She badgered Florence at every opportunity: You don't know what you're doing, she said, you're misinformed! So Florence spent as little time at home as possible. She found a secretarial job in midtown Manhattan, a few blocks from St. Patrick's Cathedral, where she attended Mass during her lunch hour. One day, she was joined by Sol Dubner. In fact, she met with him often during the six weeks that he was home on furlough.

She saw that he was in a bit of a hurry, in every way. But she could help; they spoke the same language, understood each other's minds. They talked in coffee shops, often with Gertrude, three former Jews almost giddy over their fortune of having received the gift of faith.

Florence realized how different she and Sol were. First of all, he had grown up in a religious home. What she called the Old Testament he called the Tanakh, and he knew it inside and out. All she knew was that the Old Testament contained the prophecies that proved Jesus was the Messiah. He could quote those passages by heart, even in Hebrew, and argue them back and forth. Sol was more of an intellectual than she. While she had heard of John Cardinal Newman, the nineteenth-century Anglican vicar who became a Catholic, Sol had actually read *Apologia pro Vita Sua,* the Cardinal's account of his conversion. Sol was teaching himself Latin to understand the Mass; as for the New Testament, he could retell the Gospel stories as naturally as if he'd written them himself.

And yet he seemed to think himself unworthy. Whereas Florence was unabashedly grateful for the faith she had been granted, Sol behaved as if it might be yanked away from him at any moment. Though he didn't like to talk about his past, it was clear that his spirit had been wounded over the years, nearly wrung dry of hope.

Just after New Year's of 1945, Sol's furlough was up. When he met Florence to say good-bye, he gripped her right hand with both of his, as if it belonged to the Blessed Mother herself. He would personally see to it that the war ended soon, he said, and asked if he could write to her.

Well, of course, she said, how else will I know when you've become a Catholic?

SOL was once again posted on Oahu. Florence soon received a V-mail from him:

Have been going to Mass pretty regularly, and am taking instructions now. There's a good chance of my being baptized as a Catholic at this post as the chaplain here is pretty interested in my case. My best regards to Father Conroy and to Gertrude and God bless you all.

> Sincerely,
> Sol

At the following week's Catholic Action meeting, Father Conroy told Florence that he'd gotten some good news: Sol Dubner had written to say he'd become a Catholic. Within a few days, Florence received her own letter.

> By this time, you probably know that I have been baptized and received my first Communion. Needless to say, it was a most wonderful experience and I hope to strengthen my faith in Christ each single day.
> What's extremely new out your way?
>
> Sincerely,
> Sol

During their time together in New York, Florence had not thought about Sol in a romantic way. He was a friend in the faith, she told herself, and that was all. Her friends Gertrude and Peggy were less convinced, for they had seen how Florence and Sol lit up around each other.

Still, when Florence wrote to him, she was careful to keep things on a friendship level. Her duty for now was to offer spiritual counsel. Besides, God would let her know when she'd found the man she would marry.

Sol's next letter assured her that he was on the right track:

> Dear Florence,
> By gosh—it really was swell getting your letter! Thanks a lot for the enclosures. The picture of the Consecration of Bishop

Donahue at St. Patrick's Cathedral brought back those few precious moments that we spent together there.

No, Florence, I haven't been confirmed yet—it will come the
first chance I get. In regard to religious literature, thanks for your
thoughtfulness, but please don't bother to send anything. The
truth is, there is more reading material available here than I can
handle.

I bet it would knock you for a loop to know that I am toying
with the notion of becoming a priest after the war! You know,
I've taken Paul as my Christian name, so the Paulists are the
ones that I'm going to find out more about. (sentence structure—
phooey!) If I don't have the call for the priesthood, then it will
be something like working for the Paulist Press.

                                          Yours in Christ, Sol
P.S.: Let's pray for each other!

She continued to receive Sol's letters, sometimes twice a week.
His handwriting, she had to admit, was beautiful. The letters were
more and more impassioned—about his new Catholic life and
about the Allies' growing dominance in Europe. He said he prayed
daily for the war to end and was sure that Florence did too.

Then the letters stopped. Florence told herself not to worry, but
she couldn't help wondering if something had happened to him.

The day the war in Europe ended, Florence crowded with hundreds of other Catholics into St. Patrick's Cathedral for a Mass
of thanksgiving. Her eyes were wet like the others'. She prayed
for Sol's safe return home. Now there was talk of stepping up
the Pacific campaign; perhaps he had been shipped out to the
fighting?

Still she received no word from him. At last she asked the mailman if perhaps there had been a problem with the soldiers'
V-mails getting through. Not at all, he said. In fact, I delivered a
couple of letters from your soldier friend just last week.

Florence realized that her mother had been beating her to the mailbox. When confronted, Esther admitted to intercepting Sol Dubner's letters. After reading them, she had burned them in the sink.

From that day on, Florence had her mail sent to Peggy Reilly's apartment. Peggy had recently left show business too and had gotten married, to a Navy man named Bill Wink, who was stationed overseas. She lived in the Ridgewood section of Brooklyn. Every Saturday night Peggy threw open her apartment for a gathering of Catholic friends, mostly single women and young wives whose husbands were fighting the war. They would start off with the Rosary and stay late into the night, singing and laughing and praying. Sometimes a priest friend or two dropped in after hearing Saturday confessions. They prayed as a group that God would deal with the Japanese as He'd dealt with Hitler. They prayed that He'd return to them the men they loved—or, in Florence's case, the man she would admit to seeing only as a friend in the faith.

The women were often joined by a man named Mac Lerner, whom Sol Dubner had sent their way. Mac was an Army buddy of Sol's, another Jewish fellow from Brooklyn. The time away from home had sent Mac, like Sol, into a spiral of melancholy; when he learned that Sol got some new religion, he wanted to try it too. So when he was discharged, Sol hooked him up with Florence's gang back in New York.

Every Saturday night at Peggy's, Mac put his heart into it, singing their hymns full out in his off-key voice. He read their books and attended Mass with them. But it wouldn't take root. He was wrapped in an even darker shadow than Sol: He was convinced that the FBI was trailing him, intercepting his mail, and when he demanded they stop, they shooed him out of their office like a fly.

So Mac is coming along slowly, is he? Sol wrote to Florence. *Well, considering he's been familiar with Catholic ways for so*

*short a time, we'll be very patient with him. However, you're right
in saying we must pray for him—that will never hurt.*

Sol kept Florence informed on every development in his life.
He'd been confirmed at St. Theresa's Church in Honolulu, he
wrote, with 250 boys and girls and a handful of soldiers. Now
he was looking into the different Catholic newspapers with an eye
toward a job after the war.

His next letter was dated August 11, 1945:

> Let's hope by the time you read this, there will be no more
> war. Right now we're awaiting Japan's reply to the Allies' sur-
> render terms. Hardly anyone expected us to beat Japan so soon.
> But the quicker all the shooting and killing and hating is over,
> the better. Yesterday morning about 2:30, all the boys in the
> barracks were fast asleep. Then the news came in and before
> long, all the lights were on, the boys were whooping it up and
> everybody was jubilant.

Two days later:

> Hope you don't mind my writing so often. Today Japan is
> expected to answer the Allies' surrender terms. It may be any
> minute—any hour! God help us that we may have peace again.
> If the war is over, I can expect to be discharged in a few months.
> There are two very special reasons why I'd like to be a civilian
> again. First, to try for the seminary to see whether the priesthood
> would be my vocation. Secondly, to see you again and the rest
> of the gang. You can't imagine how much I am looking forward
> to it.

It had been less than a year since Florence and Sol had met.
But the world—and their place in it—had changed dramatically.
*It's going to be hard to make my family understand why I am a
Catholic,* Sol wrote to her. *Perhaps I'll find some room and board*

in New York till I decide definitely what my future plans will be. But gosh, it's going to be great to get back and start life anew. This time, things will be different!

In Hawaii, Sol was going mad with boredom as he waited to be shipped home. In New York, Florence's vision of their reunion reshaped itself every few days. If he was thinking about becoming a priest, she told herself, there was no sense in attaching her heart to him. Her heart, though, only half listened.

8

MY father was nearly thirty years old when he returned from the war. His brothers too had come home safely. Morris returned to his wife; Martin, the youngest, was about to be married. Sol moved back into his father's house for the time being, his conversion still a secret. He spent his days in Manhattan hunting for a job and his evenings reconnecting with Florence, sharing dinner in a coffee shop or strolling through Prospect Park.

He returned home late one night to find Shepsel sitting in the dark, sobbing, his shirt torn over the heart. At his feet lay a pair of Sol's khaki pants and the rosary beads that had slipped from the pocket.

At this point, what words could possibly pass between such a father and such a son? Sol grabbed his rosary beads, packed a duffel bag, and fled.

Word of Sol's apostasy spread through the family like a rank odor. *Shloime*, Shepsel was heard to say, *du bist mer nit kein yid, du bist mer nit mein zun*—you are not a Jew anymore and you are not my son anymore. There were no words, in any language, to describe Shepsel's grief. For generations, his family had lived according to Jewish law, in fierce obedience to God; now Shepsel's own son had betrayed Him.

He had also betrayed his family. Who could do such a thing to the aunts and cousins and brothers and sisters he professed to love? Millions of Jews dead in Europe, the newspapers were reporting. And now this one from their own blood, turning his back on all of them? It was an impossibility, a perversion. This, they knew, would haunt them. In their old age, their hot, wrinkled toes poised to dunk into the blessed blue cool of a swimming pool, they would be spotted by a Brownsville neighbor: Oh, yes, the Dubners from Sutter Avenue, you had the kosher restaurant and the boy who went nuts during the war and became a Catholic.

It is true that some of Solly's cousins, particularly the female ones, were secretly aroused by what he had done: fallen so deeply in love with a Catholic ballerina in Hawaii that he had no choice but to become a Catholic himself—for that was how, in whispered snatches, the story pieced itself together, that the girl was the cake and Jesus the icing. There would be no official version or public declaration. Shepsel had made it clear that the name of his third son was never to be spoken again. Solomon Dubner, he announced, was dead. Shepsel sat shiva, but his shame was so great that he did not invite even the men from his synagogue.

Sol moved into a small Manhattan apartment with Mac Lerner, his Army friend, and found a job as an office clerk at P. J. Kenedy, a Catholic publisher near Wall Street.

Florence saw that Sol was shaken by how thoroughly his family had cut him off. She encouraged him to look forward, not back, for having found the Truth of Jesus, he had been given a brand-new life.

He took her words to heart. Indeed, he *had* been given a new life, and it was a brilliant expanse of possibility. He consulted with Father Conroy about becoming a priest; Father Conroy directed him to a Jesuit retreat, where Sol prayed for guidance. Alas, like Florence, he was directed by God not to the clergy but to the state of matrimony. It gave Sol no small measure of confidence to learn that marriage itself was one of the Seven Sacraments, as sacred as the priestly vows. By merely following his heart, he could follow Christ as well.

The matter of proposing to Florence was breathtakingly simple. Peggy Wink was still hosting her Saturday-night gatherings, and toward the end of one, Florence and Sol sat off in a corner by themselves, Florence nursing a glass of cream soda with a touch of red wine.

I'd be remiss if I didn't tell you, Sol said, that you're the girl for me.

Well, is that so? she replied.

I must say that I find myself quite in love with you, he said.

Well then, go ahead and say it, if you must.

I'm quite in love with you.

I'm quite in love with you, too.

Now isn't that symmetrical? he said, and they sealed their declaration with a kiss. A few days later, on the Feast of the Immaculate Conception, they met for Mass and he gave her a diamond solitaire that he'd bought with his mustering-out pay.

Florence went to Blessed Sacrament to seek Father Conroy's blessing. Sol had confided in the priest, she knew, as he had confided in her, about the rocky path he'd traveled before finding the Truth.

Well, Father Conroy now told her, Sol might not be such a good risk. That melancholy disposition has haunted him, you know. His soul has seen quite a few dark nights.

So you think that—

I think you should consider how sad his life has been, Father

Conroy said. I can see that you love him. But you have to ask yourself if all the love in the world can replace everything he has already lost.

Florence knew that Father Conroy was right. But she also knew that it was God's providence that had brought them together. God would not lay in their path an obstacle they could not overcome. She knew how badly Sol's spirit had been damaged before he'd found the Truth; she also knew, however, that God's mercy had begun the resurrection of that spirit. A healthy marriage, she resolved, would complete the miracle.

SOL dearly wanted Nat and Dottie to come to his wedding. He had guessed that they would stand by him no matter how viciously Shepsel had spoken, and he was right. He stopped by their candy store often, asking countless questions about the family. He was trying to get his foot in the door at a couple of newspapers, he said, but they wanted men with some experience. Dottie continued to press him to explain why he'd become a Catholic, and he continued to put her off.

Your father's been here, she told him during one visit.

He was?

Before he sat shiva. He wanted us to try to talk you out of it.

What did you say?

What do you mean, what did I say? You can't talk somebody out of something they talked themselves into. That's what I told him. Your gal's parents were here too, the Greenglasses. She's the talker of the pair. You know what she said? She said, Why'd you let him do it, why'd you let him talk our daughter into it? I said, Missus, no offense but you got it wrong. Backwards, if you ask me.

What about you coming to the wedding? Sol asked Dottie.

Much as I'd like to see you married, she answered, I can't take

Mickey to see his Uncle Solly getting married in a church. That just goes against me. I love you, and we'll never stop loving you, but that just goes against me.

The wedding took place on March 2, 1946, a Saturday afternoon, in a Brooklyn church some two miles from the house where Shepsel Dubner was sitting down for his Shabbos lunch. Florence had been careful not to tell her mother the date, for Esther's brand of hysteria was perfectly suited to sabotaging such an event.

My parents' wedding portrait shows a resplendent bride, dressed in the white satin gown she'd borrowed from Peggy Wink; the groom is wearing his Army dress uniform and a smile that betrays both a beggar's hunger and a glutton's satisfaction. They were married not as Sol and Florence but as Paul and Veronica, the Christian names they had recently taken—Paul in honor of the quintessential convert, Veronica for the woman who wiped Jesus' face as he carried his cross through Jerusalem. They promised themselves to God and each other before twenty witnesses, friends from Catholic Action and Peggy Wink's get-togethers. Not a single guest was a blood relative or a Jew or even an acquaintance from the days before Veronica and Paul had found the Truth.

They honeymooned for three days in Atlantic City, then moved into a cold-water flat in Peggy's building. Paul became the building's janitor to reduce the rent from twenty dollars a month to thirteen. Veronica painted the walls a fresh white, and they remained bare except for the crucifixes and prayer plaques the couple had received as wedding gifts. The big old coal stove was temperamental, and whenever it wouldn't fire, Veronica prayed to St. Thérèse of Lisieux, who visited without fail to fan the tinder into flame.

9

BY all accounts, my parents' marriage released an enormous amount of energy, as if two chemicals, while hardly inert in their previous forms, had in their fusion combusted in a most dramatic fashion. They befriended priests and invited them for dinner; every evening they recited the Rosary, after which my father would sit at the kitchen table writing lyric poems to the Virgin Mary. He and my mother had aligned themselves especially with Mary, for a few years earlier, Pope Pius XII had announced that all Catholics should dedicate themselves to her.

This heightened devotion stemmed from the Virgin's miraculous appearances to three young cousins, shepherd children, in the Portuguese mountain town of Fátima. The first visitation occurred on May 13, 1917, as the First World War was reaching a crescendo. The Virgin warned the children that the sins of man were destroying the world. People of faith, she said, must amend their ways and recite the Rosary daily. "The Great War is going to end," the children heard her say, "but if people do not stop offending God, another and worse one will begin. To prevent this, I shall come to ask the consecration of Russia to my Immaculate Heart. If my requests are granted, Russia will be converted and there will be peace. If not, she will scatter her errors throughout the world, provoking wars and persecution of the Church."

Paul was stationed on Christmas Island when he first read about Our Lady of Fátima, as she came to be known. Her warnings had come all too true; what was World War II if not a punishment for the sins of humanity?

Now, though, by ending the war, hadn't God granted a reprieve? Clearly the Virgin's message was a call to arms, and the time was now. Paul joined the Blue Army, a new religious organization devoted to fighting the Red Army's message of atheism; he took public speaking courses at Fordham University and began lecturing to church groups about Our Lady of Fátima. Around his neck he wore a scapular, a string affixed to two cloth squares containing the Blessed Mother's image.

Paul urged everyone he knew to say the Rosary daily and to pray for the end of Communism in Russia. He continued to jot exhortations to himself in his pocket notebook: *Evil in your country—in world? God can make good come out of evil.* When he heard that John Dessauer, a friend from the Catholic Action group, was working in a Manhattan bookstore, he called to say that the book field wasn't good for the soul—a priest friend had said so—because you never knew what was inside some of those books. A few weeks later Paul called John again, somewhat frantically: No, no, John shouldn't quit his job (not that he had intended to); Paul had misinterpreted the priest's advice. In fact, Paul now said, John could make his post a beacon of good influence.

Another priest friend offered to introduce Paul to Dorothy Day, the former radical Communist who co-founded the Catholic Worker movement. To devotees of Our Lady of Fátima, Day was a particularly blessed soul, for she had recognized that Communism, while perhaps a more brotherly economic system than capitalism, was fatally flawed by its embrace of godlessness. Day and her partner, a French peasant-philosopher named Peter Maurin, taught that the poor must be cared for and that hard work was in itself a Sacrament when used to fulfill Jesus' teachings about the destitute.

Paul visited the Catholic Worker's House of Hospitality on Mott Street. After a brief conversation with Day—as she chopped potatoes, a swarm of unfortunates elbowing their way to the free soup—Paul pledged himself to the cause. He enlisted Bill Wink, Peggy's husband, who owned a car, to help round up donated clothes.

Bill too was just back from the war, having spent his last stretch on a supply ship in the South Pacific. In civilian life he was a jazz drummer, an easygoing man more prone to wit than philosophy; he was a born Catholic and not remotely the activist sort. But Paul's enthusiasms were not easily deflected. After dropping off the clothes on Mott Street, they loaded up the trunk with copies of the Catholic Worker's newspaper to hand out on street corners in Brooklyn. The war's not over yet! Paul would shout, waving a copy above his head. The war against the poor is still raging! Read all about it in the *Catholic Worker!*

Paul and Bill were working together as carpenters on a government housing project in Canarsie. They had bluffed their way into the job—neither of them had ever built a thing—and bought tools from a pawnshop so they'd appear broken in. Now Paul read an article in a Catholic magazine about how they could earn some extra money: selling religious articles door to door.

Paul took to the pavement of Brooklyn like a shortstop drunk with the smell of first-cut grass. His five-dollar satchel bulging with samples, his tie knotted with an engineer's precision, he worked one side of the street while Bill worked the other. They skipped any doorpost with a mezuzah but attacked the rest, and soon discovered that a porcelain Infant of Prague statue lay at the very end of an extremely long postwar shopping list that included kitchen tables and easy chairs and bassinets, bassinets by the thousand.

Paul and Veronica themselves prayed for children, and God did not make them wait long. Veronica had barely gotten over the excitement of their wedding before she became pregnant. She and Paul marveled at their blessings. Their thoughts sped toward the future, toward the imminent collision of their own family and their little thirteen-dollar flat, hemmed in as it was by asphalt and brick and ragged ailanthus trees.

It wasn't only the physical impositions of New York that seemed poorly suited to family life. They and their friends—the Winks and a few other young Catholic families—had come to view capitalism in general and the city's rampant materialism in particular as bad influences on the soul. Veronica read about a Catholic Worker farm in Pennsylvania and arranged for Paul and her to visit. There, she learned to bake whole-wheat bread, holding the mixing bowl firmly against her swollen belly. Paul helped the men build a chicken coop. They slept in separate bunkhouses and held hands during the supper prayer. To their disappointment, the men and women who lived on the farm weren't particularly religious. But the Catholic Worker's back-to-the-land movement held great appeal. And so it was that the Dubners decided upon the fabric of their future: Catholicism would be their warp and healthy living their woof, woven so tightly as to be indistinguishable, and indestructible.

Back in Brooklyn, Veronica wrote to an Associated Press reporter named James Kenney:

Feast of St. Elizabeth, 1946

Dear Mr. Kenney,
Miss Dorothy Day suggested that I write to you since we have a mutual interest: Catholic farming communes.

There are at least three other couples, together with my husband and myself, who are interested in getting back to the land, as soon as possible, to raise our families in a healthful, wholesome, and Christian environment.

Two of the men (and my husband is one of them) are learning carpentry, one is a plumber, and one a stationary engineer. This seems to be a good nucleus to start. Now we should like to find the right location. Although all of the actual planning of details has to be worked out, we do have some ideas about what we want.

Firstly, our motive in moving out on the land is to keep us all God-conscious and living and working for God. This, then, is above all the reason we want to raise our families on the land, and takes precedence over all natural motives, however sensible and good they may be. So first of all, we want to be near a church so that we may live the full community life together, through Christ.

We figure on about an acre or two for each family—it is surprising, the crops that can be grown on just one acre. With too large a farm to manage, at the start, when there is so much building and other settling to be done, there would likely be the necessity of letting land lie idle, or not having time enough to harvest the crops, and the food would be wasted.

Well, perhaps this letter is too long already. If you are interested in discussing these ideas further, I should be very happy to hear from you.

Sincerely in Christ,
(Mrs.) Veronica Dubner

Mr. Kenney was good enough to offer a tour of his father's farm in upstate New York. On a chilly November morning, Paul took the train to Binghamton. Kenney walked him through the barn, the orchards and meadows, Paul shivering in his lightweight shirt. He watched in wonder as Kenney demonstrated how to prime the pump. Back inside, after a lunch of hamburgers, Paul asked for the bathroom. Kenney pointed him to the outhouse. Kenney and his father watched as Paul tiptoed around the manure piles. Your friend, the old man told his son, doesn't look like much of a farmer.

This truth became all the more evident as the day progressed. By the time Paul got back on the train, his mind had been overwhelmed by the intricacies of tree grafting and egg fertilizing and cow birthing. Their faith and zeal notwithstanding, it was clear that the Dubners and their friends were not quite ready to throw off the shackles of capitalism and get back to the land.

And then came the babies. All the mothers in their circle were prolific out of the gate, but none more so than Veronica. First came Joseph Louis, chubby and bright, and then Mary Rose and Martha Mary, each darkly beautiful, Mary with her serious eyes and Martha with an unfailingly cheery disposition. Three baptisms within thirty-six months, their very own little Trinity. Having named their first two children after Jesus' parents, Veronica and Paul vowed that every child thereafter would receive Joseph or Mary as a middle name.

Nat and Dottie sent a card when each baby was born, as did Paul's sister Bess and her husband, Sam. The rest of his family, however, seemed to believe, as Shepsel had declared, that Paul was truly dead. Paul held out hope that Shepsel might hear about his new grandchildren and perhaps end the excommunication.

Esther Greenglass meanwhile, though she was still upset about not having been invited to her daughter's wedding, could not help visiting when Joseph, her first grandchild, was born. Veronica removed all the crucifixes and prayer plaques from the walls, there hardly being need for further provocation.

What are you nursing the baby for, Esther asked the moment she walked in. You should give him the bottle. All the doctors say it's better.

Harry kissed his daughter's forehead and then the baby's. With a tired smile he shook Paul's hand and slipped an envelope into his pocket. He knew that Paul's carpentering work was unsteady and didn't pay well.

Veronica told her mother that baby formula was full of chemical preservatives. Esther parried with a twenty-minute litany of advice regarding mother's milk and various other subjects.

I'm doing all right here, Veronica finally protested, stroking the baby's head, her voice unsteady.

But just think, Esther said, how much healthier the baby would be if you just did what I told you.

Esther, who had never lacked for a target of disdain, now found in her daughter's parenting skills a subject that would never exhaust her. The apartment was much too cold, she announced, and everyone knows that a baby won't grow in the cold. She wondered aloud how Paul was going to feed the family when he didn't have a store or a trade or even an uncle who would give him a job.

After such a visit, and every visit was essentially the same, Veronica nearly imploded with anger.

Paul would counsel her: We can't let her get to us. Let's just say a prayer for her, offer up the anger to Jesus, and move on, shall we? There we go. Thattagirl.

THE deluge of babies made Veronica and Paul silly with joy. Joseph was an early talker—destined, they prayed, to become a priest. Already he was catechistically oriented. One Saturday afternoon, Paul strapped him into the stroller for some fresh air. As they passed a fire hydrant, Joseph braked the stroller with his feet, fingering the chains dangling from the caps. Wosary bees! he said. Half a block later he pointed up at a telephone pole: Cwucifix!

Veronica and Paul had seen a certain allure in tilling the earth with a baby or two strapped across their backs. With three babies already, however, the idea began to lose its appeal, and the commune idea was scrapped. Instead, Peggy and Bill Wink led a charge to the north shore of Long Island, where there was at least a little room to spread out. Paul and Veronica soon followed, settling in the town of Northport, thirty-five miles east of New York City.

It wasn't the pristine retreat they had envisioned, but it was certainly better than Brooklyn. They bought a small, boxy house on a dead-end street called Kalmia, and Paul found a job as a clerk in the personnel department at the Northport VA Hospital, which lay just through the woods from the house. It paid seventy dollars a week, enough to get by if they grew their own food. In the backyard, Veronica planted a vegetable garden and Paul banged together a chicken coop, his audience of diapered babies assembled in a rusted-out wheelbarrow.

These eggs, he would say over breakfast, sure taste an awful lot better than store-bought, don't you think, kiddos?

In fact, precious few store-bought items passed the lips of any young Dubner. Veronica had discovered the nutritionist Adelle Davis, whose regimen excluded refined sugar, white flour, all preservatives, and even a mention of candy. Veronica treated Davis's books like sacred texts. She fed the children calves' liver, washed down with goat milk (procured from a neighbor in exchange for tomatoes or corn). She bought hundred-pound sacks of whole-wheat flour (at eight cents a pound, less than half the price of a ten-pound sack!) and local apples by the bushel.

These are God's candy, she told the children, apples and pears and raisins, so perfect they don't even need a wrapper. Veronica put the children to work in the garden, teaching them how to pull weeds by the roots and shake off the dirt, how to pick beans above the stem to keep them fresh. This too was part of the Catholic Worker's back-to-the-land ideology: Children should be hands as well as mouths, and since there were always two hands for every mouth, you couldn't have too many children.

The next baby was another girl, named for St. Ann, and she was given the middle name Stella Maris, star of the sea, one of the Blessed Mother's many devotional titles. Ann was a petite child and an early walker; she looked like a windup doll, tottering among the pole beans in search of her big brother, clutching an apple nearly as big as her head.

Veronica was a strict, nervous mother, and with good reason. Joe had proved himself an able and cunning ringleader, and his sisters provided an all-too-willing constituency. Fires were set (by Joe, who had a knack for finding matches), giant holes were dug (in their own and neighbors' yards), candy and other contraband were procured (from the proceeds of gathering Coke bottles during low tide at Long Island Sound, Joe's favorite spot).

One afternoon when Joe was about seven years old, Veronica noticed that he and Mary were missing. She left Martha, who was four, in charge of Ann, who was two, and slashed through the neighborhood, pumpkin seeds spilling from her apron. On Main Street she considered asking Mrs. Brett, who ran the Northport *News*, if she had seen the children, but decided against it; however the situation worked out, it would end up on the front page. Her heart felt like a stone as she imagined telling Paul that she'd lost half their children.

She finally thought of the Sound and broke into a run. There she spotted the tiny heads of her two eldest, bobbing in a rowboat in the middle of the Sound. A young fisherman volunteered to capture them in his boat, and he did. Joe's chest was stuck out like an admiral's as he stepped from the rowboat he had plundered; Mary wore a broad grin. Veronica was too relieved to spank or even shake her children, as she would have done under normal conditions.

Veronica was the family disciplinarian, Paul the cheerful provider. He had never expected to find such joy in life. At the end of each workday he'd hurry home to kiss his wife, to toss his children in the air. The forest of unhappiness he'd been forced to trudge through—his mother's death, his father's hostilities, his own wartime melancholy—was surely the first leg of his sanctified journey toward Heaven. Suffering was part of the game. In his pocket notebook he wrote: *Disappointments? Jesus had many, many of them.* He suspected that his melancholy had been permanently vanquished, the dark blotches on his soul wiped clean by the powerful goodness of Jesus and of his wife and children. His anxieties, for the time being at least, were in remission.

10

OVER the previous decades a strange and powerful transformation had occurred in America. The Catholic Church, long the target of derision and even hatred, had become a trusted pillar of society. As World War II gave way to the Cold War, the Church's staunch opposition to Communism further strengthened its standing. All things considered, it was a good time to be a Catholic in America.

My parents, however, were not content merely to *be* Catholics. They needed to live their faith, to wield it as a carpenter wielded his hammer, as Dorothy Day used her faith, or little St. Thérèse of Lisieux, or the mighty St. Paul.

By the size of their brood, four and counting, it was obvious that God had indeed wished them to become parents, not a priest and a nun. But, they realized, this was no lesser a calling than the clergy. There were many parallels, in fact. Just as a priest must lead his congregation and minister to the sick, Veronica and Paul were beholden to lead and minister to their children. By thus dedicating themselves, they had taken a de facto vow of poverty, just as a priest would.

Paul believed that writing was the best way to spread his faith. If you've got something to say, he was always telling the children, get up on the mountaintop and shout it! He took a correspondence course with the Newspaper Institute of America, but he still couldn't find a job in journalism—he didn't have enough experience even for Mrs. Brett's local weekly. So he persevered on his own. He would jot down a thought on a napkin in the cafeteria at work—*A parent is an artist!*—and flesh it out at night once the children were asleep. In the humid summer evenings, the kitchen window propped open with a roll of newspapers, he tapped away at his typewriter:

To Catholic parents who at one time had dreamed of embracing a religious vocation only to discover that their vocations were in the married life, the following thoughts are presented to show what beauty there is in parenthood.

You—as a parent—picture yourself as an artist! God has given you a new soul to work with, which is equivalent to the artist's canvas. And through the Sacraments you are given the tools whereby you can work on that masterpiece. Just as the artist keeps dabbing meticulously with his brush on the canvas to make a more perfect painting, so you can form a more perfect soul by constantly adding to it the great virtues of charity, humility, and sanctity. Once we get our children and ourselves to Heaven, then we shall know that the masterpiece has been completed.

Occasionally Paul found a Catholic magazine that wanted to publish one of his essays. More often he was asked to try again.

Veronica too felt the need to put her ideas in writing. She had read that Communists now ruled some eight hundred million people, a full 60 percent of the world's population, and the threat of an Atomic War was all too real. In America, immorality was on the rise: One in three marriages ended in divorce; more than a million babies were being illegally aborted every year; the movies and newspapers were full of talk about sex and money. People seemed to have forgotten that it was God who was in charge of things. She was particularly disturbed by racial prejudice. How could a person go to Mass on Sunday and then on Monday call someone a nigger? She set down these feelings in a poem, "God's Paintbrush and Yours":

> To each of our brothers God gave a skin
> With his paintbrush He blended its tone
> From the darkest and lightest and most vivid shades
> He fashioned for each one his own

A Catholic magazine accepted her poem, and she immediately got to work on an essay called "Let Your Children Sanctify You!":

Like all mothers, I too love my children dearly. But three babies in three years began to play hob with my normally easy-going disposition. Somewhere along the line, I had lost my *eternal sense of values*. Immersed in the business of dishes and diapers, I was acting like a *citizen* of Earth, instead of a *pilgrim*. These children of mine with the endless duties their care imposed upon me were all meant by God, in His Plan, to be used by me to gain Heaven. That was my Revolutionary Realization!

You can let these circumstances frustrate, irritate, and annoy you. OR you can recognize them for what they really are: the many chances God is giving you to overcome the "I will" part of you. The part of you that prevents you from fulfilling what you pray for daily: "THY will be done on EARTH as it is in HEAVEN." This self-abnegation, the spiritual writers tell us, must be completed before we may enjoy the Beatific Vision.

Live all your moments in the presence of God. Irritations are inevitably bound up as part of daily living. Allow all these irritations to act on you like many tiny grains of sand, that they may serve to polish your soul and smooth away the rough edges of unconformity to the will of God, and leave you perfect and shining—ready for Heaven!

This, then, was the chief aim of life, as Veronica and Paul saw it: to prepare their family for admittance to Heaven. So while the other children of Northport were discovering the joys of television, the young Dubners were kneeling on the living room floor to recite the Rosary and to pray for the conversion of Russia. On holy days, they marched through the yard in a procession to honor the Virgin Mary, their little necks draped in scapulars, their little hands pressed together just beneath the chin in perfect prayerful formation.

Joe and Mary were now attending parochial school at St. Philip Neri, the local parish. On the sidewalk after Mass on Sunday, they watched in awe as their parents chatted with the priest as if he were just another person. Then the priest came to their house for supper! Following their mother's cue, they would execute a precise Sign of the Cross, then recite the supper prayer, enunciating every single steep and foreign sound: "Bless us, O Lord, and these, Thy gifts, which we are about to receive, from Thy bounty, through Christ, Our Lord. Amen." What wonderful children these are, the priest would say, biting into his meatloaf, which tasted quite unlike any other meatloaf he had ever been offered, thanks to the cup of wheat germ that Veronica had folded in.

Joe had by this time become an altar boy, and he liked it. The main appeal was the Latin. Although he didn't care much about the words' meaning, he admired the supremely logical manner in which the language was put together. Already Joe's mind was drawn to systems of logic, math and science in particular, especially when he realized that such systems, when placed in the hands of, say, a rocket scientist, could produce massive explosions.

Joe was enthusiastic about anything that blew up, and he followed the talk of the threatening Atomic War with a mixture of excitement and fear. Because he believed that an atomic bomb might well explode over Northport in the dead of night—it would definitely be the dead of night—he prayed that his family would be spared. His prayers seemed to work, for the Bomb didn't fall. But when he forgot to pray and the Bomb still didn't fall, he concluded that his prayers had nothing to do with it, and he stopped wasting his time.

As Joe grew older, he recognized that his family was different. His classmates at St. Philip Neri also went to Mass on Sunday, but they didn't have to say the Rosary every night or write their own Passion Plays for Easter, as Joe had to. He also realized that his family didn't have much money. Other kids had television sets and went to movies and even took vacations. In his house everything was homemade. At Christmastime he and his sisters made tree ornaments by cutting out the colored pictures in flower catalogs.

Then there was the food. Even the food that looked normal, like the meat loaf, always had something healthy hidden inside. Joe never asked his friends over for supper because the food was too weird and his father was too square. He was always whistling old-fashioned songs and didn't have a single cool thing to say about rockets or race cars or even baseball. Besides, Joe knew that his mother would try to talk Joe out of inviting the kids he wanted over for supper because they weren't good-enough Catholics or maybe weren't even Catholic at all. The only kids that were 100 percent okay to play with, he knew, were the Winks and the Burkes and the Prachers and the Kennedys.

Joe knew that his parents hadn't always been Catholic. They told him that they had once been Jewish but then became Catholic. In Joe's eyes, this was a good thing. He had learned from his classmates at St. Philip Neri that Jews were greedy and had hooked noses and that everybody hated them, just as Hitler hated them.

From what Joe knew firsthand, a Jew was very old and talked with a funny accent, like Grandma and Grandpa, his mother's parents. They visited every few months. Even though they were Jews, Joe liked them fine, in part because they brought good presents: wiggle pictures for him and change purses for his sisters. Grandma always complained about the mess in the kitchen: broken teacups waiting for glue, tubs of rising bread dough, stacks of Catholic magazines. Grandpa would just try to find somewhere comfortable to sit and hold Martha or Ann on his knee.

About once a year Joe and the others would visit their grandparents in Brooklyn. Their street was busy, and their house was dark and crowded and full of treasures: a thick oak banister to slide down when no one was looking, a miniature tea set carved from peach pits that Mary and Martha played with all day. Grandma made Jewish food like borscht, which was purple and came from beets, but Joe liked it anyway, especially how it looked like a pinwheel when you swirled in the sour cream.

One time Grandma came to Northport by herself, on the train. From this fact alone, Joe, the young master of logic, deduced that Grandpa had died. He was right.

Veronica, who had already attended her father's funeral, hadn't yet told her children the news. Perhaps, if Joe had not queried her, she might have simply let them wonder about their grandfather's absence, as she herself had been left to wonder about her grandfather Moishe when he failed to appear at the Passover table.

Harry Greenglass had lived seventy years, the last ones certainly better than the first, and he died at home without a struggle. Dr. Zatz told Veronica that he'd had diabetes and a weak heart, and was lucky to have lasted as long as he had. Still, she was shaken by his death. He was easily her closest friend in the family. She and Della had never been very sisterly, and as of late, they had practically stopped speaking. Esther was mellowing somewhat in her old age, but she was still Esther. Harry was the one person who had accepted Veronica as she was. She had always been grateful for his reaction to her conversion. She often thought about his baptism of desire, or at least what *she* considered his baptism of desire. She comforted herself with the thought that she would see him again one day in Heaven.

After Harry's death, Esther stayed with the family in Northport for several days. When Veronica put her on the train back for Brooklyn, Esther hollered out the window: Name the baby after Papa!

Veronica was indeed pregnant again, and she honored her mother's request. After a run of three girls, she finally had another son, and he was christened Peter Harry Joseph Dubner. He was a chunky baby, with gorgeous brown eyes that made even grown women blush.

The Dubners' little house on Kalmia Street had grown too small for all their children. And Paul's paycheck had a habit of going too fast. But Veronica was five children richer than she'd been just seven years ago, and she hadn't a single regret.

11

5. SHORTLY after my mother became a Catholic, she legally adopted her stage name, Florence Winters. (Esther had considered this yet another act of family betrayal.) Winters, then, and not Greenglass, was the name she used on her marriage certificate and her children's birth certificates. Even her closest friends thought her maiden name to be Winters. Many years later, when I asked why she had so thoroughly done away with Greenglass, she explained that it had nothing to do with the Jewishness of the name; Winters, she explained, was simply prettier.

True as that may be, at one point in her distant past, my mother benefited greatly from having changed her name.

Esther telephoned her one evening in mid-June of 1950 to say that David Greenglass, Uncle Barney's son, had been arrested. The FBI said he was a member of a Soviet spy ring. It seemed too ridiculous to believe—little David a Russian spy?

David was now twenty-eight years old, just a few months

younger than Veronica. He had always struck her as pleasant enough, if a bit simple. As children, he and his sister, Ethel, used to visit Harry's candy store for the free licorice, and Veronica played with them every year at their grandmother's Seder. But she had never been close to her cousins, and once she moved to Long Island, she barely heard from them.

David had married his longtime sweetheart, Ruth Printz, and they still lived on the Lower East Side. Like Uncle Barney, David was good at fixing machinery. After the war he had opened a machine shop with his brother Bernie and his brother-in-law, Julius Rosenberg.

Julie and Ethel had married years ago and had two sons. Aunt Tessie, Ethel's mother, didn't care much for any of them, especially Julie. He was an intellectual, an ardent Communist who talked on and on about how capitalism itself had brought on the Depression. Aunt Tessie might not have objected so much if Julie, way back when he and Ethel were dating, hadn't roped David into his radical politics. But David looked up to Ethel and Julie, his energetic big sister and his sophisticated brother-in-law, and like them, he joined the Young Communist League.

During the war, the Army put David to work as a machinist. In August 1944 he was transferred to Los Alamos, New Mexico. There, he wrote to his wife, he was working on something big: "a classified top secrecy project and as such I can't say anything. In fact, I am not even supposed to say this much. . . . P.S.: Not a word to anybody about anything except maybe Julie."

After the war, the family would learn that David's top-secret project really was something big: the atomic bomb that the Allies dropped on Japan.

This news in itself would have been enough to plunge the entire Greenglass family into a prolonged fit of whispered gossip. But now the FBI was saying that David was part of a Communist spy ring that had given the secrets of the atom bomb to the Soviets.

When Esther phoned Veronica, she said that the FBI had

quizzed and quizzed David, and he'd finally confessed that yes, he did it, but that his brother-in-law, Julie, had put him up to it. Within weeks David Greenglass was all over the newspapers and the FBI arrested Julie. A month later came an even greater shock: Ethel was also arrested, and her sons, Michael and Robby, were sent to stay with Aunt Tessie.

Veronica was horrified. It was hard to believe that her cousins were Soviet spies. But if the FBI had arrested them—especially Ethel, the mother of two young boys—they must have done *something* wrong. Veronica had never been proud of the fact that Ethel and Julie were Communists. Still, as often as she prayed for the conversion of Russia, Communism had always seemed a distant and theoretical enemy.

The Atomic War, though, was another matter. Joe, for one, had been having nightmares about the Russians dropping the Bomb on Kalmia Street. Now the government was saying that David, Ethel, and Julie had jeopardized the life of every man, woman, and child in America. Veronica couldn't bring herself to read the newspapers, and she refused to discuss the situation with Paul. The best she could do was to keep her children ignorant of the scandal and be thankful that no one in Northport could possibly suspect that the Dubners were in any way connected to the Greenglasses.

Within the Greenglass family, the affair grew more pitiful by the day. David's wife, Ruth, couldn't see why David should risk as harsh a punishment as Julie, who had dragged him into the mess. Ruth herself stood to be implicated; she too was in the Young Communist League and had figured prominently in David's confession. David was tortured by the possibility of Ruth's being arrested, and he told the FBI that he would kill himself if that happened. So it was decided that David would plead guilty and testify against his brother-in-law and, if necessary, his sister.

In his confession David told the FBI what had happened: In New Mexico he met with a man named Harry Gold, to whom he handed over information about a few of the Los Alamos scientists and a sketch he'd made of something called a high-explosive lens mold. Harry Gold, David said, had been sent by Julius Rosenberg.

To Veronica and everyone else, Ethel's role in the spy ring was most unclear. David, when first questioned by the FBI, said that his sister wasn't involved. But now there she was, sitting in the women's prison in Greenwich Village, her husband in the Federal House of Detention, her own brother ready to help send them to the electric chair.

Then there was Aunt Tessie. Veronica's family was well aware of Tessie's disdain for her only daughter. First Ethel had fallen in love with singing and then with Julius Rosenberg and his Communism; to Tessie, Ethel was a snob, worrying over Italian arias and Russian peasants instead of her own family. And if it weren't for Ethel, David wouldn't be in such trouble now. But he was, and everyone on the Lower East Side knew it. Tessie went to Ethel in prison and tried to drill some reality into her: If you don't talk, she screamed, you're gonna burn with your husband! Tessie was also threatening to turn over Ethel's sons to the police; they were too unruly, she said, and she was too old to care for them.

Veronica, now that Harry was dead, tried to visit her mother in Brooklyn when she could. She arrived one afternoon to find Aunt Tessie in the living room. She was tense and had put on weight. Esther made tea. The three women could muster only five minutes' worth of harmless chatter. A hard silence overtook them, and then Tessie exploded: Why can't anybody in this family talk about anything! You can't pretend it didn't happen! Everybody's afraid to talk about it, afraid to ask any questions!

They tried then to discuss David and Ethel's tragedy. Veronica and Esther offered what support they could, but the situation was relentlessly grim—especially since Tessie had by now followed through on her threat and sent Ethel's sons away, to the Hebrew Children's Home.

Ethel and Julius Rosenberg went on trial on March 6, 1951. David and Ruth Greenglass testified against them, and within a month, they were found guilty by a jury of twelve and sentenced to die.

There were many Americans who believed this to be a just outcome. While these little Jewish Communists from the Lower East Side hardly seemed capable of arranging as massive an event as the Atomic War, death was plainly the only punishment to fit their crime.

There were many others who thought that the evidence against the Rosenbergs, especially Ethel, was ludicrously thin to have produced a conviction at all, much less a death sentence.

And then there were those who believed that any scenario calling for a man to bear fatal witness against his sister, and for an old woman to dispossess her own grandchildren, was simply too bleak to contemplate.

By now it was not just America that was transfixed by the Rosenbergs' plight. In Paris and Milan and London, protesters clogged the public squares, calling for the executions to be stopped.

Veronica had a hard time working up as much enthusiasm as the protesters. According to Our Lady of Fátima, Communism was the world's most powerful demon. Whether or not Ethel and Julie were "atom spies," they were certainly Communists.

Two years dragged by until Ethel and Julie were finally killed in the electric chair. Veronica never spoke to Ethel after she was arrested, and she averted her eyes whenever she saw a headline about the affair. She felt a deep sadness, certainly, and unremitting shame—both about the crime and the manner in which her family had warred with itself—but never the outrage of so many people who hadn't even known her cousin. With any luck, the scandal would become yet another piece of Veronica's past that was best forgotten.

12

THE week after Ethel and Julius Rosenberg were sentenced to death, my father received an early-morning phone call from his brother Nat: Shepsel, who had been sick with stomach cancer, was now dead.

Paul dressed in silence and took the train into the city alone. He didn't know how he would be received. Veronica had never met most of his relatives, and the funeral of the man who had forsworn Paul's very existence hardly seemed the proper occasion.

Brownsville had fallen into decline. The empty lots were piled high with garbage; the laughter floating from doorways carried an edge of menace. The shoe store on Pitkin Avenue was boarded up, and the floor above, where the synagogue choir used to practice for Kol Nidre, had become a pool hall.

The funeral home was a squat, ugly building, the heavy chairs nicked with use, the pinkish carpeting worn to the nub in the center aisle. Up in the front rows Paul spotted his brothers and sisters, their husbands and wives, his nieces and nephews, and his stepmother, Olga. Behind them sat Tante Peshe with her family. Tante Yidis had died, and Tante Chaya, having feuded with Shepsel for years over a loan he was slow to repay, had refused to attend.

Paul made his way toward the front rows. A man from the funeral home, a tiny, hunched-over man wearing a huge yarmulke, stepped in and blocked his way. Shepsel Dubner, though he had spent the last month of his life in a hospital ward, racked by cancer, had at least had the foresight to leave instructions preventing his dead son from defiling his corpse.

Later, at the cemetery, the crooked little man again shooed Paul away as Shepsel's body was lowered into the ground, the coffin stuffed with prayer books from the synagogue, an honor reserved for the most pious men.

Paul rode with Nat and Dottie and Mickey to his sister Fanny's house, where the family was sitting shiva. Here the reception was only slightly warmer. From the sour look on Tante Peshe's face, Paul knew he shouldn't even approach her. His brother Morris scooted into the bathroom whenever Paul came near; his brother Martin finally agreed to accept the scrap of paper on which Paul had written his address, but Martin gave no indication that he would write.

When he arrived home that evening, Veronica thought he had come down with the flu. His face was gray and expressionless, his shoulders slumped. Though it was still early, he wanted to go to bed. No, he said, he didn't feel like talking about it.

What was my father feeling that night as he pulled the blankets up over his head? Remorse? Guilt? Was it pure anger, or perhaps relief?

Any answer would only be a guess, for he never told anyone. He never really spoke about his father again—for what could be said about a man who, even from the other side of life, could hurt him so?

*   *   *

THE world that my parents had created for themselves was infinitely more promising than the one they had abandoned. Had they ever harbored the slightest doubt (and they hadn't), the deaths of Shepsel and Harry, the stain of the Rosenberg tragedy, the manner in which their families were slavishly tied to a cramped and crumbling Brooklyn—all this would easily have pacified them. Their pasts reeked of the past. Esther's visits alone carried with them an entire Dark Age of claustrophobia and paranoia.

The life they had invented, meanwhile, and the future they were working toward—a future that would see them and their children enthroned in Heaven—was a boundless horizon of shimmering grace.

It was true that my father, in the wake of Shepsel's death, began once again to experience periods of deep melancholy. He was constantly worried about providing for the family. But there were other, nameless anxieties, which he couldn't or wouldn't articulate. For an entire day or even two, he would fall into a black mood, during which he kept himself in bed. It wasn't that his family's presence disturbed *him*, he told my mother; rather, he didn't want the children to see him like this, for fear they'd think he was angry with them.

It was also true that the family had outgrown Long Island. Northport had been the perfect place to launch their brood. Now, though, too many refugees from Brooklyn and Queens had gotten the same idea. The farm near St. Philip Neri where my mother and the children dug potatoes for a penny a pound had just been cleared for a supermarket. The wooded field between Kalmia Street and the VA Hospital was dotted with red plastic flags, the first signs of a housing development.

The Dubners were experiencing their own housing crunch. The three girls were getting too big for the single attic bedroom. Joe, long used to his independence, now shared a room with his baby brother Peter.

And another child was on the way. Born in May 1956, he was named David Gerard Joseph Dubner, David being a name my parents had long cherished and Gerard being a long-overdue tribute to the saint of healthy pregnancies and safe deliveries. Dave was a lively child but he almost never spoke. For some time, my mother was worried. Then she realized that he rarely spoke because he rarely had the need: He would merely point a finger or shift his eyes, and at least one of his three sisters would dart to the object of his desire and place it in his hands.

The other families in my parents' circle—the Winks, the Prachers, the Burkes, the Kennedys—had also reproduced with vigor. Once again there was talk of a communal farm. My father had grown particularly friendly with Rudy Pracher, a sheet-metal mechanic and devoted Catholic with a blazing sense of humor. The two men took a few exploratory trips, once nearly committing their meager savings to a ramshackle farm in Catskill, New York, whose chief crop was frogs' legs—which, the real-estate man assured them, were about to replace hamburgers as America's favorite food. Under further scrutiny, however, the commune plan once again fell apart.

But the urge to escape Long Island was great. My parents and the other families wanted more space for their children, more land for bigger gardens, more protection from the secular world. Northport had been a sleepy town with a solid parish and a good Catholic school, but the recent flood of New Yorkers was producing a culture of materialism and television and money, a culture of What I Have instead of What I Am. My parents didn't consider it their job to be judgmental; it was, though, their job to insulate their children from that culture.

The Winks were the first to decamp, to Florida. Peggy had developed rheumatoid arthritis and needed a warmer climate. Soon it was the Dubners' turn. After ten years of marriage and six children, after watching their family ties slacken, unravel, and fray, they were ready for yet another new beginning.

My father was by nature an enthusiastic but cautious man who, had he not met my mother and fallen so dizzyingly in love with her, might never have dared step so far outside the worn and narrow path his bloodline had bequeathed him.

My mother was by nature a kind but headstrong woman who, had she not met my father and fallen so appreciatively in love with him, might never have thought to convert her restlessness into such single-minded devotion.

As it was, they filled each other's gaps, slid into each other's grooves. Together they now conspired to throw off the inertia that was settling around the ankles of their generation, the thickening pool of complacency and vulgarity and plastic-wrapped food. All this and more they deserted, charging northward, inward, upward, charging *back to the land* (as if they'd come from it in the first place!), charging toward a place where neither the creep of modernity nor the claws of the past could reach them, a place they prayed would be nothing less than their own Eden.

Sol Dubner with family in Brooklyn, about 1923: (*from left*)
Sol, Fanny, Shepsel, Martin, Bess, Gittel, Nat, and Morris.

Sol Dubner (*second from left*) with friends in Brooklyn before World War II.

Sol Dubner during World War II in Hawaii, site of his Catholic baptism.

Shepsel Dubner, in the late 1940s.

Harry Greenglass, Florence's father.

Esther Greenglass, Florence's mother.

Florence Greenglass (*center*) with grandmother Sorah-Rukhel and sister, Della, circa 1925.

Florence and Della outside the family's home in Brooklyn, in 1943.

Florence (*second from right*) in Madame Souvorina's studio;
Gertrude Smith is at far right. (GERARD ALPHENAAR)

The wedding day of Florence and Sol, henceforth known as Veronica and Paul Dubner, March 2, 1946, with (*from left*) George Reilly, Gertrude Smith, and Bill Wink.

BOOK
TWO

Enough is as good as a feast.

—*John Heywood*

1

THE home into which I was born indeed felt like Eden, or at least what I knew about Eden as a child. There was natural bounty. There was temptation. And there was the inescapable sense that God was lurking in every quarter, at every moment.

From my earliest cognizançe, I accepted the premise that God could be everywhere at once, hovering about with paternal vigilance and pride. But I suspected, especially on those summer evenings when we all knelt on the grass to recite the Rosary, the wind rustling the cornstalks, that perhaps God hovered a bit more appreciatively over our house, like a bumblebee that can't tear itself away from a particularly succulent bloom.

I was of two minds about my family's Godfulness.

We lived on the old Gallupville Road, which was lined with hayfields and wind-bent pine trees and the occasional farmhouse like ours. It connected nothing but the tiny village of Quaker Street (one and six-tenths miles away, with one each of stoplight, general store, diner, and tavern) and Gallupville (four miles to the south, and only slightly larger). Gallupville Road, therefore, was lightly traveled. But spread out there on the lawn for our evening Rosary, I would shudder whenever the sound of a car did arise, for that car might carry a friend or classmate whose sighting of us would only reinforce the belief that the Dubners lived in the district of Devotion that bordered on Fanatical. It was one thing to be known as a churchgoing family and quite another to pray right out there on your own property.

On the other hand, our Godfulness—or the Godfulness of my parents, I should say, for while none of us would dare disobey, we were essentially actors working with an immutable script— gave our home a sense of purpose, rightfulness, safety. Ours would never be a home in which the mother sat up all night with her bottle of cherry schnapps or where a father lingered too long in his daughter's bedroom after tucking her in. Those things happened in other houses. I doubt that any of us appreciated this distinction until much later, until we got out and saw how arbitrary and vulgar the real world could be. In that regard (and that regard alone), our parents spoiled us: We expected the world to be as pure as they were.

Before I was born, when they decided to flee Long Island, my parents were drawn to the cheap land and bedrock morals of upstate New York. Esther Greenglass declared that her daughter had gone mad. Upstate New York, she said, was nothing but poisonous snakes and wild Indians, and Veronica was willfully endangering the lives of her children (not to mention moving them nearly out of visiting range).

They rented a tenant house on a dairy farm near Middleburg, a small town lodged in the Schoharie River Valley, a hundred and fifty miles north of New York City. The house could accommodate, if barely, my parents and their six children; it would do fine while they scouted for the right place to buy.

Middleburg was placid and welcoming, its Catholic priest enthusiastic, its fertile flatlands ringed by steep wooded hills. In 1957, when my parents moved there, it was still a thriving farm town. More and more men, though, had begun to commute to Schenectady, a three-hour round-trip, for the high-paying jobs at General Electric. But my father didn't like the idea of spending all that time away from the family, so he cobbled together part-time work closer to home. At the nearby Caterpillar factory, he assembled the heavy machinery and worked as the company timekeeper. He also sold an occasional article to the *Schenectady Gazette*, rural dispatches about wayward deer crashing through barbershop windows and the like. He was paid just three cents a word, but he would have done it for free, sustained by the thrill of seeing his byline in a real daily newspaper.

Within a year, my parents discovered that Eden truly lay within their reach. Twelve miles from Middleburg, they spotted a hundred-year-old farmhouse with a barn, a garage, a chicken coop, and thirty-six acres of land. The house—with five bedrooms, wideboard floors, and hand-hewn woodwork—was only slightly dilapidated, certainly no more so than the outbuildings. The land was rocky, far less fertile than in Middleburg, but it was pleasing to the sight and easily sufficient for the growing needs of one family. And, as if the farm had been stamped with a divine imprimatur, the nearest Catholic church had been named after their beloved Our Lady of Fátima. On July 1, 1958, Paul and Veronica Dubner agreed to pay $6,900 for the Ottman farm on the old Gallupville Road in the township of Duanesburg.

On my mother's birthday that year, her thirty-seventh, my father made her a card, as always. This year, though, he didn't write the usual silly rhyme or limerick. This year he wrote like a man jolted by the realization of how far he'd come, or perhaps of how his life might have otherwise unspooled:

Dear Veronica,

On this day I again want to tell you I love you with all my heart. You are a marvelous wife to me and a wonderful mother to our dear children.

God bless you with many, many more birthdays.

Love,
Paul

My mother was pregnant again by the time they settled into the farmhouse. On the February morning that she went into labor, the roads were lined with seven-foot snowbanks and there was talk of another storm. Upstate winters had proved an unpleasant surprise; the year before, the state had to airlift hay into Duanesburg for the snowed-in cattle.

Now my father panicked about driving to the hospital in Schenectady. What if he slid into a snowbank with his wife about to give birth?

So, with my mother calming him, he drove very, very slowly—he drove slowly even in the safest conditions—and Elizabeth Mary Dubner was born without a hitch. She was cheerful, affectionate, and generally satisfied to operate in the shadow of her six siblings. The farmhouse had easily found its stride—a singular, rollicking, Godful stride.

Beth remained the baby of the family until August 1963, when I assumed that position. My mother was forty-one years old, my father forty-seven, and they had procreated to their fullest. There were now eight of us, with Joe going on seventeen. The farm was so overrun by Dubners and Dubner activity that there remained but a single indicator of its previous ownership; a small white O painted near the top of the chimney. Only much later would I learn that the O had belonged to the previous owners, the Ottmans; I grew up believing it to be a halo left behind by one of the angels who ferried Santa Claus down the chimney, for in our family's telling, the reindeer were barely mentioned, serving only as brute transportation for the squadron of angels that actually directed the mission.

To me, the farmhouse was magical, it was Eden, it was life itself, and it engendered a foolhardy attachment. One summer afternoon, soon after I was old enough to bicycle into Quaker Street by myself, I was riding home when I heard the town fire siren. I knew that it was my house on fire. I stood up and pedaled in that desperate standing-up way, my thighs scorching with pain, and arrived home in tears.

The house was not on fire on that day or any other. But I lived in absolute dread that something would happen to it or, I suppose, to my family. Not that I could so easily distinguish the two: It was a temple, the house was, and while its sanctity seemed linked to my family, it never dawned on me to contemplate my family outside that house or that house without my family. Our entire history lived within its walls.

Gallupville Road bent like an elbow around our property, running the length of the hayfield and the raspberry patch, then turning to hug the garden, the cornfield, the asparagus bed, and the barn before heading up the Coles and Gluesings' Hill. The Coles and Gluesings were Mrs. Cole and Mr. Gluesing, a widow and widower who had become companions late in life. They had a fruit orchard and honeybee hives and the best catfish pond within miles, which went unfished except by us. Twice a year they came over for supper. They were white-haired, amiable, full of the tolerance of old age. After a long and noisy bout with the ten of us and a pair of roast chickens, fresh from the coop, the Coles and Gluesings would be escorted to the couch, above which hung a framed painting of the Crucifixion, and sit through a parade of our various talents: piano playing, cartwheeling, the exhibition of postage stamp and Holy Card collections, and the world-class dog tricks of Montgomery and Gustav, Montgomery performed by Beth and Gustav by me, with Dave playing the iron-willed trainer with the German accent.

We had real dogs too, of course, the first of my era being Prince, a silky black-and-white mutt with knowing eyes. My father loved Prince very much. I knew this to be true because my father, flummoxed by his number of offspring, sometimes called me Prince by mistake. "Stevie," my mother later explained, "Dad would never have called you Prince if he didn't love you, because you know how much he loves Prince, and since Prince is only a dog and you're our son, he loves you even more." I was flattered that, amid the din, anyone had bothered to notice that my feelings might have been hurt.

The dog was only a sliver of our menagerie. At one point the farm was home to twenty-three cats, all of which lived in the barn except Doxology, whose name came from a prayer in the Mass. There were also a few dozen chickens, a cow, a pair of goats, the occasional pig, and a flock of ducklings. The mother of these ducklings, who was negligent, once deserted them in a freezing downpour. This prompted a rescue by *my* mother, who, despite squawks of protest from my sisters, shoved the waterlogged ducklings into the oven on a cookie sheet to warm them up. (They lived.)

Such was her way. Poverty and eight children had forced her to become a master of risk calculation. She did not have time for indecision. She was the chief agent of our household's cooking, mending, spanking, garden weeding and vegetable canning, cow milking and chicken slaying, bedtime praying and Rosary saying, banking and bill paying, plumber calling and dentist visiting, report-card signing and Halloween-costume making, Little League–game attending and emergency-room hauling, and whatever else came up. Her position required constant invention and efficient delegation: Each week she posted a new duty roster on the pantry door, rotating the chores among the eight of us. (Entire allowances were spent to buy one's way out of shoveling chicken manure.) Above all, my mother's position demanded a zero tolerance of dissent. If anyone dared complain—about the hand-me-down clothes or the odd-duck bag lunches she packed for school (tuna fish on homemade wheat bread with bean sprouts)—she had a ready response: "We could have been rich in either money or children, and we chose the children, and if we hadn't, you wouldn't be around to complain. Dad is working very hard to put food on our table, and I'm working very hard to run this house, and if you think you can do it better, then be my guest."

Shortly after settling in Duanesburg, my father had found an accounting job at the Army Depot in Rotterdam, where he worked until about a year after I was born. The job paid ninety-five dollars a week, which, along with an extra weekly shift as a janitor, and the Army Surplus cheese and peanut butter he brought home (the cheese in massive, gelatinous bricks, the peanut butter in two-pound tin cans with an inch of oil on top), and the output of our garden and chickens and cow, and the profits from our roadside sales of tomatoes and pumpkins, and my mother's mastery of thrift, kept the family fed.

As the youngest member of this far-ranging operation, I found its momentum dazzling. I knew that my family was unlike any other, and not just because of its size. On television—my parents had finally relented after years without a set—I had seen an Apollo rocket blurring through space. I knew this to be a marvel, for everyone said so. But to me, it seemed fairly straightforward: a giant bottle rocket. My family was a far greater spectacle, an imponderably dense collection of bodies in orbit, laws and by-laws, public transactions and stolen privacies, exceptions and mysteries, all its energies directed toward a mission whose goal I couldn't articulate but that I knew to be centered on God. I wanted to know everything about this enterprise, and my want was only deepened by the realization that I never could.

In the presence of my much older, bigger, abler sisters and brothers, I felt invisible, but happily so, as if I were free to observe all they did with no one observing me. I would wander into this room or that, seeking clues, fathoming connections. I stood and

stared a lot. If challenged, I might say I was looking for my sack
of marbles, or Prince.

"Well, Prince isn't allowed in our *bed*room."

"Oh, okay."

The Girls' Room—the upstairs bedroom shared by Mary and
Martha, later by Martha and Ann—was easily the most intoxi-
cating room in the house. It had Beatles music and Aqua Net
clouds and my sisters themselves, goddesses touched equally by
Catholic virtue and feminine allure.

The house was huge, and mazy. It had been built in the Greek
Revival style. At least that is what we were told by a man who
stopped in one day. He was an architect, he said, and was taking
photographs for a book about farmhouses. My mother was skep-
tical. But since he actually took a picture of our house (there was
probably no film in the camera, my mother told us), and since it
didn't cost anything (if there *were* film, she said, he'd surely try
to sell us a print later), we believed him, and from that point on
we proudly affixed those sleek words, "Greek Revival," to any
conversation about our formerly plain white farmhouse.

For many years it had been a two-family home, and it still had
two front doors, two staircases, and two living rooms, one of
which was called the Green Room, as my mother had painted it
the color of a Granny Smith apple. The second living room was
called the Other Side, being on the other side of the house from
the kitchen, which was where my parents made all their important
decisions, late at night, once we were all asleep.

Off the kitchen was the Freezer Room. This was a small dark
space best suited for storing galoshes or perhaps a wet dog. But
it housed our gargantuan deep freezer, bought with the disability
money my father received when he smashed his finger at the Caterpillar factory. The Freezer Room was also crammed with tee-
tering pyramids of canning jars, a stand of broken broom handles
and bent curtain rods, and heaps of previous years' Christmas
wrapping, including the ribbon, rewound onto empty tomato-

paste cans. In our house there was little distinction between the sacred sins of the Ten Commandments and the secular sins taught by our parents. Of these, waste was the most dire. Pencil stubs, junk-mail envelopes, twice-used nails: None of these were thrown away. Everything had been provided by God and was therefore precious to the end; just as important, we could not afford not to recycle.

The greatest secular sin was the wasting of food. Our freezer contained hundreds of misshapen foil-wrapped objects, seldom labeled, often older than I, perhaps a slab of venison donated by a hunter who'd tromped through our woods or a clump of soup bones. On the rare occasion that someone baked cookies, my mother would wrap them in foil, label the package as liver, and toss it in the freezer.

The Freezer Room was a jungle, thick with uncertainty and mice. A trip inside bordered on punishment. If my mother were to holler out through the screen door, "Stevie, go into the Freezer Room and see if you can find some corn on the cob for supper," I would gauge whether I could afford to pretend I hadn't heard her and, if not, pull on my father's thick green rubber boots, prop open the door to let in some light, climb the step stool to reach the freezer door, and whisper the prayer my mother had taught for such occasions:

> *Saint Anthony, Saint Anthony*
> *Please come around*
> *The corn is lost*
> *And it MUST BE FOUND*

If I found some corn, Saint Anthony had successfully interceded. If not, God had intended us to eat something else that night. These, I knew, were the vagaries of prayer, and I accepted them. Prayer was as essential as food. Prayer was how we talked to God, and it was God, I knew, more than the efforts of my father and mother and all of us combined, who allowed us to survive.

The center of our house, its true heart, was the Green Room. This is where we did jigsaw puzzles on the floor, recited the Rosary in cold weather, and held family meetings, at which my father awarded a nickel for any suggestion that would improve the efficiency of the home operation.

On a small bookcase in the Green Room rested a porcelain statue of the Infant of Prague. On one wall hung the Crucifixion painting around which we congregated at three o'clock in the afternoon on Good Friday for fifteen minutes of silent prayer in commemoration of Jesus' suffering. Next to the painting was the Emergency Crucifix. If someone were to die in the house, a call would be placed to Father DiPace, and he would come and open up the Emergency Crucifix, which was hollow and contained a special candle and the rites of Extreme Unction. On the opposite wall hung a circle of photographs of all eight of us kids, and in the center, a picture of my parents in front of the church, Our Lady of Fátima, my mother with her dancer's posture, back slightly arched and one foot thrust forward, my father wearing a jowly smile, his hair clipped into a severe brush cut, thick-lensed glasses beneath his bushy gray eyebrows.

These were the only pictures on display in the house, and I never had reason to think that our family extended beyond its walls. I knew that the dour old woman who had visited once or twice was my mother's mother. But in no way did she seem like a member of my family. My family shed bright light; she cast a deep shadow. Her toenails were long and scratchy, and she was always asking Martha or Ann to trim them. When she visited, the Infant of Prague was sent to the closet and all the crucifixes and paintings had to be removed from the walls. She was the first person I ever knew to die, and because her death generated no real upset as far as I could see—even my mother did not seem very sad, and it was her own mother who had died—I assumed that death was not such a terrible thing.

The Green Room was also where, if you were feeling sick, you could sleep on the couch. From there you could hear the kitchen conversation, for the two rooms were separated by an open wall of shelves, which were overflowing with vitamin bottles and scratch paper and charity requests from the Sisters of This and the Brothers of That, all of whom would eventually receive fifty cents or a dollar.

In the kitchen, late at night, my mother and father would sit with their instant coffee, the fluorescent light buzzing, and I knew of nothing more precious than to lie sick, or claiming sickness, on that couch, drifting to sleep under the hum of their table talk, a safe gray hum about a new furnace or a new pump for the well, a conversation including snatches of Yiddish when they knew I was still awake. But I wasn't listening for content. Just to be near them, their voices, their *adultness,* was all I wanted. Years later, I would learn what sometimes happened after I fell asleep: The hum of their talk would shift from gray to desperate, my father's head in his hands, crying softly at our midnight kitchen table, my mother gripping his forearm and whispering to him, "Paul, you just do your best and let me worry about the money."

Between the Green Room and the Other Side lay a dark, twisting hallway. Inch for inch, this was the richest piece of house. At one end was the game closet: chess men stored in cookie tins, board games with missing pieces, huge blocks of playing cards, five or six decks all mixed up and rubber-banded together. Sometimes I sat on a footstool in the game-closet corner waiting for someone to pass by: "Hey, Beth, wanna do a puzzle? . . . Hey, Pete, wanna play War?"

Near the game closet, beneath the staircase, hung our coats, those very personal outer skins of my siblings and parents, aromatic with their travels: the Coles and Gluesings' spice-and-cider kitchen; the dead-flower smell of the church basement; a musty, vinegary odor I couldn't place—the firehouse? the high-school gym? cigarette smoke!

And the telephone was in the hallway. Those walls knew everything that I wanted to know. How Martha whispered her good-night I-love-you to her boyfriend, Gary from Schoharie. How Ann was talked into putting marbles—real ones, and mine—into a girlfriend's marble-food birthday cake. How Dave, the cool rebel, lined up all his cool rebel doings.

Sometimes we got a long-distance call. We had all been drilled for this possibility; we knew to scream, "Mom, long distance!" A long-distance call usually meant Joe. He had joined the Air Force right after high school and had barely been home since, so I knew him mainly from pictures and gossip.

"Joe thought he'd die if he had to stay in this house another day," I heard Mary say one time. I was bewildered. How could anyone want to leave this house, ever?

Beyond the hallway lay the Other Side, which is where we played music, read, and, very occasionally, watched television. (Lawrence Welk was the lone performer my parents wholeheartedly endorsed.) There was an old upright piano and a battered bookcase that held the family library: *Christ Is Alive!, The Silver Chalice, Profiles in Courage,* and a series of biographies about the saints, written for teenagers.

Just about everyone played the piano. My mother, when pressed, would perform her Bach étude. Peter was the best, on piano and every other instrument. Someone would bring home a trumpet or flute from school, and within half an hour Peter was playing a song on it. At Christmastime, he would take over the piano for carols, the rest of us singing, reaching for too-high harmonies, covering up with a jokey trill, the way my father trilled when he sang "My Yiddishe Mama," my mother laughing along but asking that we end with "Silent Night," sung respectfully, no joking around.

The Other Side is also where we erected the Christmas tree, which we cut down in our woods and decorated with homemade paper chains and a tiny blue angel on top. Only when the tree was finished were we allowed to lay out the miniature manger scene on top of the piano. The cradle was left empty until Christmas Eve. Other families put the Baby Jesus in his cradle from the outset, but we knew this to be historically inaccurate.

Our parents were always saying that Christmas wasn't about presents, that it was a birthday party for the Baby Jesus. That's why we had a birthday cake for him every year. That's why each of us made an Advent Tree. This was my mother's invention. After Mass on the first Sunday of Advent, a month before Christmas, you would draw the outline of a Christmas tree on school paper, then draw a hundred little stars. You got to color in a star whenever you did a good deed: red for "cheerful obedience," blue for saying the Rosary, yellow for receiving Communion. The object was to have all your stars colored in by Christmas, then hang your Advent Tree on the Christmas tree as a birthday present for Jesus.

We were all eager to give as good as we got for Christmas, especially to our parents. Once, when I was about eight years old, my mother took me Christmas shopping in a department store in Schenectady. I immediately saw a purse I knew she would like. The leather was soft and brown, not too shiny, with petite silver clasps. It looked expensive, and was: eight dollars, about seven more than I had. So I decided to steal it. I tucked the purse into the front of my pants and was immediately collared by a greasy-haired security guard. He hauled me into a back room and bopped me on the top of the skull with a heavy ring that he apparently wore for such occasions. Then he summoned my mother. She looked as if she'd been punched in the stomach. She grabbed me by the arm, thanked the security guard—*thanked* him—and practically threw me into the car. She made me sit in the backseat the whole ride home and didn't speak a word. Finally, when she was tucking me in that night, she said, "I'd rather you give me no present at all than to think you have to steal something for me. You know that, don't you?" I felt terrible for having betrayed her, and Jesus.

Midnight Mass on Christmas Eve was extra-long, and the incense made it hard to stay awake. Once we got home, though, I got to place the Baby Jesus in his manger crib (a privilege that had always gone to the youngest) and then we'd go to bed, and morning took forever to come, the older kids took forever to wake up, it took Dad forever to hand out the presents—sweat socks and long johns, dolls and baseballs, Jesus and Mary coloring books—and then it was all over before you really had a chance to take it in. For the next twelve days, I got up extra early so I could be the one to inch the little plaster wise men across the top of the piano toward the manger, where they would arrive on January 6, the Feast of the Epiphany, at which point the manger set was crated up for next year, the Christmas tree was tossed on the compost heap, and the Other Side became just another room again.

There was only one room in the house that was off-limits: my parents' room. My father might be "lying down." It was unclear what this meant—not sleeping, surely, because he would often lie down during the daytime and sometimes for a whole day or two at a stretch. Whenever he was lying down, my mother wouldn't let anyone play the piano, and she would take his supper up to him on a tray.

Their bedroom lay at the top of the staircase, as if on sentinel duty, within earshot of four more bedrooms. Over the years, while everyone swapped rooms and roommates, my parents never relinquished their strategic high ground. Perhaps it was simply too much trouble. Their room was jammed with a bed, a dresser, an oak secretary (which guarded, I knew, extremely vital documents), and a long built-in shelf. This shelf was piled mercilessly with papers and pictures and shoeboxes, a storm of miscellany broken by one clear patch of space just wide enough for . . . the typewriter!

This belonged to my father. You had to be invited to use it. If you were, happiness ensued. It was an Underwood, its ribbon sagging, its keys faded. Still, it was a typewriter; it made words. My father admired words, I knew. They were anything and everything. "There's nothing you can't do with words," he would say, "and they don't cost you a penny."

On the typewriter, he taught me my first word: f-u-n. And my second: c-h-i-c-k-e-n. I immediately raced downstairs to the kitchen. "Mom, are we having c-h-i-c-k-e-n tonight?" (We were.)

Every night at the supper table, my father would teach a new word: "melodious," "sanctify," "frustration." His favorite word, though, seemed to be *rambunctious*. Every night, as supper gave way to mayhem, our laughter barreling out of control, the dog clamoring for scraps, my mother on the edge of exasperation, he would declare in mock sternness: "You get a little food in your belly and you get *rambunctious*!"

And the very sound of the word "rambunctious" would only make us laugh more, the most uplifting sound ever invented, the laughter of a man's own children, and that, I believe, is exactly why he always said it, and why we always laughed.

2

A year after I was born, my father, at the age of forty-eight, had finally become a newspaperman. Having placed freelance articles with the *Schenectady Gazette* over the course of six years, he was offered a full-time job. No, he wouldn't be covering the Brooklyn Dodgers (they'd long defected to Los Angeles anyway). He would be an office man: a copy editor, proofreading the articles filed by reporters, writing the headlines and subheads, then hailing a copyboy to send the article to the composing room.

He was not too old to be jubilant. For the first year, he worked the second shift, fielding late-closing dispatches from ballparks and town meetings. Late at night he'd come home and slap the first edition on the kitchen table. "Hot off the presses!" he'd announce to my mother, who waited up. "Careful now, the ink's still wet!"

His colleagues came to know him as a conscientious, even fussy journalist. Copy editing appealed to him much as the Army had:

It was a system of absolutes. No gray areas, no risk of misinterpretations. The word "rape" was not to be used in a headline, ever. "Mothers Day" had no apostrophe. A "High Mass"—both words capitalized—was "sung," not "held."

Even during Saturday chores, he'd keep his Associated Press stylebook in his hip pocket and a thick black proofreading pencil tucked above his ear. These pencils were as big around as his fingers. The words they produced were thick and smeared, with the heft of importance; even his to-do lists took on a powerful new authority. The pencils wound up in all the tin-can pencil jars we kept around the house, and you couldn't possibly pick one up without feeling you were picking up a piece of him.

The top editors at the *Gazette* were Protestants, many of them Masons as well, and after a few years my father felt he was being kept down because he was a Catholic. But he couldn't bring himself to confront his superiors—conflict went against his nature— so he began looking for another job.

He jumped over to the *Schenectady Union-Star*, an afternoon paper, and things were looking up until he began to suffer from a bleeding ulcer. His insides were a constant problem. He had already had appendicitis and a hernia. He also had high blood pressure and a sinus condition that caused him to lose his sense of smell. He tried to make light of this malady. He would gather us around the kitchen table to give him a blindfolded taste test, a chunk of onion and a chunk of apple, and he swore he couldn't tell the difference.

Now he had to go into the hospital to have part of his stomach removed. When he came out, he had a huge, frowning scar across his belly and no job. The *Union-Star* had been bought out by the *Knickerbocker News*, an Albany paper, and his slot was eliminated.

While recuperating at home, he went into a slide—tormented, I later learned, about how to feed the family. "The whole world just looks black," he would tell my mother, "and I don't know how to change it." He prayed incessantly and asked all of us to pray for him. Just as things were looking desperate, he got a call from the *Times-Record,* the afternoon partner of the *Troy Record.* The *Record* was looking for an experienced copy editor. Was he available? Was he! Plus, the paper was offering him a chance to edit the weekly religion page. Troy was well past Schenectady, easily an hour's drive from Duanesburg, and Route 7 stayed icy through the winter. But the *Record* was known to be full of Catholics, from the pressmen to many of the top editors, and he took the job.

During his first winter at the *Record,* my father often spent the night in Troy. Sometimes he rented a cheap room with a hot plate; more often he'd camp out in the office, his coworkers arriving in the morning to find him asleep in his chair. My mother worried that he wasn't taking care of himself, and she was right. When he went to the hospital for a checkup after his ulcer surgery, he was found to be suffering from malnutrition. The doctors kept him in for testing and discovered that the malnutrition was just a physical symptom of an emotional problem. He was diagnosed with severe anxiety, quite likely a case of clinical depression.

Over the next several years, his depression deepened, and my father would try anything to climb out of it. He visited a psychologist at Catholic Charities, who concluded that his self-esteem was dangerously low, perhaps from the pounding he'd taken long ago at the hands of his father. He was prescribed a series of drugs that had no good effect, and then Sinequan, which helped his state of mind but badly blurred his vision. He joined Recovery, Inc., a self-help group founded by the psychiatrist Abraham Low, who preached that most people were average—neither exceptional nor hopeless—and that a depressed person's first step toward recovery was to embrace the concept of averageness. From there it was mainly a question of "moving your muscles," conquering your mental behavior with physical initiative. My father attended these Recovery meetings weekly and poured his thoughts into a special Recovery notebook, carefully alphabetized and annotated: "ATTITUDE—one cannot change situations or actions but can learn to change *attitude* toward them to curb temper and symptoms . . . PREOCCUPATION—with ideas of Insecurity (fears, inadequacy, etc.) prevents you from Deciding, Planning, and Acting to develop pride, self-reliance, self-sufficiency."

The Recovery meetings helped somewhat, but his depression would not subside. Finally his doctor suggested electroshock therapy. Over the next few years, my mother would drive him to the hospital in Albany, then pray in the waiting room as he underwent the treatments. He would emerge with a dazed, blank face. "Paul, it's me, Veronica," she would say, wrapping her arm around his rib cage to support him. His black mood was gone for the moment, but so was his memory. He knew who he was and that he had many children, but he couldn't remember their names. As my mother drove him home, he would beg her to recite the names, again and again, and he would repeat them slowly: "Joseph . . . Mary . . . Martha . . . Ann . . ."

His psychiatrist told my mother that a different man, a man without his faith and family, might well have become an alcoholic or tried to kill himself. Instead, he took to his bed, sometimes for days at a time. Mornings broke where all he could manage was a whisper to my mother: "You must think I'm a terribly weak person."

"No! I think you're very courageous. You get up when you can, you go to work when you can. That's not a weak person. I admire you very much."

One Valentine's Day he wrote her a note:

Dearest Veronica,

Here I am, a plain man with a plain sheet of paper. My hope on this day is to express my unending love for you. From the day of our marriage till now, for all eternity, my having you has been the second most wonderful experience of my life. My first—getting to know Jesus. I hope we will be together here on earth and in Heaven for all eternity. What more can I say on this Valentine's Day. I LOVE YOU.

My mother thought it was terribly unfair, what this life was putting him through. And yet, she told herself, it is often the best men who are made to suffer most. She was frustrated that she couldn't find a solution. At one point she asked Rudy Pracher, a close friend from Long Island days, to visit my father. Rudy had the sunniest disposition of anyone she knew. The Prachers had moved upstate not long after my family, as had the Burkes, the Prachers with their eight children, the Burkes with nine. They were as near to family as the Dubners had, and my mother thought that if anyone could buck up Paul, it would be Rudy.

Rudy and his family came to visit on a Sunday afternoon. Between the Prachers and the Dubners, there were a dozen kids on the lawn with an instant license for roughhousing. My father didn't come out of the house. Rudy found him in the downstairs bedroom, the blinds drawn, the kids' shouts pouring through the window. My father had managed to get himself to church that morning, but he was unshaven, and his ragged flannel shirt was untucked. He sat facing the wall, shoulders drawn in. Rudy said hello, but my father didn't, or couldn't, even turn around. Rudy pulled up a chair and sat with him through the afternoon, but nothing changed.

I knew none of this at the time. My mother kept my father's illness from all of us, covering for him in every way, bearing the load on every front. She handled the budget, the curfews, the birthday parties. If she had been allowed, I'm sure she would have commandeered my father's A.P. stylebook and black pencils and held down the *Times-Record* copy desk.

The older kids had learned to read his moods at least a bit; they knew to give him some room when he emerged from a long stretch in bed. But as the youngest child, about seven years old during his worst period, I was oblivious. I was happy with the world I knew. It never struck me to wonder why my father was only marginally inside it. I never realized that when I couldn't use his typewriter, it was because he was barricaded in his room, sobbing beneath the covers. Since he often slept over in Troy, I sometimes wouldn't see him for days at a time. Finally the weekend came. Saturday meant chores, and Sunday meant church, and it was his few leftover hours that each of us wanted to grab, knowing that it might end at any moment when my mother announced that he had to go upstairs to lie down. I wonder now what must have gone through his head then—how joyful our racket must have sounded, and how maddening, to feel that he couldn't become a part of it.

Still, my few memories of my father from that period have nothing to with his depression. There are three that are particularly strong: one recurrent, one aberrant, and one persistent, extended and dreamlike, which I have replayed hundreds of times.

The recurrent memory is of my father delivering his *rambunctious* sermon at the dinner table: "You get a little food in your belly and you get *rambunctious*!" Sometimes he bellowed the line, and sometimes he used a silly, helium voice while looking straight at me, so I'd understand that he wasn't really scolding. He would pull me into his lap and tickle my belly, the fabulous flinty smell of Sen-Sen mints on his breath: "Get a little food in your belly"—tickle-tickle, shriek-shriek—"and you get *rambunctious*!" At school, the pyramid-shaped Mrs. Elbrecht once asked me why I had thrown an open milk carton clear across the cafeteria, splattering everyone beneath its arc. "You get a little food in your belly," I explained to her, "and you get *rambunctious*!"

The aberrant memory is of my father loading us all into the pink-and-gray Rambler for Sunday Mass, Ann wrapping her arms around me like a seat belt, my father slamming his pinkie in the back door and yelling, "Shit!" I knew the word; I just didn't know that my father did.

The extended memory, the one I most often call up, is of my father taking me to New York City to see the Yankees play the Baltimore Orioles. I had never been to the City before or to a baseball game other than Little League. I was eight years old. It was a bus trip, leaving from Schenectady, just my father and I, no Dave or Peter. I understood it to be a monumental journey, a father and son in a sort of holy communion. We would be alone for hours and hours, a priceless opportunity; had his father ever taken him on such a trip?

The Orioles were my team. I had been assigned to them as an infant. My father had a rule: No two children could root for the same team. After the Dodgers left Brooklyn, he'd become a Mets fan. Ann rooted for the Red Sox, in large part because of a crush on Carl Yastrzemski. Peter liked the Dodgers, Dave the Cardinals, Beth the San Francisco Giants. There weren't many good teams left by the time I was born, and the choice was made for me.

I loved the Orioles. They were *mine* and had been *given* to me. I loved Boog Powell, tubby and jovial, and Paul Blair, who ran, as my father said, like a hot knife through butter. I loved Brooks Robinson, the human vacuum cleaner, and Frank Robinson and Jim Palmer and even Merv Rettenmund, the leadoff man with the ridiculous name, Merv, as if he should have been a turtle or a make of car but not an Oriole.

The bus left from Schenectady in the dawny dark. There was a bathroom in the back, and I had to use it three or four times. The sky was a nasty gray, and raindrops streaked the bus windows at a sharp angle. We finally stopped at a diner for lunch. The bus driver said we were in Yonkers, but it looked like New York City to me: one building after the next, cars everywhere, parking meters, pay phones.

We sat in a booth, my father and I, just the two of us. I had only been in Gibby's Diner, in Quaker Street. Here there must have been a hundred people eating at once. The man behind me smelled like Father DiPace but when I turned around, I saw that he wasn't a priest at all.

Our waiter was in a big hurry. My father flagged him down and ordered a tongue sandwich. A *tongue* sandwich? "Give it a try, Stevie," my father said. "Maybe you'll like it."

I wanted to but couldn't. I ordered pancakes.

My father ate differently from the way he ate at home, stabbing his teeth into the bread, wiping his mouth with his sleeve. He wore a big smile.

"How about this," he said, "huh, Stevie? How about this? Things sure move fast down here, wouldn't you say?"

"Yeah!"

"Yeah. You gotta keep an eye out." He shoved the last corner of sandwich into his mouth, wiped his lips one last time. I had just started on my pancakes. "The clouds are gonna blow over, I'm telling you. It's gonna be a perfect day for a ball game. Perfect day."

He said he had to go to the bathroom. Then he cleared his throat, looked at me intently. "Don't let that waiter take away my coffee!" he said, and then gave a big laugh for some reason, and disappeared.

Within about three seconds the waiter swooped in and cleared my father's place, including his coffee. By the time I aroused the nerve to say anything, he had dashed through the swinging doors.

Many years later, reading *The Great Gatsby,* I got a good laugh myself. "Don't let that waiter take away my coffee!"—that's what Rosy Rosenthal says to Meyer Wolfshiem before he steps outside the old Metropole into a hail of bullets. In a diner in Yonkers with his eight-year-old son, my father was quoting Fitzgerald. Perhaps he had even set me up, sending the waiter over to test my mettle?

Now he returned from the bathroom. "What happened to the coffee?" he said.

I told him, and he laughed harder than I'd ever heard him laugh, the sound bouncing around the shiny diner, embarrassing me. Then he grabbed our waiter again. "Another cup of coffee. And let me finish this one, will ya, bub?"

Sure enough, the clouds had blown over by the time we got to Yankee Stadium, and we found our seats, miles and miles from the field.

"Will you look at that!" my father said. I tried to see what he meant, but he was just looking around at everything, arms across his chest, nostrils turned up, sniffing the air: hot dogs, city sky, our too-heavy coats. "Will you look at that!" he said, and again: "Will you look at that!"

I too started looking around, folding my arms across my chest like him, and my eyes finally landed on the huge outfield scoreboard. It said that Merv Rettenmund was the batter and that there was one ball and one strike. The game had started already! This wasn't at all like baseball on TV, with the announcers giving the starting lineups after the beer commercial. I looked all the way down to the field and spotted Rettenmund, tiny and faceless.

Suddenly I became sharply aware of the moment I was inhabiting. Something made me say to myself, Freeze this moment in your mind, for if you do, it will last forever, and I did: Merv Rettenmund leaning over the plate for the one-and-one pitch, my father sitting back in the narrow wooden seat with his arms crossed, chewing on a Sen-Sen, a broad smile tattooed on his face, my father as happy as I would ever see him, our bellies both full, our minds a little rambunctious.

3

―

▣. BY the time I was a child, my parents' reinvention of themselves was essentially complete. We were such a full-throttle Catholic family, living in such a Jewless land, that only a crackpot would have thought to challenge our provenance. Even our name, to the ears of our neighbors at least, was serendipitously un-Jewish: Dubner, pronounced with a short *u,* faintly German perhaps, a bit of a mumble but solid enough, a safe ratio of consonant to vowel.

It is true that some of my father's friends and coworkers knew he had been Jewish. He wouldn't go out of the way to hide this fact, and, bred in the Little Jerusalem bustle of Brownsville, he carried in him far more of the Brooklyn Jew than did my mother, whose years in Madame Souvorina's ballet studio had wrung out whatever ethnic or cultural giveaways she might have once possessed. Even she, though, would not deny her past. If the topic of Jews were to arise, perhaps at doughnut hour after Mass, my mother would say, "Oh, I was born into a Jewish family, you know, but later on I became a Catholic." Beyond that, however, she didn't have much to say. My brother Dave, when he was seven years old, asked my mother why they had converted. "Because we were young and we were searching for the Truth, and we found it," she told him.

As a child I had no awareness whatsoever of Jews, what they were, what they did, where they came from. I knew that my father had some strange habits—eating gefilte fish, for instance, or, when he was feeling particularly expansive, singing "My Yiddishe Mama"—but these I attributed to the sheer exotica of a Brooklyn background.

When it came to important matters, matters of Mass and Heaven and the Holy Trinity, my father's embrace of his adoptive faith was unwavering. I have since come to wonder: Did he feel no pang of dissonance as Yom Kippur approached each year? Did he never hear in his memory the cry of the cantor from his father's synagogue? Did he not think of his father at all?

If so, he kept it entirely to himself.

By the time of my First Communion, at the age of seven, my parents had been Catholic for a quarter of a century. Their past was ancient history, inaccessible and irrelevant, a distant, faded star overshadowed by the glow of the world they had created.

The center of this world was the Church of Our Lady of Fátima. It had been built in 1954, a long, white, rather graceless structure with tan wooden pews, cracked gray linoleum, and too-colorful stained-glass windows. The church was in Delanson, across the street from the high school my brothers and sisters attended. Long ago, Delanson had been a booming railroad town; my father had written an article about its history for the *Gazette*. Now it boasted nothing but the church, the school, a post office, Bernie Duszkiewicz's barbershop, and Lenny Van Buren's funeral home.

My father, when he was feeling well, directed most of his spare energy toward Our Lady of Fátima. He started a parish library and headed up the St. Vincent de Paul Society, which gave anonymous charity to hard-luck families. He taught catechism and sometimes served as a lector at Mass, self-consciously adjusting his eyeglasses and clearing his throat before leaning into the microphone with pride—"A reading from the first letter of St. Paul to the Thessalonians"—enunciating each word with care.

My mother was also a force within the church. She taught catechism, baked pies for church suppers, and held down a link on the parish's prayer chain, one woman phoning the next to offer prayers when someone got sick. As the legalization of abortion crept near, she reacted as if war had broken out. She helped launch the local Right to Life chapter, peppering state legislators with letters and attending marches on Albany. She enlisted Beth and me to stuff envelopes and draw up "Abortion Is Murder" posters, using Magic Marker on yellow cardboard, that we'd parade in front of the capitol.

I didn't like going to church. But I knew my parents did, and I knew it to be a force for the good. There was nothing to be done about it anyway; it was as inevitable as rain. Even at the moment of liberation, after Mass and catechism, after Mrs. Ferry had slipped me that precious stick of Doublemint gum, I could think of nothing but the fact that I would be returning the following Sunday. Church was a chore that could never be completed.

In catechism, I learned that if Adam had not eaten the apple that Eve offered him, we would all have been born pristine. Jesus would not have had to sacrifice himself. Mothers would have felt no pain during childbirth. We would not have had to go to school—or, I gathered, to church.

I once approached Sister Agnes after catechism for a clarification: "Do you think that if Adam just took the apple and threw it back into the Garden, we wouldn't even have to go to Sunday School?"

"That," Sister Agnes said, "is not the kind of question with which we need concern ourselves."

I cursed Adam for all the trouble he had caused. I considered him a real person who, presented with a not-so-difficult dilemma, had blown it. For all of us. How good could the apple have looked? I thought of Eve, lovely naked Eve, offering me the Coles and Gluesings' best apple, a huge pale yellow apple called a pound sweet, with a taste as mellow as honey. "No, thank you, Eve," I would have said. "We're not supposed to eat that one, you know that, don't you?"

But Adam ate it. The resulting arrangement felt arbitrary and unfair. We all stood a good chance of plummeting into the fires of Hell, far too grave a punishment for the crime Adam had committed.

Yet that punishment is what motivated my every action. The fires of Hell kept me from winging a fastball at Richard LaPoint's head the next time he came to bat after hitting a home run. The fires of Hell kept me from letting Dale Schaeffer cheat off my math test even though he offered me first a dollar and then a skull-bashing. When we recited the Rosary at home, there was only one line I prayed with true feeling: "O my Jesus, forgive us our sins, save us from the fires of Hell."

There was nothing more upsetting than inadvertently taking a step down the path toward Hell. One day after school, I was playing out in the front yard by myself. I was good at this; I had a lot of practice. My sisters and brothers had begun abandoning home with alarming regularity, bound for college and jobs. By the time I was eight, only Dave, Beth, and I remained, and Dave being a tough high-schooler and Beth being a girl, I mainly entertained myself.

On this day, I was playing an intricate solo version of baseball in which I performed the role of every batter as well as the pitcher, umpire, and sportscaster.

A car slowed down and stopped in front of the house. Inside

the car were two nuns. I had never seen a nun driving before. I would have been less surprised to see our dog, Prince, behind the wheel.

"Hello there," said the driving nun.

I considered how to address her—"Yes, ma'am?" or "Hello, Sister"—but just stood there dumb until she spoke again.

"I'm afraid we're lost," she said. "Can you tell us how to get to the Catholic church in Delanson?"

The Catholic church in Delanson! My church! Nuns at my house, on my road, going to my church! This was nothing less than a visitation.

The directions were simple, only three turns. I spoke clearly and slowly, as one spoke to nuns, proud of my knowledge and of the opportunity to serve. The driving nun thanked me as she pulled away.

Their car had just disappeared over the rise when I realized I'd flubbed the directions. I forgot to tell them to turn left in Quaker Street. Instead they would go straight, down Route 7, into Schenectady, then Troy. From there? Maybe Massachusetts, to the ocean, all the way to England.

I had sent a pair of lost nuns to England, and my soul was surely bound for Hell.

I knew now how Adam must have felt. He thought he was just eating an apple; I thought I was just giving directions to a pair of nuns. We each had made a terrible mistake.

That night I vomited in my sleep. My mother told me I had the flu, but I knew I was getting an early taste of Hell. So I prayed to God, as savagely as I knew how, vowing to follow His path for all eternity. And for a few days I did. But I soon found myself slipping off, as always, committing errors that had less to do with evil than mischief, errors whose penalties I hoped could be erased by my diligent service within the walls of Our Lady of Fátima.

* * *

I had become an altar boy at the age of six. Father DiPace offered me fifty cents to serve my first Mass. I assumed that to be the standard pay and was ecstatic, as my weekly allowance was a dime. By the time I realized that the fifty cents was a one-time sign-up bonus, I was listed on the weekly altar-boy schedule, and it would have been uncouth to withdraw. I liked Father DiPace. He was solemn but kind, with heavy black eyebrows the shape of caterpillars. He told me I was the youngest altar boy in the history of Our Lady of Fatima, and that it was only fitting since I was a Dubner.

Reluctant at first, I came to love it. An altar boy was the policeman of the church world: vaguely above the law, a uniformed executor of ceremonial duties, with special access to the highest authorities, if necessary. There were other perks. Serving a wedding Mass usually meant five dollars from the father of the bride, more than I could earn mowing lawns all week. Several times, I became an emergency godfather. Father DiPace would phone our house and my mother would toss me in the car and we'd hurry down to the church. We'd meet a woman with a baby, always young and nervous, and in the dark and empty church my mother and I recited the godparents' vows as Father DiPace doused the baby's head with cold Holy Water. Even though the job didn't pay, and even though I knew I wasn't *really* a godfather the way Peter was my godfather, I couldn't wait for the next call to come, for although no one would tell me anything, I understood this to be an invitation to witness an imperfection that was not my own.

Another perk was that altar boys didn't have to sing the hymns during Mass. At home I loved to sing and play the piano, writing little blues songs after Dave had taught me a few riffs. But the songs at church didn't fit my throat somehow. They were too high, or too low, too slow, too dry; they made me feel as if I were drowning, and I enjoyed hearing everyone else struggle with them as I attended to my altar-boy chores.

But best of all, an altar boy was a junior member of the priestly cult. He was one step closer to God and one step farther from the fires of Hell. Therefore I took my position seriously.

An altar boy's tasks were varied and often intricate. Ten minutes before Mass, you lit the candles, then helped Father DiPace pull on his chasuble. When he was ready, you signaled the organist to start the processional hymn, then marched in the lead, clutching the tall wood-handled crucifix, eyes fixed forward but listening for the silky rustle of Father DiPace's chasuble to make sure you didn't get too far ahead.

The early part of the Mass consisted of what I thought of as the warm-up prayers. They were colorless call-and-response affairs between Father DiPace and the congregation, and my main duty was to stand or sit at the appropriate time, which signaled the congregation to do the same. Some of the older parishioners still mumbled the Mass in Latin, but everything was in English now. I ardently memorized the entire liturgy, even the long and tricky Apostles' Creed, because an altar boy resorting to his prayer missal was bush league, like a policeman having to whip out the owner's manual of his gun.

Next came the Scripture readings. I tried to pay attention, especially if my father was the lector, but often failed. I would be thinking about the previous week's Little League game or scouring the pews for kids from my class. Father DiPace's sermons, too, usually passed me by. Once, though, he dispensed what struck me as pure wisdom. "We all spend our lives," he said, "waiting for *the next good thing* to happen. The next job, the next vacation, the next grade of school. But that goes against what Christ taught us: There is no time to wait. The time—for everything—is now. Now is when we live, and now is what we must live for."

I immediately knew that even I, a child, was guilty of Father DiPace's charge, waiting for the next good thing, though I had no idea what that might be.

The action picked up toward the Consecration, when the bread and wine would become the Body and Blood of Christ. I presented Father DiPace with the cruets of water and wine, handles facing him. Then, from a kneeling position, I would ring the handbells as he blessed the host of bread ("This is my Body, which was given up for you. Eat it in memory of me"), then the chalice of wine ("This is my Blood, the Blood of the new and everlasting covenant. It is shed for you and for all men so that sins may be forgiven. Drink it in memory of me").

A moment later I would ring the bells again—three short rings, timed to Father DiPace's recitation of "Holy, Holy, Holy." Sometimes the three rings would overlap, producing a shimmering harmonic overtone—the voice of angels, I thought, singing their approval of my precision.

For the distribution of Communion, I accompanied Father DiPace to the edge of the altar and slid the gold-plated paten under each communicant's chin. To reach the tallest men, I stood on tiptoes. In the hundreds of Masses I served, not a single host ever fell from Father DiPace's fingers or a communicant's mouth. Still, I acted as if each one might be the first, for that was the Body of Christ he was placing on their tongues, and to let the Body of Christ plummet to the cracked gray linoleum floor was unthinkable.

But was it really the Body of Christ? An hour earlier I had seen that each Body of Christ was one of a hundred plain wafers in a crinkly plastic package—the same kind of plastic in which my ball and jacks had been wrapped—that Father DiPace fished out of a cabinet.

It was the miracle of transubstantiation, I knew, that changed each wafer into the Body of Christ. In catechism we learned the definition of "transubstantiation": "the changing of one substance into another substance while retaining the accidents of the former thing." Sister Agnes had forced me to memorize this definition because I once said that transubstantiation sounded like a magic trick that didn't quite work.

I would never have joked like that with my mother or father. Sister Agnes was a professional; my parents took things more personally. I knew how they felt about the Body of Christ: Without it, life would not be worth living.

I tried to believe as they believed. Every Sunday, I let the communion wafer dissolve on my tongue undisturbed, as Sister Agnes had taught. I waited to feel God filling up my body. I longed for that sensation, longed to understand how my parents felt when they spoke of being filled by God. Their faces shone when they talked like that; they became warriors, saints, keepers of the key to the universe. But Sunday after Sunday it wouldn't happen for me.

Was it my fault? Obviously. It worked for plenty of other people. I was clearly unworthy. Whenever I tried to concentrate on Jesus, my mind wandered. Perhaps my soul was born even less pristine than others'. Perhaps I had racked up too much spiritual debt—the lost nuns, the shoplifted purse—ever to hope for a true connection with God.

Deep down, though, I didn't know if I really wanted the Body of Christ in my mouth. It was one thing to be filled by God—God was everywhere, practically gaseous, and He could just as easily be inside me as I could be inside Him.

Jesus, though, made me uncomfortable, especially how we prayed to him—*Praise to you, Lord Jesus Christ*—because Jesus was a man, as real as my father, and I saw his face when I prayed to him, just as I saw his face every time I finally swallowed the Communion wafer, thin and pulpy from having dissolved on my tongue, and inviting the long, sad face of this man inside my body simply felt unnatural.

I kept these thoughts to myself, of course. My mother took great pride in the vigor I exhibited as an altar boy. In turn, I took great pride in pleasing her. As a rule she was stingy in her praise. Especially with the older kids, she did not refrain from yelling and had been known to smack them on the side of the head or the backside. Thus far I had escaped such wrath. So, having found myself in her good graces, I would do anything within reason to stay there.

I also sensed that my mother had placed a lot of her hopes in me and in my sister Beth. It was clear by now that none of the older kids was going to be a priest or a nun, not by a long shot. Joe was still in the Air Force, with a wife and a baby daughter, happy to be far away. Mary, oppressed by the virtue of her very name, had taken to calling herself Mona. She was living out near Rochester and had married a man who was not a Catholic and who, from what I could gather, possessed an even more serious flaw than that. (Many years later I learned it: He hadn't fully broken off with his first wife when he took Mona as his second.) Martha was in college at Brockport, still dating Gary from Scoharie, also talking about marriage. (She too had rebelled against her saintly name, but only going so far as to spell it differently, with an *e* at the end instead of an *a*.) Ann and Peter both lived near Duanesburg but didn't go to church anymore, and from the tone of voice my mother used when she spoke of them, I knew they were doing other things she didn't approve of. I was too young to comprehend the brand of rebellion that some of my siblings embraced, their wanton abuse of one Sacrament after the next: pot smoking and premarital sex and who knew what else. All I knew was that my mother sometimes slammed down the phone after talking to one of them, looking as if she wanted to hit something. Once, she ran outside, grabbed a scythe, and began hacking down weeds like a madwoman.

So I went along with all of it—the altar-boy service, the Advent trees, the Rosary recitation. There was just one thing I truly dreaded: the Wednesday-night prayer meeting that my parents ran. This was part of something called the Charismatic Christian Renewal, and I was foggy as to how it fitted in with Our Lady of Fátima. The meeting was held in the church hall, but Father DiPace didn't come; the songs they sang were different from the regular church songs, and so were the people. There was Mrs.

Pracher and Mrs. O'Sullivan and the McNamaras, all friends of my parents, and only a few parishioners from our church.

I was usually the only one who wasn't a grown-up. They gathered in a circle of metal folding chairs under glaring fluorescent lights. They would begin with a song from a pale blue booklet, songs about Yahweh, whom I'd never heard of, songs with strange, curvy melodies. They clapped as they sang, in that circular, folksinger way, like mashing hamburger patties. When the song was over, they'd close their eyes tight and pray, quietly at first, not together like in church but each of them on his own, voices swarming like bees—*Praise you, Lord Jesus . . . Lift us up, Jesus, lift us, lift us up . . . We praise you and love you, Lord Jesus . . . Alleluia! Alleluia!* Louder and louder, and soon it would begin: one voice, then a second, jagged outbursts of the strangest syllables, their faces twisted into what looked like pain, their strange syllables then blossoming into shouts, some of them standing as they shouted, a dozen grown-ups, my mother and father among them, crying into the air—and me, petrified, peeking through half-shut eyelids. I prayed from the heart: *Please, God, make me invisible.*

Why were they making up this ridiculous language? Was I supposed to know it too?

Afterward they all behaved as if nothing happened. That was the most upsetting part. One night, as the grown-ups were having their coffee and day-old doughnuts, someone said the words "speaking in tongues," and I understood that to be the name for what they had just done, but as for how it came about and what it meant, I was utterly in the dark and too rattled to ask questions.

In church, though my father always sang too loud, he and my mother were composed and attentive. They stood straight, knew every prayer, sang every song. When my mother knelt to pray after Communion—head slightly bowed, eyelids closed, her ten fingertips pressed delicately together—she looked as proper as the lady on the cover of my catechism book.

In these prayer meetings, though, my parents went wild. They were the chief clappers and shriekers, and then, riding home through the dark, they were totally calm. I would stew in the backseat, angry at the inexplicable madness that had transpired. Up front, my mother would squeeze in close to my father, which she never, ever did, and rest her head on his shoulder.

"It really just grabs your heart, doesn't it?" she would say to him.

The Charismatic Renewal meetings really had grabbed my father's heart, much more than I knew at the time. They were, in fact, a lifesaver.

My father was fifty-four by now and had tried everything to fight his depression, most recently the electroshock treatments. He was desperate for a healing, and through the Charismatics he finally found it.

It had all begun months earlier in Albany. My father had heard that as many as five hundred Charismatics met there every week, in the gymnasium of a Catholic girls' school. They were called the Emmanuel Community and what they sought was direct access to the Holy Spirit, the most fiery element of the Trinity. The Holy Spirit was thought to be a great healing power; for that reason it could be easily abused, and this had made the Vatican nervous about the Charismatics. But when my father heard that the Emmanuel meeting was moderated by a Catholic priest, he decided to give it a try.

My parents didn't make me go to the Emmanuel meetings. They were held on Sunday nights, and Albany, the way my father drove, was easily an hour each way. So I would stay home with Beth and Dave. Beth would do her homework, and Dave would keep to himself. I would generally mope, wandering from the piano to the TV to the kitchen window, where I would sit and watch the road for my parents' car. Sunday nights were the saddest: the whole day spent strapped into God's world, the crush of school lurking in the darkness, my parents off on some strange spiritual mission.

As I later learned, the healing took hold of my father almost immediately. At his first Emmanuel meeting he stood up and asked the group to lay hands on him, and within a few weeks he received the gift of tongues. Soon after, my mother also began speaking in tongues. They both were ecstatic that God had allowed them to taste the Holy Spirit and its healing powers.

These prayer meetings instantly changed my parents' lives. They had always agreed that a truly spiritual life should include any number of conversions, not just one; the soul, like a battery, could always afford a recharging. They now began to experience their faith at a deeper level. With the hand of the Holy Spirit upon their backs, they felt themselves slipping past the scrim that had always kept God one dimension removed from life on earth. Jesus in particular became ever more real, as if he were accompanying them step for step, breath for breath. And with Jesus so resolutely at his side, my father discovered that the black moods that had troubled him for much of his life did not have the audacity to trouble him anymore.

Suddenly the world opened back up to him. He kept taking Sinequan, the antidepressant, but he hardly needed it. His depression, like a claw at the back of his neck, was easing its grip. Every week he couldn't wait for Sunday night to come around.

He also couldn't wait to spread his good fortune. All these years, he had hated his dependency, his helplessness. He was a Christian, a man, a father; his role was to help others. Now he set out to reconnect with his children, especially Dave, who was sixteen years old and unhappy, on the cusp of the sort of trouble that happens to bright young men in too-small towns. My father also joined the volunteer fire company and raised money for a youth recreation program. He wrote countless letters to the editor, one of which suggested that a new shopping mall in Troy should include a chapel—"for all those who wish to stop for five or ten minutes to say hello to God. This proposed chapel could perhaps be built in three sections—Protestant, Jewish, and Catholic."

Now he brought the Charismatic Renewal movement home, to Our Lady of Fátima, establishing the Wednesday-night group. It wasn't easy to replicate the Emmanuel meetings. In Albany, with hundreds of worshipers and eight or ten musicians, the spontaneous prayer was practically apocalyptic, the silences deep and mysterious. At Our Lady of Fátima, my father could rarely round up more than a dozen people. One of the parishioners he did recruit was named John Jorgensen. He was in his thirties and lived in Duanesburg with his wife and three children. John had started to sour on the rigors of the Catholic Church; when he heard about the Charismatic Renewal meetings, he latched on hungrily and began to see my father and mother as parent figures.

As John told me many years later, neither he nor anyone else who met my father during this time had any idea that he had ever been depressed. He didn't talk about himself all that much, but when he did, it was clear that he was in love with life, aglow with possibility.

As the circle of light around my father widened, we were all eager to climb into it. Around the house, he was his old self— better than his old self, really. We had all adjusted to having a fragile father. Even I had learned by now to tiptoe through the Green Room when he was lying down upstairs; I knew better than to throw myself around his waist when he finally resurfaced.

Now he was up for anything. He took us to Gibby's Diner and to stamp-collecting fairs; he even got down in a three-point stance with me and Dave to play football.

The older kids could feel it too. That year, they were all excited about Thanksgiving. Everyone except Joe was coming home: Mary, a.k.a. Mona, who now had two baby daughters; Marthe and Gary from Schoharie, who had gotten married and were living in Milwaukee; Ann, who had also gotten married; Peter and his girlfriend; and then there were the three of us still at home.

On Wednesday night it started snowing hard, and I was scared they would all cancel. I woke up early to watch the road through the kitchen window. By late morning, the snow already reached the first strand of barbed wire on the hayfield fence. Ann and her husband and Peter and his girlfriend all drove up together, their Volkswagen fishtailing up the hill, and I ran outside. Ann was the only sister I wasn't too shy to hug. My mother hollered for me to put some shoes on, that I should know better than to run around in the snow with bare feet.

The snow was up to the second strand of wire by the time Mona arrived, and everyone ran out to look at her two baby girls. Mona had the kind of voice that made the house sound full even if she was the only one there, and I hoped she'd stay for a long time.

Still no Marthe and Gary, and the road was starting to drift in. I hadn't seen any headlights for close to an hour. They were driving in all the way from Milwaukee.

Finally a car poked its lights through the snow, made the long haul up Gallupville Road, over the rise, and then—yes!—it turned in. We descended on them, my father leading the way. Marthe was the sister most like Mom, always looking out for everyone, and Gary was already solid, the way fathers were.

The only sad part about everyone being home was knowing they'd leave. As we sat down for supper, we said the regular grace, and then my father kept going, thanking God for all his children. The kitchen was full again, and so noisy that the dog started howling. Mom had so much food going that she had to use the woodstove to keep things warm. We had two turkeys and all kinds of vegetables. As usual, we started playing with the olives. Dad stuffed four or five in his upper lip and staggered around like a beaten-up boxer. I stuck an olive on every finger, and Marthe bit them off, like a fish taking the worm. Beth jammed a carrot stick between the gap in her front teeth and wiggled it with her tongue. When Mom turned to get the sweet potatoes from the stove, Dave fed a big chunk of turkey to Doxology, the cat.

"You get a little food in your belly," my father roared at all of us, "and you get—"

"*Rambunctious*!" we all roared back.

We played War that night, with two decks of cards, and Monopoly and Scrabble. We cracked walnuts and threw the shells into the woodstove. We settled around the piano, Peter and Ann with their guitars, Beth running upstairs to get her flute, and played "Somebody Robbed the Glendale Train" and "When the Saints Go Marching In." Finally I got to sit in on the piano. I started up a blues in C, playing too loud and too fast as always, even when Peter told me to watch his foot beating out the time, everyone else rushing to keep up, Dad on the couch, cradling Mona's two little girls against his chest, both of them sleeping against our din somehow, me pumping the piano's sustain pedal and begging my left hand to keep up with my right, my father surveying his rambunctious offspring with grateful eyes, the eyes of a man who knew that after such a long and searing drought, Heaven had at long last bestowed all its love upon him.

ON the Sunday night after Thanksgiving, with the family having scattered, my mother and father drove into Albany for the Emmanuel meeting. Even though they'd had their own Charismatic Renewal group for over a year, they still liked to go to Emmanuel at least once a month. John Jorgensen would be there tonight, as well as Sister June Szumowski, a nun from Albany whom my parents had befriended.

The force of what happened that night was so great that John, Sister June, my mother, and several others remembered it in great detail, and, many years later, told me about it.

At least three hundred worshipers packed the gymnasium. With Christmas in sight, the mood was celebratory. My father and John found seats halfway back from the center of the circle, my mother sitting behind them with Joan O'Sullivan, a friend from Schoharie. For several months my father had been inviting Wally Hebert, a parishioner at Our Lady of Fátima, to the Emmanuel meeting. Now Wally turned up, smiling shyly at my father.

"Wally, you made it!" He threw his arms around Wally. "You're in for a treat, let me tell you."

The singing began, first a gentle hymn, then a roof-raiser. The priest, Father Tammany, asked for a few moments of silent reflection. All but for a few stray coughs, the room fell still.

At last Father Tammany broke the quiet. "Who would like to share with us tonight?"

My father rose to his feet. "Praise the Lord," he said.

"Praise the Lord!" came the answer, hundreds strong. Sister June, sitting nearby, looked up at my father and noticed how strong he seemed, and peaceful. He wore his gray suit, a white shirt, a dark tie.

"I'd like to offer a reading tonight, from the first letter of St. Paul to the Corinthians," he announced. "It's about something I'm very grateful for." He held a Bible in his left hand, straightened his glasses with the right. He squared his shoulders, cleared his throat.

"Love is patient and kind," he read. "Love is not jealous or boastful; it is not arrogant or rude. . . . Love never ends; as for prophecies, they will pass away; as for tongues, they will cease; as for knowledge, it will pass away. For our knowledge is imperfect and our prophecy is imperfect; but when the perfect comes, the imperfect will pass away. When I was a child, I spoke like a child; I thought like a child, I reasoned like a child; when I became a man, I gave up childish ways. For now we see in a mirror dimly, but then face to face. Now I know in part; then I shall understand fully, even as I have been fully understood. So faith, hope, love abide, these three; but the greatest of these is love."

He closed the Bible. "Some of us," he said, "cannot love others because we don't truly love ourselves. And Jesus is the only one who can teach us to love ourselves. Praise the Lord."

"Praise the Lord!"

He sat down, closed his eyes. Again the hush descended. His shoulders relaxed, and his head settled softly on John Jorgensen's shoulder. Wordlessly, John embraced him. The deep quiet sustained itself, and my father did not move.

"Paul?" John finally said. Then, louder: "Paul. Paul!"

"What's wrong, John?" my mother asked from behind them.

"I don't know."

She jumped to her feet. "Something's happened to my husband! He's been stricken! Is there a doctor or nurse here?"

A nun named Sister Kathleen came forward. With John and the others, she laid him out on a coat and began mouth-to-mouth resuscitation. John, on his knees, watched Paul's face change from white to a light gray to a darker, greenish gray, the color of a filing cabinet. He heard a raspy gurgle cross his lips.

My mother stood over his body. "Have I lost him?" she asked her friend Joan.

"No."

"Is he dying?"

"Yes, he's dying."

Sister Kathleen began to cry over his body and stopped the mouth-to-mouth. She looked up at John: "John, he's gone."

Another nun, who was a nurse from a nearby hospital, moved in, ripped open his shirt, and began thumping his chest with interlocked hands.

Shrill voices broke the uneasy silence in the big room.

"Call an ambulance!"

"We called—they're coming!"

"Where's Father Tammany?"

"He went for his bag!"

Father Tammany hurried back inside and knelt at the body. He anointed the forehead with oil, recited the rites of Extreme Unction.

A loose circle had formed around the body, and now they began to sing: "Praise to you, Lord Jesus Christ! Praise to you, that your will be done." The nurse, still straddling his chest, again pounded his heart.

The ambulance had still not come. Another call was made. The dispatcher said the driver couldn't find the gymnasium; someone should go out to the main road and flag him.

Lying on the floor, the corpse—for by now it surely was a corpse, they all knew—slowly lost its greenish-gray color. The face receded gradually to the light gray, then white, then the faintest of pinks.

Was there a pulse? No. Wait: maybe.

Finally the ambulance came. It took him to Albany Medical Center, my mother and Sister June riding in the back. They began to pray the Rosary and continued as he was wheeled into the emergency room, where he was swallowed up in a clot of doctors and nurses. By now John Jorgensen and several of the others had arrived. They joined my mother and Sister June, assembling just outside the emergency-room door, praying that God's will be done, whatever that might be.

Several minutes later they heard a shout inside: "Lie still!"

He had begun to thrash about. For forty minutes he had been unconscious and apparently quite dead. Now he had returned.

One of the doctors asked the patient his name. He moved his lips, soundlessly, to say, "Paul."

Within an hour he was taken upstairs to a critical-care ward. My mother followed to thank the doctors. One of them took her aside. "Your husband had a serious attack of some sort, perhaps a heart attack, and he may have suffered some permanent brain damage," he said. "We won't know for sure until we run some tests. And he's got two broken ribs from the C.P.R., which is to be expected. But this is no small thing that we got him back after he was out so long. This is like a miracle."

No, my mother said to herself, still clutching her rosary beads, this isn't *like* a miracle at all.

*   *   *

A few of the older kids went to visit him in the hospital. I didn't. My mother said that I shouldn't miss school and that if all went well he'd be home soon. I didn't really want to go to the hospital anyway. If my father is sick, I thought, let him get better and come home.

My mother visited often, as did Sister June, whose convent was nearby. To both of them, Paul was scarcely recognizable: the personality seemed to have been drained from his face; his eyes, my mother noticed, seemed to betray the old melancholy.

On one of her first visits my mother jotted down notes on his progress:

> E.E.G. test remarkably shows no brain damage.
> Depression is treatable, brain damage is not.
> He walked up and down the hall today.
> Talked—When they got him out of bed this morning, he wanted to go back. The nurse asked him, "Do you want to go back to bed?" He nodded "yes." She said, "Well, if you want to go back to bed, say, 'I want to go back to bed.' " And he said, "I want to go back to bed."
> Kissed my cheek.

The doctors were unsure if he would recover completely. He was having a hard time speaking. My mother, having learned long ago to read him, could see what he was thinking: *What a mess I've made. I'm supposed to be the caretaker of this family, and now I'll just be one more burden.*

His improvement was marginal but steady, and there was talk that he'd be home by Christmas.

Before dawn on the morning of December 21, Sister June awoke with a strong urge to visit my father. It was silly, she told herself; she'd seen him just the day before. But a voice inside her kept saying, "Go to Paul," and as she had never before experienced such a voice, she heeded.

She dressed, left a note on the kitchen table for the other sisters, and drove to Albany Medical Center. She arrived at seven o'clock, just as the nurse shift was changing.

"How's Paul this morning?" she asked the departing nurse.

"Well, he's breathing pretty heavily."

Sister June took up at his bedside. His breathing was indeed labored. She began to pray: "Lord, we prayed before and he got well. How do you want me to pray now? What should I ask for?"

She thought about God, and about Paul. She knew well his devotion to the Blessed Mother. On the night they first met, he had pulled out his wallet to show her pictures of his children; the last picture in the wallet was of the Virgin Mary. So now she prayed: "Hail Mary, full of grace, the Lord is with thee. Blessed art thou amongst women and blessed is the fruit of thy womb, Jesus."

His breathing suddenly became normal, and he opened his eyes. He seemed to recognize her. He lifted his eyes toward the ceiling and smiled, as if he had seen a pleasant vision.

He closed his eyes. Sister June leaned over and whispered in a soft rhythm the words she knew he wanted to hear: "Jesus . . . Jesus . . . Jesus."

And then he died.

CONCERNING the death of my father: Everything that I was not aware of, and everything that I do not recall, easily overwhelms the few sad specks that did manage to cling to my memory.

December 21, the day he died, was a half day of school, the last before Christmas break. In the fifth grade, we had a grab-bag gift exchange, and I came away with an extremely deluxe bingo set. It was an octagonal console, made of sky-blue plastic, with berths for eight cards and in the center a shiny silver roulette wheel for calling the numbers. This was a caliber of toy well beyond the reach of our family; I immediately knew it would be my favorite for a long time.

After school, I spread it out on the Green Room floor, hoping to lure Beth or, even more remotely, Dave into a game. Neither of them wanted to play, so as I often did, I pulled down the Infant of Prague statue—about two feet tall, his eyes glassy and calm, his milky-white fingers raised in a salute of peace—and installed him across the board as my opponent.

When I heard the car in the driveway, I put the Infant back in his place. My mother came inside but didn't take off her coat. She asked me to go get Beth and Dave. I did, and she told us that Dad had passed away, that he was with God in Heaven now, and that she needed to go upstairs and lie down.

As they all dispersed, I knew this to be bad, bad news, but I was also troubled by the thought of a ruined Christmas. And I knew that my bingo set would be forever tainted by this sudden circumstance.

That, essentially, is what I recall about my father's death, when he was fifty-seven and I was ten.

His funeral Mass was held on the morning of Christmas Eve, and I am told that I served as the altar boy while my family sat in the front pews. I don't recall if my father's body was in the church. I am quite sure that I never saw his corpse; I would like to think that I would remember having seen his face that last time.

I was not aware then of my mother's opinion of his miraculous resuscitation: She believed that God had allowed him to undergo expiation during his hospital stay instead of visiting Purgatory, and he would thereby go straight to Heaven. Nor was I aware that she was rejoicing over his death, insofar as it released him from a world of suffering into a world of peace, or that she had refused to wear black to the funeral, sending my sisters to Carl's department store in Schenectady to buy her a blue-and-gray outfit, and that she hadn't given them enough money but when they explained what the outfit was for, the clerk gave it to them anyway; or that when my mother cleaned out my father's safety-deposit box shortly after his death, she found a letter dated three years earlier:

> Dear Veronica:
> In case I die before you do, I want you to know you made heaven-on-earth for me during our married lifetime.
> Death may bring sadness to families, but you and I are happy to know that we shall meet again for all eternity, God willing— you and I and our wonderful, loving eight children.
> Again, thanks for being you, and providing the children and me with such wonderful happiness.
> > With love for all eternity,
> > Your Paul

Nor would I learn until many years later that relatives of mine, Jewish relatives from New York City, had come to the funeral, Uncle Nat and Aunt Dottie and their son, Mickey, forty years old by now, and Aunt Bess and Uncle Sam; or that Mickey cried in his car afterward, angry that Father DiPace had encouraged everyone to be happy for his Uncle Solly up in Heaven, wondering how in hell you're supposed to be *happy* about that; or that, back at our house, which was freezing cold because the furnace had broken again, these relatives walked in to find a big group of my parents' friends holding hands and singing hymns.

I was also not aware that, in the days after my father collapsed at the prayer meeting, hundreds of people telephoned the priests who ran the Charismatic Renewal group, and even the Albany bishop, wanting to hear more about the miraculous resuscitation of this man who plainly had been dead; or that once he finally did die, certain members of the Emmanuel prayer meeting were disconcerted that the Holy Spirit's healing power seemed to have abandoned him, prompting Father Tammany to speak of death as "the final healing," upsetting them even more; or that because of the frozen ground, my father's body couldn't be buried until the spring, at which time only my mother and a few of her Charismatic partners stood over his grave, my mother reading from St. Paul's second letter to Timothy: "I have fought the good fight, I have finished the race, I have kept the faith. From now on a merited crown awaits me."

Of all these events and emotions, I was completely unaware or would fail to remember. I took cues, certainly, from my mother's behavior. I did not cry, for instance, over my father's death. I did not dwell on it or even wish it hadn't happened.

Still, it hung over me, like a toxic cloud blocking the sun. Whenever it finally seemed about to lift, my mother or someone in her Charismatic crowd would mention how deeply God must have loved my father to have taken him from us and how proud and happy I should be, the son of a man so loved by God.

And that is where I stepped off that train. For while I was not interested in blaming God for killing my father, I certainly wasn't about to thank Him for it either.

5

MY actual participation in the church did not diminish in the six years between my father's death and my leaving for college. I was too unsophisticated for heresy and too obedient—toward my mother and, frankly, toward God—to betray even a hint of the empty-heartedness that had taken root inside me.

My fear of Hell had gradually worn off. Perhaps all the talk of my father's surefire ascension to Heaven persuaded me I'd be entitled to the same by virtue of kinship. Even in church I was having a hard time sensing God's presence, and I began to wonder if I'd ever sensed it at all or only imagined it, the way you imagined that the felt-footed Ouija palette was moving across the board on its own, whereas it was the encouragement of your mind and fingers that actually made it move. I didn't so much break up with God as put Him off for a while: I figured I'd make up with Him once I got married and had children, to keep us all safe from whatever damnation might or might not lie at the end of our days.

At the moment, I was far more interested in avoiding man-made punishment. Adults in general and authority figures in particular terrified me. One Saturday afternoon, Mr. Guyder, the school principal, came into Wolfe's Market in Quaker Street, where I worked as a stock boy. He was buying a half gallon of milk. As he did so, I trembled at the punishment he might suddenly choose to mete out. Adults were gatekeepers, disciplinarians, throttlers of desire. Their purpose in life, as I saw it, was to withhold from children all privilege and knowledge that would threaten their own supremacy. In the early grades of school, I was a pants wetter, a condition so debilitating that I would do anything to avoid it—pouring my milk down the sink at breakfast when my mother wasn't looking, fabricating excuses to leave the classroom—as long as it didn't involve confiding in an adult. Where adults were concerned, the less attention I could call to myself, the better.

This strategy, however, was at odds with another trait I had grown into: a steep desire to distinguish myself—not for the sake of excellence necessarily but for the attention that excellence would produce. Hitting a home run in Little League felt good because of the back-thumping I'd receive after crossing the plate. Afterward, the feat itself floated off, worthless. The same went for history tests and playing the piano in talent shows and being selected by Father DiPace to serve the bishop's Mass.

Even as I chased it, I sensed that this need for attention was unseemly. It ran counter to the brand of obedience I had been raised on. I knew what I *should* have done after hitting a home run: accept the congratulations far less eagerly than I did, then attribute the home run to God's will. But I could not act this way because I did not believe that God had played any greater role in the home run than in creating me in the first place, for which I was grateful but which did not convince me that my every flicker of muscle or syllable of speech was a result of His intervention, as my mother seemed to believe.

So I tamped down my aggressive, ambitious, unseemly desires as best as I could, presenting to my mother the son I assumed she wanted: polite, industrious, cheerful, obedient.

I saw that she mistook my obedience for religious devotion, and I let her. I didn't have the language to tell her otherwise, and I doubt she had the ear to hear it. We both were floundering, she without a husband and me without the family I'd grown up admiring. By the time I was twelve, only Beth and I were still living at home. Beth, truly virtuous, truly considerate, truly worshipful, and I, going through the motions. My mother sometimes sent us off on a weekend Catholic youth retreat in Albany. Beth would return inspired, energized. I'd come home almost broken. I hated sitting around in that circle, Indian-style, surrounded by felt banners ("We are all Lambs of God!"), talking about how Jesus was working in my life, because he wasn't and I didn't want him to. The year I was thirteen, Beth went off to college in Cortland, to become a teacher, and it was just my mother and me.

She threw herself ever more zestfully into her causes: the Right to Life movement, the prayer chain, the Charismatic Renewal meetings in Albany. On those late Sunday nights, I would sit at the window over the kitchen sink staring down the blackness of Gallupville Road, the old house painfully quiet but for the groaning of the windbreak trees in the winter wind. Whenever a pair of headlights broke through the dark, I'd run to the Green Room, willing them to turn into our driveway. When they didn't, I'd return to the kitchen, my throat tight, waiting not so much for the next set of headlights as for the phone to ring, with some volunteer ambulance man on the line asking if this was the home of Mrs. Veronica Dubner, saying, I hate to tell you this, son, but Route 7 was awful icy tonight, and there's been an accident.

But she always made it home, and I would scamper onto the

Green Room couch with my algebra homework, trying to look as if I hadn't been scared out of my skull thinking that the same place that had stolen my father had stolen her too.

She could tell, though. She would ask if I wanted to play a game—my choice. She'd pretend it wasn't already an hour past my bedtime and we'd play poker, five-card draw, using the Coles and Gluesings' cherries for poker chips, eating our way through the bank in fifteen minutes, always splitting the last pot. I'd bring in some wood from the back porch, bashing the ice off each piece, and we'd bank the woodstove and go to bed. She'd get up at five-thirty and wake me at six. We ate breakfast in silence, like an old married couple, oatmeal with wheat germ and molasses, then a dozen vitamin pills. I had to be at Wolfe's Market by six-forty-five. I hitchhiked in front of our house. Over the years, I caught rides with the same five or six men again and again, early-shifters at General Electric. I spoke only to answer their questions, never learned any of their names. At Wolfe's, I stocked shelves and mopped floors until eight-fifteen, then walked down Delanson Hill to school. After school there was Drama Club rehearsal in the fall, baseball in the spring, then home by seven for another cold night in a house built for ten, not two, the pair of us rattling around like the last two coins in some old man's pocket, or maybe God's.

My mother wasn't happy with this arrangement either. She began taking on foster children, one or two at a time. They went to church with us; my mother taught them to recite the Rosary, to say bedtime prayers, to hold their tongues if they were even thinking about saying anything negative about anything, and to appreciate whatever slim good fortune their leaky lives held. Once we had a brother and sister whose mother was Japanese and whose father was an American soldier. Then there was Jerome, just two years younger than I was, the only black kid in Duanesburg.

"You've got a lot to be grateful for, Jerome," my mother would say at supper, the three of us stuck for conversation.

"Yes, ma'am," Jerome would mumble through his meat loaf.

"God loves you, Jerome. He made you, He loves you, and He always will love you."

"Yes, ma'am." And then Jerome, from months of training, would take a deep breath and say, "The supper is very delicious," words that could be neither less sincere nor more untrue.

My mother would smile at his effort and say, as if responding to the Queen of England, "Why, thank you very much, Jerome."

My mother, loath to waste anything, had thought it a shame to waste all her parenting experience. That, at least, is why she told me she signed on as a foster parent. But the state stipend helped. Although our house was paid off, we were strapped, living on my father's VA and Social Security death benefits. Once the Arab oil embargo hit in 1973, we couldn't afford to run the furnace, so we shut down half the house and relied on the wood-stove. We bought a piglet to raise for our winter's meat, planted a half-acre garden to sell the surplus.

I didn't object to any of this. Such enterprise carried me further from childhood, closer to freedom, and working side by side with my mother, I began to admire her grim determination and utter lack of self-pity. Not once did I hear her complain or bemoan the lot she'd inherited. It was plainly she, not my father, who had kept the family so strong for so long. Her physical strength too was astonishing. One night, as I was washing the supper dishes, she commented on how tall I'd gotten and wondered if she could still lift me up. She came up behind me, wrapped her arms around my torso, and hoisted me into the air—cracking two of my ribs.

Around late September, when the weather forecast was calling for the first frost, I would come home straight from school to help her strip the garden. We would haul rickety bushel baskets up from the cellar and stuff them with corn and zucchini and pole beans, all of which we'd can or freeze in the coming weeks. I'd lay an old blanket on the ground beneath the Seckel pear tree, then climb it to shake down the fruit. There were too many tomatoes to pick by hand, and the green ones might still ripen if given a chance, so we'd uproot the plants, haul them into the cellar, and tie them upside down from the crossbeams. As darkness unfolded, we'd use flashlights to pick the last of the cucumbers, our noses running, fingers burning with the chill, the clear black sky pushing its first kiss of winter upon our sacred soil, the two of us scrambling like some eastern cousins of Ma and Tom Joad, prying from the land every last bit God would allow. Too exhausted to eat supper, we'd just sit in the kitchen with a pot of coffee, leaning in toward the woodstove.

It was clear that there would be no college money for me, just as there had been none for my brothers and sisters. This had provoked some grumbling, especially when my siblings' half-assmart classmates went off to Union College or Colgate or even Notre Dame. My mother was intolerant of such complaining. "It's easy for parents with one or two children to give them everything," she'd say. "We gave the gift of life to eight of you. We gave all of you the opportunity to work for whatever you want, and if you want to go to college, you'll just have to figure out how to work your way through."

They all did go, sooner or later, to state universities or community colleges. Nobody begged, nobody stole. Nor, though, did anybody try to leap over the very modest bar that our parents had set on personal ambition. Only Joe, whose will seemed forged from a harder material than the rest of ours, had taken his life and run. By now he was flying F-111s for the Air Force. Most of the others meandered a bit, through hippie boyfriends and macrobiotics and free jazz. Dave, once he got out of the house, rarely visited and, I later learned, was living on a farm where nudism was the rule.

They had all graduated from the same high school that I was now attending, across the street from Our Lady of Fátima. When the family first moved to Duanesburg, Joe and Mona and Marthe were sent to Catholic school in Schenectady. But between the expense, the long commute, and an indiscretion concerning dandelion wine that led to Mona's expulsion, they were soon transferred to the public school closer to home.

There, all my siblings had done something to distinguish themselves. They were prom queens and valedictorians, class clowns and sought-after sweethearts. They played sports, performed in the school choir and band, acted in Drama Club, ran the school newspaper and the student council. Peter was a legacy unto himself: smart enough for the slide-rulers, cool enough for the motorheads, athletic enough for the jocks, and probably the best musician and actor in the school. Peter was the guy everyone wanted to be like, myself included, when I arrived ten years after he'd blazed through.

Among the teachers, I was looked upon as the last of a minor dynasty. "Another Dubner, I see," said Mr. Davis, eyeballing me, on the first day of ninth-grade English. "Your brother Peter was one of the few excellent writers I've had the privilege of teaching who didn't deem it beneath himself to learn to diagram a sentence properly, for which I've remembered him fondly since, and which I hope you'll be wise enough to master as well."

I talked back to my teachers and made trouble for myself. But my genes rescued me. Writing came easily, especially the kind of writing that teachers wanted, as did the bald memorization that yielded high dividends on tests. Every time I stepped into a new class, I felt as if I'd already been there: For years, our supper table had buzzed with high-school Latin and French; with the lightning-quick alphabetical recitation, as required in ninth-grade history, of all the counties in New York State; with sedimentary and igneous and metamorphic and dangling participles and pi—"an irrational and transcendental number."

School was bearable only because of the extracurriculars, especially sports. I was smaller than average but also faster, and having been a baseball zealot since birth, I managed to play well enough by now to lead the high-school team. Basketball, though, was the money sport. Four hundred people would jam the bleachers for home games. Road games were even better, those long, dark, delicious bus rides home with a freshly exercised cheerleader shrugging off your clumsy embrace. So I joined the basketball team, too.

In the school band I played French horn, then trombone; in choir I sang a shaky tenor. Every fall I'd spend two months wrapped up in Drama Club, feasting on a plucky role like the Artful Dodger but primarily interested in getting Irene Swidersky, with that pertly inviting Czechoslovakian mouth of hers, alone behind the velvet curtains. I never got as far as I wanted with her; I knew, though, that even our dry kisses would go down as demerits on my soul.

Talent Night came each spring, another grab for attention. I'd practice for weeks, a hard-charging piano blues from the Otis Spann record Dave had given me or a howlingly bad "Jumpin' Jack Flash." I was constantly forming and dismantling rock bands. I hated the music my friends wanted to play—Journey, Elton John, the Bee Gees' pap from *Saturday Night Fever*—but I was a snob without a solution. Jazz, I knew, was ultracool, but I hadn't a clue to how it was played. The blues were more within my reach, and I loved how the Rolling Stones had updated Slim Harpo and Robert Johnson, but I sounded like a fool when I tried it.

The school newspaper had gone dead in Beth's era, so I started a new one, *Impact*. This immediately felt like a calling. My father had once helped us publish a family paper, the *Quaker Street Quacker*, which included hard news (Chicaboom, a family cat, getting hold of the Thanksgiving turkey as it thawed in the cellar), community updates (Marthe making the dean's list at college), and church announcements ("the establishment of a parish library by Mr. Paul Dubner, a.k.a. Dad").

The *Quacker* was, in some ways, a better paper than *Impact*. Now I was writing turgid editorials criticizing the school administration and breathless features touting the conscientious objector movement (I was already looking ahead to the possibility of being drafted). I was a greedy editor, writing half the stories and re-writing the rest, marking them up with one of the heavy black pencils my father had left behind. I learned to keep the pencil tucked behind my ear, to wet its tip with my tongue, just as he had done; what I didn't learn was to hide my dismay over the sluggish copy my colleagues filed.

I didn't have the nerve to be arrogant, so I became aloof, and not just with the newspaper. I didn't want any help from anyone. If I couldn't learn to do something for myself, then I wouldn't do it. Since my father had died, my brothers and sisters kept trying to draw me out; Peter or Ann would stop by the house on a Saturday to bring me books or just to horse around. But I couldn't get close to any of them. I liked them all fine, but they intimidated me, and their visits felt like charity.

Up through junior high school, I'd generally been a popular kid, with at least a few close friends. At about fourteen, though, I began to drift off. I felt miscast. I simply had a different engine under my hood—not better necessarily, in fact quite likely not, but certainly different, anxious about frequencies my friends didn't seem to hear, puzzled by the ease and satisfaction with which they cast their lives into the mainstream. My friends worked on their fathers' cars, drew up plans for the perfect hay-baler. I was the most unmechanical boy in school. Had I not played sports, I would surely have been considered a churchgoing namby wasting his time on frilly pursuits: music, the newspaper, and girls.

Girls made up a strange and special stratum of high-school life. They were our friends, classmates, neighbors; they were also, though, dearly guarded treasure vaults from which you would try to procure, at great odds and risk, a priceless, life-changing prize.

As for the particulars of this prize, I was largely in the dark. My parents had been extremely chastity-minded; I would have died of nerves trying to hide a dirty magazine in the house. My friends and I cobbled together misinformation, imaginings, and horror stories, much of it concerning Walter and Wanda Blanton, a brother and sister who lived on a dairy farm. Walter was said to have been caught "bawling" a cow. Wanda had allegedly used a frozen hot dog to "do" herself, and because it broke off inside, she was rushed to the emergency room. We were more reluctant to discuss the gropings we ourselves attempted, or said we attempted, those tense little wrestling matches smelling of denim and Prell. I knew only that each encounter might lead me nearer the fires of Hell, if they actually existed, but that I could not resist.

AS it turned out, my mother and I grew restless with our lives at the same time. I was fifteen, and she was fifty-seven. The older kids were coming home less often, the winters were longer, the house was colder. I was the man of the house, as it were, but powerless to recapture its old energy. It was hard to believe that the kitchen table where my mother and I now ate our glum suppers was the same table that had been so alive just seven or eight years earlier. We were poor, but it wasn't poverty that tortured us; it was depletion.

A family we knew from church had moved to Asheville, North Carolina, and said we should come visit. We did—my first plane trip—and my mother liked it well enough to move there. We made a plan: She would put the farm up for sale and I'd combine my last two years of school into one, then go to college somewhere in North Carolina.

There was a school up in the mountains, Appalachian State University, that offered me a full academic scholarship. I accepted and decided to study journalism; perhaps I could become a newspaperman or a sportscaster. For my last year of high school, I doubled up on a few courses and cut back on the extracurriculars. I still worked mornings at Wolfe's and served as an altar boy every Sunday, even though the cassock barely reached my knee by now.

I hadn't yet undergone confirmation, the Sacrament by which a young Catholic becomes a mature member of the Church. This happened in the eleventh grade. Every year the bishop would come out from Albany for a special ceremony at Our Lady of Fátima. But now the diocese announced a change: In the rural parishes, the bishop would be performing confirmations every *other* year. So he wouldn't be coming this year at all, and by the next year I'd be gone. Through a freak of scheduling, I would go unconfirmed in the parish where I had spent my entire life. I didn't much care, but my mother was distraught. She made me promise to take instruction and be confirmed at the Catholic church near my college. Of course, I said.

Another piece of our getaway plan soon went astray. By the late 1970s, the recession had pushed mortgage rates toward twenty percent. Suddenly no one was buying any houses, much less a windblown farmhouse with thirty-six acres on a bumpy road many miles from anywhere. It would be four years before my mother finally found a buyer. She would be alone much of those last four years, alone in the Eden she had created, its spirit intact, its flesh diminished.

I too would be alone, or at least on my own, and I was grateful. I was sixteen years old, eager for reinvention. The world I knew— my house, my family, my town—was a fraction of a shard of reality. The God I knew was finite, rigid, distant. My mother warned me that I might have some trouble down South, being a Catholic in the Bible Belt. They might run their hands through my curly black hair, she said, feeling for the nubs of Satan's horns.

Satan's horns? On me, a Catholic? This news shocked me. From the gossip I'd heard at school and church, the Jews were the ones with devil horns. Catholics were the most chosen of all people. Perhaps my mother had misspoken? Or had she and my father somehow passed on to me the gene for devil horns? But since they weren't even Jewish by the time I was born, how could that be? Surely they had been Catholic long enough to eradicate whatever ill side effects the Jews might possess. Surely I had nothing to do with the Jews, whoever they were.

6

APPALACHIAN State University had been founded around the turn of the century as a teacher's academy in the tiny mountain town of Boone, North Carolina. By 1980, when I arrived, there were ten thousand students. The campus, having insinuated itself into the middle of town, was a patchwork of brick and stone buildings laced together by steep stairways cut into the red-dirt hills.

There were in general three types of student: the well-dressed children of textile and tobacco executives, often blond, with plenty of money for Duke or Wake Forest but insufficient grades or a pressing desire to spend their college years piloting a BMW from one mountaintop keg party to the next; the well-behaved children of southern Christians, often Baptists, who would study elementary education or chorale music or forestry, meet a like-minded future spouse, and return four years later to Mount Airy or Raleigh to lead the same carefully constructed lives their parents had led; and the well-read children of teachers and southern intellectuals, often stoned, who quoted Flannery O'Connor and Woody Allen and listened to Lynyrd Skynyrd (but with ironic detachment) and who boasted no discernible future plans. It was this third group, a slim minority, that I fell in with. Schoolwork was at best our second priority; we were too busy gently expanding our minds, whether watching *Citizen Kane* for the fourteenth time or climbing a mountain to gaze down on the classes we were cutting.

My roommate, Patrick Tamer, came from a Lebanese Catholic family. They owned a grocery store in Winston-Salem. Patrick was a math major and had a lame leg. He spent every night in the library, the five-minute walk taking him fifteen, dragging his dead foot up and down a dozen of those rocky staircases. Yet Patrick was never late for anything. He woke early on Sunday mornings to walk the half mile to Mass. The first few weeks, I went with him. And then I stopped, as casually as one might stop attending a weekly lecture series that had grown tiresome. When my mother called to ask how my confirmation instructions were coming along, I told her that, Well, you know, Mom, things move slow down South. Every conversation with my mother eventually got around to God: I should pray before every exam, I should ask God for career counsel. I generally let her speak her piece, mumbled in agreement, then ignored her advice.

At Appalachian, there were roughly fifty times the number of young women that I had known in high school. During the fall semester, I fell in love with perhaps a dozen of them. These were southern girls, soft of voice, soft to the touch, pastel clouds of bare shoulder and cashmere, so unlike the farm girls back home with their thin, chapped lips and thick woolen sweaters. A few of these college women were titillated by the thought of a New Yorker in their midst; I did not reveal that my part of New York made Mount Airy look like a big city. With unruly dark hair and a strange accent, I was as good as a Frenchman. To them, I seemed dangerous—which in a sense I was, overwhelmed by the sudden limitlessness of a heretofore precious commodity and by the license to acquire it.

Halfway through the fall semester, I was well on my way to losing my scholarship. But the day I failed my first midterm, I envisioned spending the next few years cooped up in the cold farmhouse back in Duanesburg with my mother and decided to change my ways. I began going to my classes, reading the books.

Early one morning I was heading for class with David Pugh, a good and roguish friend who called himself Stinky. We came upon a slight, blond, bleary-eyed fellow, crunching over the icy sidewalk with a halting sort of delicacy.

"Jeffrey Foster!" Stinky called out.

Jeffrey squinted up at him, spoke lightly: "Hey, Stinky."

"Jeffrey Foster, you look like something too goddamn sorry for the goddamn cat to even bother dragging in."

Jeffrey smiled. "I just drove up from Greensboro. Elvis Costello played last night."

"Elvis Costello! And how was Mr. Costello?"

"He was good. He was real good. His band is incredible." Jeffrey had icy blue eyes and a soft country accent.

Stinky introduced us, we shook hands, and Stinky and I walked on.

"Was he stoned?" I asked him.

"No, he's not into that at all. That's just the way he looks. Jeffrey Goddamn Foster!"

I had seen some hand-lettered signs around campus: WANTED: GUITARIST AND DRUMMER TO START BAND. ORIGINALS, PLUS ELVIS COSTELLO, BRUCE SPRINGSTEEN, BUDDY HOLLY, THE CLASH. I'd thought about calling—it would be nice, I thought, to be in a band again—but I was a piano player. A week later, though, I ran into Jeffrey again, and he told me that those hand-lettered signs were his and that what he really wanted *was* a piano player, like Roy Bittan in Bruce Springsteen's band. He said he was worried that if he'd advertised for a piano player, he'd get calls from everyone who'd ever taken a few lessons in his parents' parlor.

The next night, we let ourselves into the music building. Jeffrey had a friend, Tim Fleming, who was learning to play bass. Neither of them had ever been in a band before. They both had guitars, though, and a little Fender amp, and we taped a microphone to a broom handle and stuck it through the slats of a chair to hold it straight. We played about thirty songs that first night, a few that Jeffrey had written and everything else we could think of: Buddy Holly, the Rolling Stones, Bruce Springsteen, Bob Dylan. At the end of each song we'd come down on the last chord with a big crash, sweating and grinning.

The semester ended, and I went home for Christmas break. My mother looked half her size, as if the cold had shriveled her. Beth came home too, but even the three of us were no match for the memories of the house. They overpowered us, sent us to bed early, made our supper conversation timid. On Christmas Eve we all went to Midnight Mass. The church looked tiny and gray, and so did Father DiPace. As an altar boy, I had thought of Midnight Mass as the big show—the packed pews, the well-rehearsed choir, the altar decked in pine boughs and white tapers. But now the whole scene had lost its magic. Even the incense, that dark aroma I had once thought of as God's very breath, seemed like just another prop in an ostentatious floor show. I was impatient for Christmas to end and to get back to school.

Jeffrey and I had agreed to meet in Boone a week early so we'd have the run of the music building. Every day we'd play for a few hours, then listen to records and plot our impending greatness. We came up with a name for the band, The Right Profile, and when the semester began, we found a drummer. Within a month we unveiled ourselves in a concert at the student union, thrashing and leaping and singing from the center of our guts, and we were instantly taken to heart by the hundred or so discerning fans who believed, like us, that three loud chords and unbridled emotion could defeat even the most serious musical deficiencies.

That first show was all we needed. We were to spend the next several years in the bosom of this band we'd created, this exclusive club of high ideals and higher ambitions. I had never been happier. If either Jeffrey or I had been a woman, I'm sure we would have gotten married on the spot. We had come together like the last two pieces of a jigsaw puzzle.

Jeffrey projected an odd air—precious, people called him—and he thought quite highly of himself, even in the beginning, when there wasn't much reason to. But he also had a deep sense of right. His parents, Wanda and Larry, were rock-solid Lutherans from Winston-Salem, among the most decent people I'd ever met. We often slept at their house when we played a concert nearby, and if we wound up there on a Sunday morning, we'd go to church with them. We weren't enthusiastic exactly, and they didn't push us, but it just seemed the right thing to do.

Our appearances to the contrary—we had begun to cultivate the requisite scraggly rock-band look—we were straight arrows. Jeffrey rarely drank, had never smoked pot. Without intending to, he helped me back onto solid ground. He knew what he wanted to do with his life, and I was grateful to have wandered into his dream.

Spending time with Jeffrey and his parents also made me begin to appreciate my mother again. I still didn't enjoy her advice, which she dispensed at every opportunity. But now that she was no longer governing my daily behavior, I felt that her standards were admirable, if unrealistic. I felt myself swinging back toward her, wanting to stand beside her as much for my sake as for hers. For all her heavy-handedness, she was a good influence.

Not that I could voice any of this to her. We simply didn't talk that way. She was forty-two years older than I was; she was my mother. But her wisdom worked its way inside me. At one point,

I was ready to quit college for the band. "Well, if you think that's really the right thing to do, you should do it," she said. "But I wish you'd think it over. Someday you'll be happy to have that degree. You may want to go to graduate school."

Graduate school? Please. I was eighteen years old, interested only in writing songs, learning the guitar, achieving international stardom. But I sensed that my mother truly understood my situation. She too had been an artist, a ballerina. We had barely talked about it, but I'd seen the pictures: my young and quite beautiful mother, a thoroughly different person, leaping through the air in a shiny silk outfit, her fingers pointed delicately skyward, a glow of ecstasy around her eyes. When the older kids were still at home, my mother had set up summer school around the kitchen table: a little math, a little French, a little painting. Then we'd all troop into the Green Room for a ballet lesson. My mother's entire manner would change, from harried mom to focused artiste, straightening the small of Ann's back with a firm hand, showing us how to extend our arms so they flowed gracefully from our torsos, like branches from a tree—like Jesus on the cross. She let me feel the muscles in her stomach, still firm, and the strange muscle just above her shin. "That's a ballet muscle," she said. "There's no other way to get it."

So my mother, I knew, had some idea of the life I was trying to put together. I stayed in college.

Every weekend, The Right Profile played wherever we could get a booking. Close to home we'd draw five hundred people, who sang along with every song. We also played roadhouses in Tennessee and South Carolina and Alabama, where the reception was considerably cooler. Once, the end of our set brought a shower of empty beer bottles. "That's what they do sometimes when they're really into the band," the bartender told us matter-of-factly. "When they don't like it, they just find the power cord and rip it out of the wall."

Jeffrey and I were each writing dozens of songs. He sang

his and I sang mine, more Lennon and McCartney than Jagger and Richards. The Rolling Stones, though, were our heroes, along with Bob Dylan. They did what we wanted to do: build a foundation of country and blues and folk music and add that mysterious, heart-stopping layer of raw emotion, equal parts tenderness and arrogance. We filled our songs with lovers seeking redemption, with lonely, desperate souls trying to break out of their hardscrabble world. The strange thing was, God was also inside a lot of our songs—often unnamed, as I suppose He was inside me at the time, but there He was, the irrepressible force that broke and fixed lives. Meanwhile we read book after book about the Rolling Stones and Dylan. They too had been schoolboys once. What kind of Faustian deal had they struck to climb the mountain?

I was astounded to learn that Bob Dylan had been born in Duluth, Minnesota, as Robert Zimmerman—a Jew! *This* was a Jew? By now, Dylan had famously become a born-again Christian. His conversion made me think of my father: What did he and Bob Dylan possibly have in common? Dylan was caustic, judgmental, with an acid wit; my father was gentle, with a low opinion of himself, and hopelessly corny. I couldn't even begin to make a connection.

I did, though, begin to pay a bit more attention to things Jewish, at least the Jewish things available to me in the mountains of North Carolina, which consisted primarily of Woody Allen movies and, once, a staged reading of *The Dybbuk*. Then I came across a book of Isaac Bashevis Singer's short stories and found such a great line in "Gimpel the Fool" that I stole it for a song I was writing. The song told the story of a young man whose one brief burst of evil lands him on death row. In Singer's story, a rabbi delivered the line; I gave it to the young man's mother— *my* mother: "My mama used to say/ Better a fool all your days/ Than to be evil for one hour."

Along with that unnamed God, my mother, or someone a lot like her, floated through many of my songs. The mother stood for wisdom and tradition and righteousness; her son, meanwhile, piled up transgressions. He didn't mean to, necessarily—sins just seemed to *happen* to him. Afterward his conscience would torture him. Yet he couldn't handle all that wisdom and tradition and righteousness his mother had tried to pass on. It was all too heavy, or he was simply too weak.

MY mother still hadn't been able to sell the farmhouse. But at sixty-one she could no longer stand the winters. Her friends Peggy and Bill Wink encouraged her to come to Florida, where they lived. Thanks to her nurse's training, and having raised eight children, she got herself qualified as a home aide, then found an elderly, wealthy woman in West Palm Beach who had broken a hip and needed live-in assistance. This woman, my mother told me, had plenty of floor space for me to sleep on. I should come visit during spring break, stick my toes in the warm ocean.

I caught a ride south with a student named Sean who was driving to Miami in an orange Jeep. But when we reached Tampa Bay, he pulled off the highway and announced that we were spending two nights there because he had to go to his grandfather's eightieth birthday party.

"There's an extra bedroom at my aunt's house," he said. "The party'll be cool. My grandfather's loaded."

I didn't have the money for a bus ticket, so I called my mother and told her I was running late.

Sean went out that night with some old friends, leaving me at his aunt's house. The grandfather's birthday was apparently a big deal. All sorts of relatives had made their way to Tampa Bay, including a family who was also staying in the aunt's house. The father of this family was named Irving. He was in his late thirties, with a wife and two young daughters. They were all sitting and talking in the living room. Irving was a bit sloppy, with a loose smile and big, fluttering hands.

"What's *your* connection to the Judge?" Irving asked me.

"Who's the Judge?"

Irving smiled at me. "Well, he's not really a judge. We just call him that. The birthday boy. He's our uncle—well, not my uncle, my wife's uncle." He gestured to her, and she smiled too.

"The Judge is my *great*-uncle," said the younger of the little girls.

"Mine too," said the other.

"We're from *Brooklyn*," said the first girl.

"The Judge is *rich*," said the older one.

"He paid for our flight," Irving said, as if he really appreciated it. "It's extra nice, because I get to see my mother. She lives nearby."

"My parents are from Brooklyn," I said.

"Whereabouts?"

"I don't know. I think my mother lived near Ebbets Field."

"You've never been back?" Irving asked.

"No."

"Not even to visit your bubbe?"

"What's a bubbe?"

Irving blinked, twice, and scratched the top of his head, which was going bald. "Aren't you Jewish?" he asked.

I had no idea why he said that. No, I explained, I wasn't Jewish, but my parents had been, before they became Catholic.

Irving looked at me as one might look at a dog that had suddenly stood up and begun to tap-dance. "Anyway, once a Jew, always a Jew," he said after a moment, chuckling, and I laughed too and nodded, as if I understood.

We kept talking, and then, since there was a piano in the room, I played for a while, showing off on the fastest blues I knew.

"You play the piano like you're Jewish," Irving said.

"Is that a good thing or a bad thing?"

"From where I sit," he said, "it's a very good thing indeed."

I usually felt uncomfortable with strangers, even with my own brothers and sisters, but Irving and his family relaxed me. I kept playing, and we all sang: "When the Saints Go Marching In," the little girls singing too, and "St. Louis Blues" and, because I couldn't think of anything else, "Happy Birthday," in honor of the Judge. We sang harmonies, high and true, Irving throwing his arms out the way my father used to when he sang "My Yiddishe Mama."

"Whew!" Irving laughed when we finished. "The Judge will sure be sorry he missed that one. Kiddos, I hate to say it, but we're *way* past bedtime." Irving turned to me. "See you in the morning, okey-doke?"

For some reason, I threw myself at Irving in a clumsy hug, and Irving, surprised, hugged me back. The little girls giggled, but then Irving's wife, sensing my embarrassment, hugged me too.

IN the morning, Sean's aunt loaned me some too-big dress-up clothes and gave me a ride to the Judge's estate. It curved around a huge piece of bay, acres of deeply shaded lawn and a long, spread-out house, very fancy. The living room was an expanse of dark, polished wood. The only light-colored object in it was a gleaming white grand piano, which I did not even think about approaching, surrounded as it was by intimidatingly well-dressed, well-postured adults, a wall of twinkling jewelry and brilliant white teeth and bony wrists cocked around wineglasses.

I was introduced to the Judge—he was small, wrinkled, extremely tanned, with a gray goatee, like a retired conquistador—then shuttled outside, where the other teenagers were standing around.

Sean, whom I hadn't seen since he abandoned me the night before, strode over. "Hey, my cousin has a huge bag of coke," he said. "We'll be in the pool house." He walked off toward the bay, his cousin, a big-boned blond girl, hurrying to catch up.

Irving found me standing alone and brought me over to meet his mother. Her name was Mimi. She was at least my mother's age. She looked like my mother too—the same full lips, a certain brightness around the eyes—but Mimi wore her hair long, a thick caramel brown trailing down her back. She had on a silky dress with a blue scarf around her shoulders.

"Irving told me all about you," she said. "You should have phoned me up last night, such a party you were having."

Irving went off to get Mimi something to drink.

"He's a very nice man, Irving is," I said, nervous suddenly. "But he'd have to be, with a mother like you."

"Oh! Flattery will get you everywhere."

A black waiter in a white uniform, excusing himself, told us that lunch was being served. All guests under twenty-five were invited to eat in the rec room.

"Twenty-five? I just missed the cut," Mimi said with a smile, taking my hand in hers. "Until we meet again, yes?"

In the rec room, Sean was sitting between the big-boned blonde and a pretty dark-haired girl with watery eyes. He looked up but didn't wave me over, so I sat at the other end of the table with Irving's two daughters. A waiter served us shrimp and crab legs, then sliced pork with candied apple.

Afterward I went looking for Mimi. She was standing alone at the edge of the empty dance floor. The band—six musicians, about Mimi's age—was just tuning up.

"Hey, young fella," the drummer shouted over, "you get away from her now, she's mine!"

"What are you, Max, crazy?" the piano player said. "You didn't hear me talking with the lady? We made a date already."

Mimi clasped my hand, smiled at me. "They're *all* talk," she said.

The band started playing "Strangers in the Night," and Mimi led me onto the floor. I hated to dance, and I didn't know how. The last time I'd tried was at Marthe's wedding, with my mother, and I had felt awkward touching her that way. But now my right hand slid easily into the small of Mimi's back, my left hand locking comfortably around her right. We moved in a small, serene circle.

Between songs Mimi told Charlie, the piano player, that I played piano too.

"Get over here, kid," he said. "Let me take the doll for a spin."

I sat in on "Summertime" and "My Funny Valentine," making nervous three-note chords and trying to keep a cigarette burning in the corner of my mouth like Max, the drummer. I watched Mimi and Charlie dancing, too closely for my taste, beneath a sad willow tree. Max handed me five bucks when I got up. "I've heard worse," he said.

Mimi and I danced three more songs, still the only couple on the floor. In the distance we watched the entire birthday party, some two hundred people, tramp in one thick stream toward the water's edge. They stopped out of our sight. Mimi whispered something that I didn't hear, and I tilted my ear down as she reached up to whisper again, and we laughed at the lovely collision. Then she said, "I think we're missing the Judge's birthday cake."

We danced two more songs. "Well," Mimi said, "I do believe I've had my fun." She shook the musicians' hands, all six of them, and asked if I would call a taxi for her.

"I can take you," I said. "Wait right here."

I wasn't much of a driver, and was particularly nervous about unfamiliar roads. But I found Sean, standing at the outer edge of the big group, his arm locked around the blond cousin's shoulder, and asked if I could borrow his car. He dug into his pocket for the keys. I gathered up Mimi, opened the passenger door of Sean's orange Jeep, helped her up. She directed me to her apartment, and I didn't even think to panic about how I would find my way back.

We passed the security booth at her apartment complex, then navigated a twisty drive past flower gardens and fountains. Her apartment was on the second floor, purple fuchsias hanging along the overhead rail. She turned the key, stepped inside, pirouetted to face me.

"Well," she said.

A breeze caught the fuchsias and spun them about, a merry-go-round of magenta flashing onto Mimi's face. Her lipstick, a creamy red, was fresh; she must have touched up while I was getting Sean's keys. She also seemed smaller now, more pixieish. When we danced, her lips had rested just below the curve of my jaw. Now her lips would reach only my Adam's apple. And mine were no longer level with the bridge of her nose, but with her widow's peak. I saw that she was holding her shoes in her hand. When had she taken them off?

Finally I leaned toward her. She turned her face just so, my lips meeting not her lips but her cheek, as warm and soft as rose petals. Reluctantly I let my lips finish their kiss, and pulled away.

"I had a wonderful time, and I thank you," Mimi said. She looked into my eyes, as if to say, Yes yes yes but no, and I commanded my eyes to say, No no no, of course, and we clasped hands for the last time.

Driving back to the Judge's estate—I got severely lost, it took me an hour, and Sean yelled at me—I tried to make sense of what had happened. I had never felt so instantly attracted to another person. But the feeling went beyond attraction. It was as if I were a piece of her somehow, or as if within her dwelled a piece of me that I had been searching for. But what could possibly dwell within a sixty-year-old Jewish woman that would stir me so?

I never saw Mimi again, but I would think of her often, and dream about her, such tender, glorious dreams that they almost, but not quite, came to overpower the memory of the day I fell in love with her.

7

THE Right Profile, by the time we all finished college, had become my family. Like a family, we quarreled and scrapped for attention, but we were bound by a common pursuit and attacked it with a singleness of vision, almost unthinkingly. Who in his right mind, after all, wouldn't want to be a rock star?

We moved to Winston-Salem, Jeffrey's hometown, and rented an old clapboard house. On rainy nights the entire sky stank of tobacco, as though a thousand old men were working their chaws on the same front porch. Jeffrey's father owned a store that sold fishing gear and installed car mufflers. We rehearsed in its basement, the clatter of our guitars and drums rattling the tailpipes that hung from the ceiling like a row of giant silvery fish.

Jeffrey and I were writing good songs by now, and music hounds were tracking down bootlegged tapes of our concerts. When we went to the mall, teenage girls would trail us; we'd get fan letters from England and Sweden and South Africa. We had graduated from playing roadhouses to first-tier nightclubs and college auditoriums. This was power, this was release: hundreds of hungry eyes straining upward, waiting for you to slash the guitar strings, to lean into the microphone and tell your tales of curdled love and crazy dreams. For the next two years we practically lived in our van, a tribe of desperate troubadours, waiting to be beckoned into the big time the way some of the bands we were friendly with, R.E.M. and the Del Fuegos, had been beckoned.

Finally it came: a call from a New York management company. These people had heard our tapes, followed our ascent, and didn't see any reason why we couldn't get a record contract.

In the middle of a bitterly cold February, they brought us to New York City to play C.B.G.B., the cramped, dank temple of hard-edged rock music. Encamped in the darkness, beyond the throw of the stage lights, sat the keepers of our fate, a cordon of producers and record-label scouts. Among them, our managers told us, was Clive Davis, the legendary former president of Columbia Records who now ran Arista Records.

We played as we always played, as though on this, or any given night, we might possibly be the best rock band in the world.

We weren't, of course. Jeffrey had a good voice but lacked a killer instinct; I had the killer instinct but a voice prone to great breaches of melody. Our guitars were too twangy, our drums too brash, our energy too reckless. But the same alchemy that had visited us that first night we'd played together, in the college music building, had never vanished. At the end of our set, we collapsed giddily in our tiny dressing room, drenched in sweat and expectation, the black walls around us graffitied with the names of the hundreds of bands that had made this same pilgrimage.

We were told that Clive Davis wanted to speak with us. We met him out on the sidewalk, an icy stretch of panhandlers and spent needles. He was a trim little man, bald, in a long blue overcoat.

"I enjoyed your music very much," he said. "I understand good songwriting when I hear it. I understood Bob Dylan, and I understood Bruce Springsteen. Your people tell me you're in New York for a few days. Why don't we talk things over in my office?" He looked at me, a stupid grin on my face, sweating and shivering in the rank, brittle air. He unwrapped his scarf—dark, mottled, expensive silk—and tied it around my neck. "We can't have our new band catching pneumonia now," he said, and climbed into his limousine.

I had to return the scarf when we met, but Davis gave us our record contract. Five years of toil had led to the promised land. We would make our record, score hit singles, tour the world, stick fame and wealth in our pockets, and do it all over again, until we were ancient, like Bob Dylan himself.

Over the years, Jeffrey and I had formed an intense relationship. We were soul mates, practically with our own language. Whenever I wrote a song, I would bring a guitar up to his room and play it through; we'd add and subtract, try some harmonies, talk through how the band should play it. And he would do the same. Whether a song was born in his fingers or mine, it soon belonged to both of us.

Now, though, as we plotted our first record, our egos turned proprietary. *Seven* of his songs and only *three* of mine? Worse yet, Arista asked us to consider recording *someone else's* song for our first single. Our songs were great, they told us, but maybe not commercial enough for radio.

It was decided that we should move to New York for a year, to write more songs and meet with the producers that Arista was foisting on us. We rented a house in Cliffside Park, New Jersey, just across the George Washington Bridge from Manhattan. Jeffrey and I sat in our rooms all night writing, then tromped out to the garage the next afternoon to rehearse with the band. We'd stop only when the police came. It was a quiet neighborhood, full of retired mafia men, and our noise was unwelcome.

For entertainment, we took the bus into Manhattan to prowl record stores and used bookshops. New York mystified and frightened me. Our trip to C.B.G.B. had been my first time back since the Yankee Stadium trip with my father. I knew my parents had grown up here, but I couldn't square their image with C.B.G.B. and the subway winos and the clog of businessmen on Fifty-seventh Street, where Arista had its offices. My parents were country folk, as was I. The city devoured people like me. Its rhythm was unsolvable, its density incomprehensible.

At the same time, it called out to me, and I felt compelled to peel its layers. It was, after all, my parents' homeland—though I couldn't even begin to imagine what sort of lives they had led here, some forty years earlier.

I began exploring Manhattan more and more, especially after I met a girl by the name of Abigail Seymour. Her older sister, a journalist in North Carolina, had written an article about our band just before we moved north. "I have a sister who studies photography at NYU," she'd said. "She's absolutely beautiful and very talented and lovely in every way. Why don't I give you her number?"

She did, and while I had generally found older sisters' testimonials to be vastly overstated, this one was not. Abigail was a Sargent painting come to life, a classic beauty, with fair coloring and delicate features and a spirit as vibrant as any I had ever encountered.

I had known Abigail a few months when it was time for the band to move again. We had gotten our way with Arista: We would record our songs and our songs only, with a producer of our choosing, who worked out of Memphis. His name was Jim Dickinson, a minor legend of Deep South rock and roll who, most impressively, had played piano on the Rolling Stones' "Wild Horses." He was old pals with Keith Richards. This association placed him, however marginally, in the pantheon we were so desperate to join.

We flew to Memphis, the air already sticky by early June, to start recording. It was the first time we'd ever gotten on an airplane with our guitars; it was enormously satisfying to stack them in the storage bin near the front of the plane, among the businessmen's lifeless garment bags.

Jim Dickinson was friendly enough, and seemed to have a good feel for our music. He had, we knew, not only played with the Rolling Stones but partaken, rather fully, of their druggy lifestyle. As if to offer proof, he gave me a photo of himself and Keith Richards in a hotel room, their glazed eyes peering through a cloud of cigarette smoke, Keith's trademark bottle of Jack Daniel's nestled between them. I taped the picture inside my guitar case. Let the rock gods watch over me, I thought.

We had recorded enough demo tapes by now to know how slow and inorganic the process could be. This, though, was ten times worse. Dickinson's vibe settled over us, and it was miasmic. Our rock-hero producer had endured major stomach trouble, and his diet now consisted mainly of marijuana and Coca-Cola. This seemed to soothe him, but it also put him severely out of sync with us, his admirers and dependents. Sitting at the mixing console with Dickinson, listening to the playback at a thundering volume, I would remind myself that this was indeed the promised land we'd been dying to enter. We returned to our hotel every night exhausted from inactivity.

Late one night, after the ninth consecutive room-service dinner, I sat with my guitar and composition book, trying to sharpen the lyrics to the song we'd be recording the next day. My hand, without any instruction I was aware of, printed on the page: *What do I want?*

I stared it down. What kind of question was that? I knew what I wanted.

Are you sure? one half of me asked the other.

Of course I'm sure.

So what is this thing you want?

What I am doing now. Writing music, singing songs.

Why?

Because it's important. Well, it's fun. F-u-n. I'm doing it be-cause it's what I want to do.

You don't look like you're having fun.

Well, I am.

You look like you're watching Jim Dickinson, with his half a stomach and his cloud of pot smoke, and thinking, Maybe I don't want this after all.

Shut up, please, I said. And then, because I was sick of arguing with myself, and was sick of myself in general, I got into bed.

I had considered quitting the band before. But such thoughts were generally precipitated by a string of lousy concerts or an-other twelve-hour van ride or a long, silent standoff with Jeffrey over some perceived slight.

Now, though, I had no legitimate complaint. We had arrived; we were doing exactly what I'd dreamed of doing for five years. Lying in bed that night, to my great surprise, I found myself think-ing about Father DiPace's sermon from my childhood, about the dangers of waiting for the next good thing to happen.

When I awoke the next morning, I asked myself the same ques-tion: What do I want? And the answer came to me, in a Ramada Inn in muggy Memphis, with the force of a revelation: Not this.

I tried to think my way out of it. The band was all I had; the band was all I *was*. But the voice inside me would not be quelled. I spent the rest of our recording session in a state of secret mourn-ing. Every day, as I became ever more convinced that I needed to get out, I grew more disappointed that my own mind was forcing me to abandon the one passion I had ever owned.

We finished our work in Memphis and returned to Winston-Salem. I must have had a lousy poker face, for when I finally told Jeffrey and the others, they didn't seem all that surprised. The phone rang steadily the next few days: our managers, Arista ex-ecutives, friends from other bands. Some tried to talk me out of it; others let me know I was a heretic or a fool, or both. I admitted that I couldn't really explain why I was leaving. I would mumble that I'd had second thoughts about wanting to be famous, which was true, but incomplete. I didn't have the courage to say, *Well, I heard a kind of voice, and it told me that this whole band thing isn't healthy for me—not physically unhealthy, but unhealthy for my soul somehow.*

How odd this was. In our lyrics, Jeffrey and I both used the word "soul" with abandon. It packed an enormous wallop, that one little word (plus it was easy to rhyme with). But in these conversations I couldn't bring myself to speak it.

I didn't know it at the time, but at twenty-two, I was the same age as my mother when she quit ballet. Truth be told, I barely knew anything about my mother. But as I later learned, we both had removed ourselves from the one pursuit we cared about; we both felt, momentarily at least, that our lives were over. We had both asked ourselves an unanswerable question and, hearing nothing but a still, small voice from within, a feathery voice of encouragement, had taken the leap.

She, of course, leaped into the arms of Jesus Christ. I wound up leaping into the arms of Abigail Seymour. But I could hardly have known that Abigail—my Sargent vision, a college junior, the daughter of a stalwart Yankee family—would lead me into a reckoning with my Jewish blood.

8

SIX months earlier, on our first date, I had taken Abigail to the Ritz to hear a swing band led by Charlie Watts, the Rolling Stones' drummer. As I was still an aspiring rock star, this was the coolest ticket imaginable. Keith Richards was supposed to be in the house, maybe Mick Jagger as well. But Abigail and I never even ventured into the main hall. We sat all night on the worn marble staircase leading down to the cloakroom, talking about our families.

Abigail's father, Thaddeus, was the president of Rollins College in Florida. Her late grandfather Whitney North Seymour was an esteemed lawyer, a president of the American Bar Association who had argued more than a hundred cases before the U.S. Supreme Court. Abigail spoke admiringly of Whit; among his many involvements, he'd been a warden at Grace Episcopal Church, which was just a few blocks from the Ritz. In a more plaintive tone, she told me about her other grandfather, an artist named

Jon Gnagy, the host of television's first learn-to-draw program. He'd led a tumultuous life, his mind full of disquiet and demons. "But you can't run from your roots," Abigail said, "so you may as well untangle them."

In turn, I told Abigail about my rural Catholic upbringing and what little I knew about my parents' lives.

"What were your grandparents' names?" she asked.

Thud. I didn't know. "I guess I should look into it," I said, "but as far as I know, everyone's dead. I don't think my father had much contact with his family after he converted. I barely knew *him*, really."

Abigail and I both were the babies of our families—she had two brothers and two sisters—which, we agreed, was significant, perhaps even fateful. Although she was a photography major in college, what she really wanted to be was an actress. She studied with a man named Ivan Kronenfeld. "He's more than an acting teacher," she said. "It's very hard to put into words what he does. He's crazy but he's brilliant. Not crazy—*mad*. Mad with wisdom, and incredibly difficult, but the way he teaches you to see beneath the surface, it's amazing. And really, under all his bluster, he's got a huge heart. But he scares the shit out of me."

I'd had a few steady girlfriends during college, but from the outset Abigail and I roamed a higher plane. We traipsed around New York, visiting bookstores and bars and museums, discussing, only half in jest, what our children would look like (her features, we hoped, and my coloring).

After my awakening in Memphis, and after I quit the band, Abigail offered to find an apartment in New York for the two of us. Within a week, I sold my guitars, packed a U-Haul, and left North Carolina for good.

I arrived in New York in October 1987. Abigail had found a fourth-floor walkup in Chelsea. She had caught me on the rebound, as it were, from the band, and we nested like a pair of blissful birds. Under her direction, I painted the apartment and put up some antique molding. We blanketed the living-room walls with flea-market paintings, filled our shelves with old volumes of Thurber and Mencken and Shakespeare that her mother sent us. For our first Christmas, Abigail gave me a book of early Brooklyn photographs. "To better understand your roots," she wrote inside.

Abigail was spending her days at NYU, three nights a week at Ivan Kronenfeld's studio, and another two nights waitressing. I found daytime work as an office temp, and began writing short stories at night. From the window I'd watch the drug dealers slip in and out of the shadows; when Abigail was on her way home, she would call from a pay phone so I could meet her at the corner.

As for the future, I was baffled. All I knew was that I wouldn't return to music. The band, I'd heard, had finished the record without me, but Arista didn't like it and was preparing to drop them; over time I would fall out of touch with Jeffrey and the others.

I considered becoming a psychologist (Abigail deemed this a terrible idea), and then I thought about writing novels and teaching college (a plan she approved). We looked into graduate writing programs. Columbia was the best but horribly expensive, and with my credentials—Appalachian State University and a few amateurish short stories—it seemed a waste of money to apply. At root, I felt undeserving. Abigail, though, had different roots. "You should go to Columbia," she said. "We'll borrow the money. If you have a choice, you should choose the best—like Ivan's always teaching, your *choice* is your talent." So I applied to Columbia.

I had yet to meet this Ivan, this shaper of my girlfriend's mind. One Sunday morning, as we pawed through a stack of old photographs at a flea market, Abigail froze.

"Oh, my God!" she said. "There's Ivan. With Anne."

"Where?"

"Oh, God, he sees us. He's coming this way."

"All right. What's the big deal?"

"It's *Ivan*," she whispered tersely.

They walked toward us slowly, Ivan low to the ground, his wife, Anne, seeming to float above it. Abigail had told me that Anne used to be a ballerina, but I would have known anyway; her line was graceful and erect, straight hair pulled back from her long Irish face. Ivan meanwhile carried himself with a sort of bullish insistence, just shy of a swagger. He wore a wool vest over a gray shirt and maroon tie, with a brown fedora cocked low. His face too was tough, a wide nose and high cheekbones, with far more wear than forty years' worth would warrant, though that is how old he was.

"Well, well, well," Ivan said, "if it isn't Abigail Seymour and her rock-star boyfriend. *He exists! He exists!* With Abigail, you're never quite sure if she's making it up."

"Hello, Ivan," Abigail said, nervously. "This is Stephen. Anne, this is Stephen."

"So why'd you quit with the rock and roll?" Ivan asked.

"I guess I decided I didn't want to try to be famous anymore," I answered.

"So why'd you start with it in the first place?"

"I was so much older then, I'm younger than that now."

Ivan laughed. "Very good. Now there's a strange and interesting Jewish boy, Mr. Bob Dylan. Maybe not as strange and interesting as *you*, from what Abigail tells us." Now he turned to Abigail. "Why have you been hiding him? He's not *totally* unpresentable. He's not a *monster*. I was expecting much worse. Come on over to the house, we're heading back."

Abigail quailed. "To the house?"

"Anne, is there a problem with my voice? Abigail can't seem to hear me."

"I don't think you've *ever* had a problem with your voice, Ivan," Anne said. She laughed, as if in apology to Abigail, and I laughed too. I liked this Ivan.

We walked through the West Village. Ivan locked his arm in

mine, and I didn't mind. Anne and Abigail followed a few steps behind.

"So, you going to marry this girl?" he asked me.

"I haven't really thought about it yet."

"*Excuse* me, I thought you were living together."

"No, we are."

"And you haven't *thought* about it yet?"

Ivan and Anne lived in a stately little building on West Twelfth Street. Their apartment was utterly enveloping. It wasn't luxurious, quite, but beautiful: the wine-dark dining room with its claw-footed table and silver candlesticks, the living-room walls thick with oil paintings and floor-to-ceiling bookshelves, neat stacks of sheet music and a cluster of photographs splayed atop the grand piano. The coffee table was stacked with books about Jewish mysticism and boxing and the Irish famine; a spare bedroom was filled with even more books. This apartment, obviously, was what Abigail had been trying to replicate in our little walkup. It felt like home but more than home: It made you want to live up to its embrace of achievement.

As Abigail trailed Anne into the kitchen, Ivan sat me down in the living room. The air quivered with the promise of an inquisition, but I found myself looking forward to it.

"So Abigail told me about your parents," Ivan said. "That's some story."

"I guess so."

"You *guess* so? You think it was easy for them to do what they did? You think a Jewish father was happy to hear that his son was becoming a Catholic?"

"I guess not."

"So what are you doing about it?"

"About what?"

"You go to church, you go to synagogue?"

"We go to church once in a while. Grace Church—Episcopalian. I've never been to a synagogue. I'm not Jewish."

"Son, you'd have been *plenty* Jewish enough for Hitler. You've got the map of Poland written all over your face. You could have worn a crucifix down to your knees, and they still would have thrown you in the ovens, you understand?"

I was stunned. I had never considered myself remotely connected to the Jews in that regard.

Ivan's tone eased up. "Not that you should let the Nazis define you, or anyone else. But *you* should figure it out. So you're not *really* Jewish and you're not *really* being a Christian. It's not my job to tell you what to do"—he said this in a tone that contradicted his words—"but I don't think it's such a brilliant idea to live with *nothing*, you understand? You like the world the way it is now? You like all this crime, you like this utter disregard for ethical behavior? What you're looking at, darling, is called the breakdown of Judeo-Christian society. Maybe you're a fan of that, but I'm not. You think your parents did what they did so you'd just walk away from it?"

Ivan, as I would learn, was the kind of man who could slap you across the face and leave you wanting to thank him.

"I'm not saying, 'Boy, oh, boy, we've got to recruit this Jew,' " he continued. "Look, I'm a Jew who married two Catholic women, although Anne's converting. I'm just saying, What *are* you? This is no small thing, coming from a family like yours. And if you're going to get married and have children, you better figure it out."

He paused, but his pause was clearly not an invitation to respond. "You're an interesting case," he said. "According to halakha, the Jewish law, you're probably Jewish because your mother was a Jew. But I'm not sure, since she converted before you were born. I'm no expert. I know some rabbis, though—let me look into it."

Leaving their apartment that afternoon, I felt as if a rough hand had clamped my shoulders and hoisted me high above the earth to peer down on myself. From above, my smallness rattled me, and left me dizzy with an ache to grow. This vortex I had stumbled into, this Ivan Kronenfeld, would prod and shape me no less than Madame Souvorina had prodded and shaped my mother fifty years earlier, and I knew it right away. It wasn't that I felt powerless to resist; I simply felt that resisting would have gone against my better interests. Ivan was a strong-arm man, almost comically pushy, in love with the sound of his voice—but I was in love with it too, because for all its bluster, his words settled upon me with the comfortable weight of truth.

A week later, Anne and Ivan invited us to their house for dinner. "I put together a beit din the other day," Ivan announced as we walked in. "Three rabbis, all Orthodox, no bullshit. They voted two to one: According to halakha, you're a Jew, even though your mother converted. You don't need to know what the third rabbi said—the majority rules. Now, that's not to say you can't be a Christian, but you sure ought to be *something*."

What did this mean? How could a religion be transmitted through the blood? By what right, by what bizarre law, had these rabbis declared me one of theirs?

Abigail and I walked home in silence that night. She studied me as if I'd just stepped out of a time-travel machine: Had my cells been irrevocably scrambled, or had they reconstituted themselves into what I was before? What *was* I before?

As we crossed Seventh Avenue, my legs felt numb. I wondered: Are my legs Jewish? I tried to smile, and Abigail tried to smile back.

ABIGAIL had begun talking about marriage as a foregone conclusion, and as I liked the idea fine, I proposed, quite casually, over dinner one night. She accepted. A few days later the mailman brought me an envelope from the writing school at Columbia University. "Congratulations," it began, and we went out to celebrate all our good fortune.

We were married in June on the campus of the Massachusetts boarding school that Abigail had attended. The service was officiated by the school's headmaster, an Episcopalian minister and a Seymour family friend. To compensate, my mother invited Father Victor Donovan, an old friend of *hers*, as if to consecrate the union properly if only from the pews.

In September, I entered the fiction-writing master's program at Columbia. Abigail was starting her final year at NYU, though she was more fully immersed as an aspiring actress under the totalitarian regime of Ivan Kronenfeld.

Ivan told me I should study with him too. "You want to be a writer, you've got a lot to learn," he said. "I won't make you get up on the stage—we don't want to *kill* you—but the truth in writing is the same as the truth in acting or singing or painting, and if you don't want to be a dummy your whole life, you'll get your ass down here."

He taught in a cramped studio apartment on Christopher Street. The stage was a raised dining area. Sometimes Ivan would work as many as ten actors during one class. ("That's *puke*!" he'd shout. "Work on it, bring it back, don't waste my time.") Sometimes he'd have the whole class sing "Amazing Grace." ("Now *that's* a piece of writing," he'd growl at me.) And sometimes Ivan would hold forth the entire session, perched on the edge of the couch in his vest and tie and fedora, tamping a pipe with his pinkie. He preached that an actor, and an action, must be truthful to the circumstance, that circumstance is everything, and you can't know the circumstance if you don't understand the play's social-historical context, whether it's Shakespeare or Arthur Miller or, God forbid, Harold Pinter. His discourses ranged from Max Weber to Alfred North Whitehead to Maimonides, Spinoza, Sandy Koufax, anything to make his point, a circuitous, dazzling, infuriating monologue stuffed with inflated truths, dire warnings, and, I began to realize, Jews, Jews, and more Jews—countless citations from Torah, Talmud, Hasidic parables. "This isn't a

Jewish acting class," he'd say, "but I'm a Jew, and there's nothing I can do about it. And if you think we'd be sitting in this room studying the theater without the Jews, then you've got a lot to learn, darlings."

Ivan had grown up in the East Flatbush section of Brooklyn. His parents lost their share of relatives in the Holocaust. Ivan had idolized his father, who drove a fruit truck in Manhattan. Ivan started hauling fruit too, when he was twelve. His route to acting was indirect: He first ran a day-care center in the Bedford-Stuyvesant ghetto, studied parapsychology, hosted a radio talk show, and, somehow, became dean of students at the College of Staten Island. He read books by the bushel and sat at the feet of any number of teachers, from longshoremen to aeronautical engineers to rabbis. When he finally came to acting, he fell hard, studying ballet, painting, and opera singing as well, each with a teacher who, he now claimed, represented a height of achievement from which my generation had fallen so far that we were too stupid even to know to look up.

His acting teacher was Stella Adler, a disciple of Constantin Stanislavsky and a daughter of the legendary Yiddish stage star Jacob Adler. Stella, as Ivan reminded us at least three times each class, was a brilliant actor and teacher, smarter than all of us and him put together. Compared with Stella, Ivan promised, he was a pussycat. "If I brought up on stage the puke you brought up tonight," he'd say, "the Old Broad wouldn't let me back in class for a month."

Now it was Ivan's duty to rescue all of us from our own stupidity. He conceived his duty toward me a bit more loosely—in part because I was a writer, in part because I was an inchoate Jew. The phone might ring at any time: "How soon can you get over here? There's this rabbi in Brooklyn, Avigdor Miller, totally whacked-out and totally brilliant, he's teaching at seven o'clock." And we'd hustle out to Miller's storefront synagogue, where a hundred Orthodox men, sweltering in long black coats and broad-brimmed hats, were packed in on backless benches. The gnomish Miller sat up front, teaching a piece of Torah. Ivan pulled two yarmulkes from a box and handed me one. It felt like a strange crown upon my head. I tried to soak up Miller's words—only half of which were in English, the rest in Yiddish— but my cheeks burned with the cold stares directed our way. Ivan was perfectly oblivious, and entranced; on the subway home, he expounded on Miller's teaching as if he'd recorded it in his head.

One Saturday morning, Ivan called to ask if Abigail and I wanted to go to shul. We didn't, really, but we threw on our church clothes. It was a tiny Orthodox synagogue that he and Anne attended, perched innocuously on the corner of Charles Street. I was surprised at how little it felt like a church. It was a mess, for one thing, with sloppy piles of prayer shawls and yarmulkes in the entryway. Several lightbulbs were burned out. The air felt dense, milky, as if exhausted. I followed Ivan into the pew, while Anne and Abigail sat together in the women's section.

The yarmulke felt slightly less foreign on my head this time. The service, though, was baffling: standing, bowing, moaning, no one in unison, cloudbursts of Hebrew, as intelligible to me as a coughing fit, as bewildering as my parents' speaking in tongues. What was I doing here? Ivan chanted the prayers in a blaring, tone-deaf Hebrew, but no one seemed to care. I felt at least like an intruder, perhaps an impostor, and I was utterly forlorn.

And then the Torah was brought out. Suddenly, all the jabbering was reduced to an appreciative murmur. The air itself seemed to grow lighter, easier to breathe. The bulky Torah scroll, swaddled in its glittering cover like a child of royalty, was liberated from the ark and escorted down the aisle by an old man struggling happily beneath its weight, and as the men and boys up front hurried to greet it, pressing the fringes of their prayer shawls to its cover and then kissing the fringes, I tumbled into a bone-deep understanding. I too threw myself at the Torah, awkwardly scraping it with my fingers, lifting my fingers to my lips. A resonance—a gratefulness, a relief—blistered its way inside me: It is the *book* they are venerating here. They are not eating the Body and drinking the Blood of the Christ, that sad-faced messenger and martyr of my youth.

Oh, how I had tried to believe in him! How I'd prayed to share in my parents' treasure! And how shabbily he had treated me, leaving me to trudge between the mountains of belief and disbelief, too uninspired to climb the first, too timid to climb the latter.

Hope, though, on this day, came to rest inside me. The way a Jew greeted the Torah—as though it contained everything he would ever need, everything that had ever been known and everything that could never be known.

But what would it mean to become a Jew? How could I overcome all the attendant foreignness? What, above all, would my mother think?

She had finally sold the farmhouse and settled in Florida. She still asked regularly if I went to church, and I answered, truthfully, that we often did. Abigail and I had taken to heart Ivan's exhortations against a Godless life. Most Sundays we attended either Grace Church or Holy Cross, a cavernous Catholic church on West Forty-second Street. The pews of Holy Cross were sprinkled with bent, sorrowful Italian widows, shivering homeless men, and Abigail and me, ramrod straight, desperate to eke from the wisdom of our predecessors that which would make us stronger, larger, kinder. My revelation in Ivan's synagogue notwithstanding, I was still more comfortable in a church, if only because I understood what happened there.

I did continue to study with Ivan faithfully. For my benefit, he began teaching script interpretation. This was my first taste, though I didn't realize it, of Talmudic enterprise. A handful of us would pore over *Death of a Salesman* for months, seeking to worm our way beneath the lines on the page. "Here is Willy Loman," Ivan would bark, "a *salesman*, once a respected and important man in our society, now standing at the very threshold of despair. Now, you *sophisticates,* you *college graduates,* you scoff at a *salesman.* He's *ordinary.* That's where you're stupid. Let me tell you, one of the best exercises the Old Broad ever had us do was to take five things that you think are ordinary and that have gone on for generations and see where they're not ordinary at all. *A man walking up the steps to the church.* I mean, you want to talk about an extraordinary event?"

For all his hyperbole and browbeating, I trusted Ivan and believed in him. I tried to apply his thinking to my writing, with limited success. I had already banished one unfinished novel—about a former rock-and-roller—to a desk drawer. My second attempt was going just as badly. The Columbia writing program didn't seem to be helping much, and, already ten thousand dollars in debt, I was ready to quit after the first year. But then I won a fellowship: In exchange for teaching two semesters of freshman comp, I would receive full tuition exemption.

Ah, teaching—my chance to become Ivan! I baldly stole from him, assigning essays on the difference between truth and fact, on the significance of the cathedral in postmodern society. I even began dressing like Ivan, woolen vests over thrift-shop neckties. In the classroom, I found myself mimicking his cadence—a resolutely Jewish cadence, which came so easily that I began wondering what other vestigial Jewish attributes might be roaming around inside me.

I tried, like Ivan, to simultaneously inspire and badger my students, though they were only a few years younger than I and, in some cases, far better educated. In the spring semester, I had one particularly bright student, a modern Orthodox Jew named Eli. He wasn't a stylish writer, but the clarity of his thinking left me awestruck, and a bit envious. Whenever I taught from a piece of Jewish writing, which was often, Eli sat up a little straighter. He sometimes wanted to talk after class, hovering uneasily until the other students had left. One day he told me that he was writing a short story. Would I mind taking a look? I'd love to, I said.

On the morning of Ash Wednesday, I went to early Mass with Abigail before heading up to Columbia. Walking through the quad, I suddenly became self-conscious about the cross of ashes on my forehead. It was Eli I was worried about. I was quite sure he took me to be a Jew. I had certainly encouraged this perception; in what sort of warped flirtation had I trapped myself?

Eli slipped into his desk about thirty seconds before the hour, as always. He bent to stow his backpack, and I watched his knitted yarmulke dangle from the clip that fastened it to his hair. Then he looked up, saw my forehead, and blanched.

I was distracted during class and decided to have a talk with Eli afterward. But he left quickly that day, and every day from that point forward. He never did bring in his short story. At the end of the semester I nearly wrote him a note: "Dear Eli, about this seeming contradiction . . ." But I didn't know what to write after that, for I was as confused as he was.

Anne and Ivan invited us to their Passover Seder that year. We were both nervous—Abigail because Ivan, for all his generosities, still petrified her, and I because I was daunted by any ritual that was not my own. As an altar boy I had always delighted in knowing the *procedure,* the cues and landmarks that allowed me to navigate the Mass with ease. Without them I would have felt like an intruder in a sacred place, a voyeur, a miscreant.

When we arrived, Anne and Ivan's apartment was already roaring with conversation. Ivan had a knack for collecting disparate friends, and as we found our places around the table, the plates and glasses glimmering beneath dancing candle flames, he realized—and promptly announced—that he was the only born Jew in the room. He circled the table, pausing behind each person to give a rapid-fire introduction: a Russian Orthodox couple (a schoolteacher and a restaurateur), a Swedenborg married to a

Turkish Muslim (an actress and a heart surgeon), a few wanderers like Abigail and me (all of them actors), and a Catholic priest, Father Joe Dispenza, a quick-tongued, high-spirited man whom Ivan instructed me to sit beside. I watched Father Joe don his yarmulke with a practiced hand; mine was thickly embroidered, as substantial as a fez, and it felt solid and strangely comfortable. For the next two hours Ivan held a *Haggadah* in his hand but rarely referred to it, spinning tales and extrapolating wildly on the Passover story, which I remembered well from all the Easter services of my youth. As we broke matzo again and again, I thought of my father, eating his matzo-and-gefilte-fish sandwiches after Mass. By the fourth glass of wine, though my discomfort had been fully vanquished, perplexity danced in my mind. Had I stopped being a Catholic? Had I become a Jew? Why had my Catholic father clung to his Jewish matzo? As the meal was finally served, Father Joe clamped a warm, meaty hand on my shoulder. "I heard your parents' story," he said. "That's some choice you have. But you've got a good rabbi here, this Mr. Kronenfeld, and if he steers you wrong, drop a dime to me, will you?" I promised that I would.

That summer, Ivan and I began writing a screenplay about the late Moe Berg, a brilliant and eccentric New York Jew who became a professional baseball player and, during World War II, an American spy. Ivan and I worked on Berg's character from the ground up. We listened to tapes of Avigdor Miller, the Brooklyn rabbi, describing Jewish shtetl life in Russia, where Berg's family had emigrated from. We tracked down Berg's brother, a retired doctor, in Newark, and a flock of his cousins. We dug deep into the character of Berg's father, who was so disgusted that Moe would waste his formidable mind on baseball that he practically excommunicated his son.

"You've got to understand, this was a terrible, terrible thing for the father," Ivan lectured me one afternoon in his living room. "To have survived the Czar's pogroms as a Jew, to have made it to America as a Jew—*America*! the *goldene medina*!—and then to have your son turn against the family's way of life. A *baseball* player? This was not what a Jewish father wanted for his son. This was not nothing, you understand me?"

The father's anger moved me. But I was also moved by Moe's desire to do what he loved.

I had never given any thought to such a dynamic, a father and son at such great odds. I hadn't had much occasion to think about fathers and sons at all. But now I began to wonder: How did my father's father, whatever his name was, react when his son became a Catholic?

I didn't know. I didn't know anything, really—about my father, my mother, why they'd converted, what it meant for me. This ignorance was beginning to gnaw at me. Spending time with Ivan had awakened in me the idea of a father. It wasn't that I wanted *him* as my father. I had my own; I just didn't know him yet. But Ivan had awakened something else in me: an appetite for the Jewish wisdom he dispensed. It was kaleidoscopic, baffling, thrilling; it spoke to me as nothing ever had. Did it speak to me, though, on its own merit? Or because my long-lost father had been nourished on the same wisdom? Or perhaps it was because curling around somewhere inside me was a Jewish *neshuma*, a Jewish soul?

I had grown restless. For too long already I had been snooping around the periphery, peering through windows into Moe Berg's family, Willy Loman's family, Ivan Kronenfeld's family. The time had come to find my own.

The family way: Paul and Veronica in 1953 with a priest friend and the first five of their eight children: (*counterclockwise from upper left*) Peter (*in Paul's arms*), Mary, Joe, Martha, and Ann.

On the farm: Paul with Mary and Peter in 1959.

Paul Dubner, now forty-seven, and Veronica, forty-one, had by 1963 procreated to their fullest. Outside Our Lady of Fátima Church with Beth, four, and Stephen, on the day of his baptism.

(*from left*) Mary, Peter, Dave, Beth, and Stephen

Eden's heyday: (*from left*) Stephen, Mary, Ann, Martha, Gary (from Schoharie), Paul, Peter, Patty (Joe's wife), Joe, and Beth.

Stephen in the Green Room with the Infant of Prague, 1967.

Paul, wearing a scapular as always, serenading Stephen, 1967.

In Eden's waning light: Veronica and Paul.

Veronica Dubner, 1996. (SCOTT THODE)

The first meeting of the Catholic and Jewish branches of the Dubner family, June 1996. (SCOTT THODE)

BOOK THREE

We are not so virtuous as the angels, or so beautiful or powerful, but we are much more interesting.

—*Paul Johnson*

1

MY family reclamation project began in Lake Worth, Florida. My mother had settled there, in a retirement community of white stuccoed buildings fringed with thick greenery. Peggy and Bill Wink lived just ten minutes away. Reunited after thirty years, my mother and Peggy had quickly fallen back in sync: attending daily Mass together, protesting at abortion clinics, preaching to their grown children the restorative powers of wheat germ and lecithin and shark cartilage.

I had told my mother I wanted to interview her about the family's past. When I arrived, she hugged me hard, as she always did, and said—somewhat anxiously, I thought—that we might as well get right to it.

In her one-bedroom apartment she had effortlessly re-created the tangle of our farmhouse. Every horizontal surface was overrun with newspaper clippings, vitamin coupons, Catholic magazines. Pictures of Jesus and the Virgin Mary and the Pope gazed down from the walls, along with family photographs—the eight children and, to date, eleven grandchildren.

We sat across from each other at the kitchen table, her hands folded primly before her, my fingers nervously popping a cassette into the recorder. This, I sensed, was the beginning of history.

I hadn't told her anything about my Jewish explorations. Even uttering the word "Jewish" to her would have felt vaguely profane. So I said that I wanted to begin by roughing out a family tree. Then, surprising myself, I told my mother that what I really wanted to hear was the story of her religious conversion.

Her face shimmered. "Well, the priest was talking, and he said, 'God said, This is my beloved son in whom I am well pleased. Hear him.' *Hear* him. Those words were the key to my conversion actually."

What priest? How had she come to him? What had she been looking for?

And then she told me about studying ballet with Madame Souvorina, who in turn led her to the epistles of St. Paul, and how she had been puzzling over the meaning of life ever since that day as a little girl when she lay in bed, taunted by the sounds of her friends at play. "I said to myself, boy, life goes on without me, whether I'm there or not." She laughed at the memory. "And *that's* what started me wondering." She paused, then said with deep satisfaction, "That was probably a little glimmer of the grace of God right there."

She described her parents, Esther and Harry, and how they worked seven days a week at the candy store. She described her grandparents, old Moishe with the bristly beard and sweet old Sorah-Rukhel, whom she adored.

When I wanted to know more about her parents—how they treated each other, how they saw this New World they'd landed in, if they'd had any reservations about working on the Sabbath—her mouth drew tight. She said she didn't know. I made a mental judgment: How myopic she is! She saw her parents only as parents, not as people. She didn't care about any part of their lives that lay outside the arc of hers.

It failed to enter my mind that I was equally myopic: Why had I waited until my mid-twenties to ask my mother a single significant question about her life?

She then explained, a hint of sorrow working its way into her voice, how vigorously her mother had disapproved of ballet. "But I was very headstrong," she said, "which has two sides to it. It's good, because you follow through with things, but it also makes it very hard for your parents." She told me about the Radio City Music Hall audition—which thrilled me, to think of my mother on the brink of stardom—and then her broken foot and how she took the injury as a sign from God to reevaluate her life. I tried, unsuccessfully, I'm sure, to hide my grimace.

Then she slowed down, and something like pride crept into her voice as she talked about her decision to become a Catholic. "I looked into a few other things," she said, "Christian Science and whatnot, but the Catholic Church rang a bell with me. I had a conviction very strongly that this was the *true* Church and that they couldn't all be true because they differed so much. I must tell you, I was very grateful. I just always considered it a special gift, this grace of conversion."

She grew somber when I asked how her parents took the news. "My mother was very annoyed with me, angry and annoyed." Now her eyes lit up. "But my father, when I explained to him, he *listened,* and then he said—I thought this was beautiful—he said, 'I wish I *could* believe.' That's what you would call the baptism of desire because he said, 'I wish I *could* believe,' and he really meant it."

I tried to steer the conversation back toward her mother's wrath, but she refused to relinquish the ecstasy. "You see, this whole thing was calculated," she said. "You know what you're going to have to give up. And to me it was worth it. It's like the story in Scripture, where you sell everything you have to buy that one pearl of great value. That's what you do when you find that pearl, you pay the price. And I could not have lived with myself if I hadn't done it."

This was the mother I was accustomed to, the one so confident of her faith, so enmeshed in it that she seemed to shut out the rest of the world. I was determined to untrack her. Just a few weeks earlier, my sister Mona had told me about our mother's connection to Ethel and Julius Rosenberg. None of us had known this; Mona had put the pieces together after reading about David Greenglass and recalling that Greenglass, not Winters, was our mother's real maiden name. Mona and I agreed that since our mother had never revealed the connection, it must have hurt her terribly and that we shouldn't bring it up. But here I was, curious and petulant.

"Can we talk about Julius and Ethel Rosenberg?" I asked. "How were you related? How well did you know them?"

My mother made a small waving motion with her hand, as if shooing a fly. She didn't speak. Again she fluttered her hand—at the tape recorder, I realized. I shut it off. Even then she would only say that she didn't want to discuss the Rosenbergs.

I clicked the tape recorder back on. "Even though your family wasn't religious," I said, "you were still Jews. How did the Holocaust affect you?"

She responded by telling me about Edith Stein, a Polish Jew who converted to Catholicism and became a Carmelite nun. "She was tremendously intellectual. I don't remember the whole story, but I can give you some literature. The Nazis took her out of her convent and put her in Auschwitz. She was martyred there. She offered her life for the Jews. I don't remember if it was for the *conversion* of Jews, but it was definitely for the Jewish people."

"But what about *you*? How did the Holocaust affect *you*?"

"It didn't affect our family because we didn't have anyone there."

What I wanted to say next was this: Are you trying to tell me that you're a Jew in the middle of World War II and you decide to become a Catholic and it has *nothing* to do with what's happening to the Jews in Europe?

But I could not bring my tongue to form that question. "What about Dad?" I asked. "Did he have relatives in Europe?

"No, not overseas, no, no. Not to my knowledge."

"So tell me how you met Dad," I said.

She had only a foggy memory of the Catholic Action gathering where they met; that story would have to be filled in later by others who attended. She said that my father never explained in any real detail what had led to his conversion, only that it transpired overseas and that by the time he came to Father Conroy, he was one step away from Catholicism. He had some questions about the Virgin Mary, she explained; he was so attracted to her that he almost seemed to believe that she belonged in the Holy Trinity. Concerning his life before that point, she knew only the wispiest details: His father was an Orthodox Jew, she said, for whom a son's conversion was unthinkable. "They sat shiva for him, as far as I know," she said. "That's what they did, and that was the end of that. Dad just accepted it."

He just *accepted* it? Again I wanted to challenge her; again I found it impossible to do so.

We meandered for a while, and when the conversation wound back to Edith Stein, I shut off the tape recorder. We had been going at it for nearly four hours, and were both drained. This first interview would set the tone for the coming years: reluctance alternating with exuberance, yawning gaps of knowledge or interest, patches of tension that threatened to derail not only the conversation but our entire relationship.

Later, listening to the tape, I recognized a pattern in my mother's storytelling. For the recitation of straight biography, she spoke in a nonchalant, almost bored tone; when she relived the highlights of her conversion, her speech took on an ecstatic surge. The first voice was for fact, the second for the Truth.

I noticed that my voice too fell into a two-tone fluctuation. As my mother narrated her discovery of Jesus, my responses were reserved, polite, bordering on indifferent. When she mentioned my father, though, my voice shot into an upper register, eager and plaintive. At one point she named a book that had influenced her conversion. "Did Dad read that too?" I jumped in.

This first interview left me parched for information about my father. My mother told me that only two of his siblings, Nat and Bess, had kept in touch after his conversion. All of them had died by now, she said, except for Bess—who, my mother thought, might still live in Brooklyn with her husband Sam. And that news, coupled with the fact that I would be spending three nights on my mother's lumpy fold-out couch under the too-watchful eyes of Jesus and Mary, made me impatient to get home.

ABIGAIL was excited that I was on my family's trail. Her own ancestors, generations of Seymours, were all present and accounted for. She pushed me now to unearth my own history, standing over me as I placed a call to Aunt Bess and Uncle Sam.

"Well, how do you like that!" Sam rasped. "Stephen Dubner!" He pronounced the name *Doobner*. "How the heck are you? How's your mommy? How's all the children?"

"They're great," I said. "My mom's doing well. She sends her love. Listen, Sam, I wonder if it'd be all right if I came out to visit you and Bess sometime."

"What are you, kidding me? It's better than all right! You're like my own blood—hell, what am I saying? You *are* my blood, you're my nephew! How the hell are you? Where are you living? What are you doing?"

I told him I was living in Manhattan, near Carnegie Hall. (Abigail and I had recently moved.) I was twenty-six years old and married. No, she wasn't Jewish; she was high-WASP, and an actress, or at least trying to be one. And I was trying to be a writer. After graduate school, I told Sam, I had gotten a job at *New York* magazine. It was a bottom-of-the-ladder position, calling up theaters to put together the movie listings, but I'd also have the opportunity to write.

"A writer, just like Daddy, huh? Well, God bless! When are you coming?"

"When's a good time?"

"As soon as you can."

"How about Sunday?"

"You can't come sooner?"

"Sunday would be good. Do you want me to hold while you check with Bess?"

"What are you, kidding me? She'll be here, don't worry. Carol and Harriet too, we'll all be here."

Who were Carol and Harriet? Sam gave me directions from the D train.

"I tell you, this is a happy day," Sam said. "Your Aunt Bess can't wait to see you. *Zei gezunt.* That means 'Be well,' okay? So *zei gezunt* from your Uncle Sam, who loves you very much."

As I was on the brink of tears by now, I squeaked out my own *zei gezunt* and hung up the phone.

SUNDAY broke crisp and sunny, the first legitimate day of spring. Aunt Bess and Uncle Sam lived in the Midwood section of Brooklyn, small apartment buildings and cramped storefronts full of Pakistanis, Syrians, Russian Jews. I was early, and my stomach was churning with anxiety, so I stopped and bought a can of apricot nectar. In front of Bess and Sam's building, a cluster of old folks were sunning themselves like turtles.

The elevator shimmied its way upstairs. On their floor, I noticed that every doorframe had a mezuzah. I'd only recently begun to look for them. My closest friend, Adam Reingold, had given Abigail and me a mezuzah for our apartment. I mounted it backward and had to pry it up and nail it down again.

Now, as I reached for Bess and Sam's mezuzah, I saw my fingers shaking. I was nervous about meeting my family, about plundering their memories. I touched the mezuzah, kissed my fingertips, rang the bell. My nervousness was shattered the moment Sam wrapped me in a bear hug.

"Oh, boy, look at you!" he said. "Bessie, look at what we got here!"

Aunt Bess, tiny, white-haired, grinning like a pixie, was sitting on the couch. She was well into her seventies, as was Sam. He was barrel-chested and hale, with a rubbery, animated face and a booming voice, just how I'd pictured a Jewish uncle. Bess, though, looked fragile, and I bent down to hug her carefully. I felt her warm tears on my cheek.

"What took you so long?" she choked out.

Everyone laughed—I was right on time, plus or minus twenty-some years.

"Come on, Ma, don't use up all your tears. He just got here."

This was Carol, in her mid-forties, one of their daughters, I realized. She hugged me next. And then Harriet, another daughter.

"I can't get over it," Bess said. "How long are you here? I don't want you to go. Because we once had a big family, and now the family is hardly around. You see the picture of my great-grandson?" Harriet was holding out a photograph.

Sam grabbed me by the shoulders, spun me around to face him. "You look a lot like your mommy, I can tell right away," he said. "Your daddy, Sol, Bess's brother, he had a short face. Your mommy, God bless her, she was a lovely young lady."

I sat beside Bess on the couch. They fired questions at me: How old is Mommy now? Sixty-nine. How's Joey, the Air Force man? He just retired from the service, and he's living in Idaho. Did Dave become a carpenter, like he wanted to? He did, and he moved out west too.

I was happy to tell them about my brothers and sisters. None of them had been permanently scarred by their rebellious years; they'd all straightened out, and flourished. But I was surprised at how much Bess and Sam knew about my family when I'd never *heard* of theirs. My father must have written them, at least a few times, and they must have sifted his letters the way an anthropologist would sift his notes about a strange and distant tribe.

And then, from Bess: "Why are you the first one to come see us?"

"Well," I said, "I didn't really know my dad all that well when he died, and I've been thinking a lot about him lately. So I wanted to meet you all and find out what I could."

"What do you want to know?" Sam asked. "Where do you want to start?"

Sam, although he had married into the Dubners, in 1934, was the family's institutional memory. He began with Sol and Bess's parents, Shepsel and Gittel—such Jewish names!—and told me how they came to America with two children, Nat and Fanny.

"Do you know where they came from?" I asked.

"Poland, for sure," Sam said, "but I don't know which town. Your grandpa Shepsel married his cousin. She was a Dubner too."

"That's why we're all nuts," Carol said.

"Your grandma Gittel had three sisters that came over," Sam continued. "Tante Peshe, Tante Yidis in Philadelphia, and Tante Chaya."

"Tante Chaya, that's the one we didn't like," Carol said.

Carol was tough, sassy, sharp. She taught at a public school in Bedford-Stuyvesant, one of New York's toughest neighborhoods. I immediately liked her. I immediately liked all of them. They were my aunt and my uncle and my cousins—a new concept for me. They talked about the Dubners' restaurant, about Gittel's premature death and my father's learning this news from a neighbor shouting out the window. "He took that real hard, let me tell you," Sam said. "He loved his mommy very much." They told me then about Shepsel, a man in love with his religion, a good man as long as you did things exactly as he prescribed. My father, they said, was obedient, did well in school, knew the Torah inside and out, but he had too many ambitions that Shepsel wouldn't allow.

"Solly loved baseball," Sam said. "He wanted to be a sportswriter."

"What were Sol's hobbies besides sports?" I asked. It was a strange sensation, unleashing this new name from my lips, *Sol*.

"Sports and music and writing," Bess said.

"He played baseball, he played punchball," Sam said.

"Was he—was he one of the best in the neighborhood?" I asked.

"He was good," Sam answered, generously, "very good."

Bess clasped my hand. "So you're a writer. Are you making this into a book?"

"Maybe. I'm really just starting. I've been interviewing my mom because I'm curious about why she and my dad converted. But I don't really—"

"Does she open up with you?" Sam asked.

"Yes and no," I said. "Not really. What I really want to know is why—"

"The *why*," Sam said, "is a never-known. Because Mommy will not tell you why. She may have been sorry for something she did, or she may not want anybody to know why she did it. If she told you why, it would show maybe that she was a little weak-minded."

"Did Sol ever talk to you about why he converted?" I asked.

"No," Bess said.

"No," Sam said. "He may have talked to Aunt Dottie and Uncle Nat, because they were very close. When your daddy had an argument with his daddy, he'd go to Uncle Nat's for a couple days, then Uncle Nat would send him home. Your Uncle Nat died some years ago, God rest his soul, but Dottie is still alive, sharp as a tack."

"The converting, that was the hard part for my mom," Carol said, rubbing Bess's shoulder. "Because Grandpa Shepsel sat shiva and said that no one in the family was allowed to mention Uncle Solly's name anymore."

"Do you think he ever regretted sitting shiva?" I asked.

"No," Bess said. "That was the right thing to do."

"Did they ever talk again?"

"No," Sam said. "It broke his heart."

I was not sure whose heart he meant: Shepsel's or Sol's. Maybe both.

"A lot of times," Carol said, "even as a kid, I would ask my grandpa Shepsel, why are you doing this or that Jewish thing? And he'd just say, 'Because you're supposed to.' I think your father would ask questions, and the answer was just 'Because.' "

"Because *I say so*," Sam added. "They clashed. You don't question your parents, in any religion, because what the parents say is supposed to be right, whether Catholic, Jewish—"

"Your father was always very inquisitive," Carol said, "learning and reading."

Suddenly Bess squeezed my hand hard. "So what are you, a Catholic or a Jew?"

"I'm still trying to figure that one out," I said, and everyone laughed. I asked Bess who had kept in touch with my father after he converted.

Sam answered for her. "In the beginning we kept in touch, and Uncle Nat and Aunt Dottie, but the others—*ech*. After your daddy got married, he went to Northport, then moved up to Duanesburg. He didn't have money enough even to call. He was working hard, trying to scrape money together to feed a big family. We knew he was having a tough time. And there must have been a helluva lot of pain. Don't forget, in the house he grew up in, the whole Dubner family ate together at every holiday, the whole family blessed the Lord by the table. And he couldn't have none of that anymore."

Sam looked as if he were about to cry. "He had a tough life, your father," he said, "a very, very tough life."

It was nearly dark outside. No one had turned on a light, and we all sat in the shadows, as if in mourning. Bess hadn't spoken in some time. I was still holding her hand; I wondered if she'd fallen asleep. I turned toward her and saw a lone tear working its way down her cheek, her mouth drawn in as if she'd swallowed something bitter.

At the door, we exchanged kisses and *zei gezunt*s and promises for another visit. Sam told me I should get in touch with Aunt Dottie if I wanted to know more about my father. "Dottie knows everything," he said.

The subway home stank of urine, but I didn't have the energy to change cars. I was wrung dry, and overwrought. Maybe this was too much: receiving an aunt and uncle and cousins, even a sliver of my father, like some too-extravagant gift that I hadn't quite expected, and didn't know what to do with.

<h1 style="text-align: center;">2</h1>

I was in no hurry to forge the next connection, to Aunt Dottie. What was I looking for? My father was dead. He would stay dead. At Bess and Sam's, I had turned over the first spadeful of dirt. It was exhilarating but frightening. I didn't want to exhume my father. It was too much work, and too sad. I had neatly avoided ever grieving over his death by consigning it—and his life—to a sealed corner at the edge of my memory. There he couldn't hurt me. To get to know him was to get to love him perhaps, and to love him might mean grieving over him, which I was not eager to do.

Besides, I was busy. *New York* magazine turned out to be a good home for me. I got to explore the city and write about whatever I found. More and more, I was finding Jewish stories. Jewish actors, Jewish cops, Jewish hustlers: I studied their names and their faces, and I listened to their stories, wondering all the while if even the slightest strand of connective tissue linked me to them. My eyes had been realigned. It was as if all New York City were a Rorschach blot, and the harder I looked, the more Jewishness I saw.

The city was still reeling from the 1987 stock-market crash, and crime seemed to be on an endless uprise. *New York* magazine's solution was a special issue called "How to Save New York." Looking for good people to interview, I asked Ivan to put me in touch with a Hasidic rabbi he'd told me about. His name was Simon Jacobson, and he was one of Rabbi Menachem Mendel Schneerson's "oral scribes." Schneerson, the leader of the Lubavitcher Hasidim, was known as the Rebbe and was thought by some of his followers to be *Moshiach,* the Messiah. Schneerson often taught his Hasidim on Shabbos, when Jewish law forbade writing or recording, so it was Jacobson's job to memorize the talk and set it down on paper the following day. What sort of mind, I wondered, was capable of such a feat?

Ivan tracked down Jacobson's number. I expected to be brushed off; a holy man like Jacobson certainly wouldn't want to waste time chatting with a reporter about New York's troubles. But I was wrong. Jacobson was smart and wry, more up-to-date on city affairs than the self-professed civic leaders I'd been interviewing, and our conversation turned into a surprisingly good short feature.

Not long after, I started working on an article about a thirteen-year-old boy named Shai Fhima, an Israeli whose family now lived in New Jersey. His mother, who wasn't religious, sent him for bar mitzvah instructions to a Hasidic rabbi in Brooklyn. Shai was smitten with the rabbi and wanted to stay with him. His parents had to drag him home, crying. Before long, Shai disappeared. His parents were sure that the rabbi had kidnapped him and stashed him in a yeshiva in upstate New York or Toronto. The rabbi, Shlomo Helbrans, denied everything. The police investigated but couldn't prove a kidnapping.

All along, Helbrans had refused to grant me an interview. Finally, a few hours before my deadline, his lawyer persuaded him to talk.

I had never sat down with a rabbi before. When I was an altar boy, I would get nervous being alone with Father DiPace. He represented God; I represented human shortcoming. Now I was to meet with another representative of God, this one suspected of grave human shortcoming himself. I didn't yet have the imagination to conceive of both extremes fitting inside the same person.

Helbrans wouldn't let me come straight to his house. I was to drive to a certain street corner in the Borough Park section of Brooklyn. It was a cold November night. Two young men in broad-brimmed black hats, students from Helbrans's yeshiva, stepped from the darkness and escorted me to his house, wordlessly.

I had been picturing a wizened old man, a Woody Allen caricature of a rabbi. But beneath Helbrans's beard and side curls and thick glasses, I saw the pinkish face of a man barely older than I was. His lawyer sat beside him. Helbrans wore a black caftan of brocaded silk and a black felt hat. He smiled at me, fiddled with a paper clip, then began drumming his fingers on a leather-bound book with Hebrew lettering. The door was ajar, and the rabbi's young son peered inside—at me, I realized, a hostile, freakishly dressed invader of his sanctified world.

Helbrans maintained, almost nonchalantly, that he knew nothing about Shai's disappearance. Yes, the boy was fond of him, and yes, he had wanted to get away from his family—who, the rabbi hinted, had mistreated the boy. But that, he said, was all he knew.

I questioned him for another hour. His answers were rehearsed, detached, full of soft-pedaling and contradiction. It didn't take much of a journalist to guess that Helbrans was lying. By the time I left, I was deflated—in part because legally I couldn't write what I thought had really happened to Shai Fhima but also because I hadn't wanted to believe that a representative of God could do such a thing. I wrote the article with a heavy heart, seeding between the lines as much skepticism as I could. It would be many months before Helbrans was finally arrested—for doing exactly what Shai's parents had charged. He was convicted of kidnapping and sent to jail. Shai finally resurfaced, sporting his own black hat and side curls, and testified in defense of his beloved rabbi.

The whole affair shook me. It was a nasty peek into the crazily divisive nature of religious fanaticism. Shai's parents were probably no saints; neither, obviously, was the rabbi. Unfortunately they were all Jews. This was the tribe I was so keen to join?

My next awakening was another story of fraud. A new documentary film, *The Liberators,* told the tale of a black Army battalion that had liberated the Buchenwald concentration camp at the end of World War II. As it turned out, the filmmakers, a Jewish woman and a black man, had stretched the truth: The black battalion had performed heroically, all right, but they hadn't liberated Buchenwald.

I interviewed the parties involved—it was the usual swarm of calumny and finger pointing—and studied the history of the concentration camps. I was jarred by the photographs. I had never been schooled in the Holocaust. To me it was a distant calamity, faceless and bleak. Now I stared at the pictures of the dead Jews. They were hardly faceless. No two looked remotely the same. Their corpses, stacked high, reminded me of the icy woodpile on the back porch of our farmhouse.

FINALLY, fitfully, I had begun to grow up. I had begun to realize the depth to which my parents' Eden had penetrated and insulated me. I had been sheltered from vast realities, taught simply to embrace goodness and run from evil. Nuance was for philosophers, or Protestants.

Now, as a journalist in New York City in the early 1990s, I was beginning to view the mores of our Eden as simplistic, corny.

Everything then was black and white; everything now was turning gray.

This too was unsettling. Having been raised on absolutism, I found comfort in it. I craved clear-cut boundaries, a code of conduct. Without boundaries, life was limitless; without limits, life would paralyze me.

But I feared absolutism as well. My parents' Catholic version of it had nearly suffocated me, and what I had seen so far of Jewish absolutism left me queasy.

Still, I was my parents' son. In the early mornings, as Abigail slept, I spent an hour reading the Bible. I began with Genesis and crawled my way through. It felt like a fever dream. Many of the stories were intensely familiar, but at home we had never treated the Old Testament like a *Bible;* it was a filing cabinet full of rough drafts and scattered notes, from which the New Testament plucked citations and precedents in order to lay down an official version of the Truth.

Now I was meeting these characters on their own turf. Rebecca and Jacob, tricking poor old Isaac into forfeiting Esau's birthright. Bratty Joseph and his hateful brothers. Moses! *Moishe rabbeinu,* Ivan called him, Moses our teacher. Such an imperfect man, a murderer, a stammerer, full of doubt and, occasionally, loathing. No wonder my family never looked too closely at this book. Even God was irascible, and horribly inconsistent.

I began dreaming dreams as Joseph had, full of portent and drama. In one, Ivan was taking me to synagogue, but the service was being held at Our Lady of Fátima. My mother and brothers and sisters, all smiling broadly, met us at the door. Had they come to join us or to block our way? My father, I noted, was not with them; my father never appeared in my dreams.

Did such dreams mean I wanted to be a Jew? *Was* I a Jew? I couldn't tell. I was Jew-*ish,* to be sure, though what I mainly was, day and night, was confused.

There were, however, other forces at work. Abigail had by now decided not only that I should become a Jew but that she should too. Anne, Ivan's wife, had converted by now, and Abigail revered Anne as much as she feared Ivan. Abigail saw no reason why she and I couldn't be just like them. She began bringing home armloads of Jewish books. She spoke of the day she would enter the mikveh, the ritual bath. She promised to name our first son Solomon, after my father.

When Anne and Ivan invited us to a Shabbos dinner, Abigail baked a challah. It was the most pernicious loaf of bread any of us had ever encountered, but we all adored her for making the effort. Together, Abigail and Anne lit the Shabbos candles, their lovely faces lapping up the golden flame, their long fingers so graceful, their carriage so stately. In the wine-dark dining room, they seemed an apparition from some long-ago DAR ceremony, all but for the pair of Jewish men, appreciative and vain, crowding the periphery.

I was somewhat daunted by the bear hug that Abigail had thrown around the faith of my fathers. The rituals of Judaism were lovely, the traditions alluring, the philosophies engaging, but none of it was *mine*. And it all felt compulsory, too much like the religion I had been suckled on. I still believed that God was hovering out there somewhere. The Jews had built doorways that led to Him, as had the Catholics. But I wasn't ready to walk through any of them. Perhaps I never would be.

Abigail was untroubled by such ambivalence. She had taken to Judaism as she had taken to any number of secular enthusiasms. One day, she brought home an abused puppy from the animal shelter and then, suddenly, another puppy, and then a tubercular cat. On the career front, Abigail had devoted herself to becoming a movie star and then, in quick succession, a schoolteacher, a photographer, a theater producer.

Her various passions generally lasted between one and six months. Judaism, however, proved to have remarkable staying power. She stuck with it while I dragged my feet, my earthbound

Jewish feet, which had been given every conceivable motivation now to rush toward the God of Abraham, Isaac, and Jacob, the God of Shepsel and Solomon.

Only after a few determined years did Abigail finally abandon her Jewish quest. Not long after, she decided to abandon me as well. This news she delivered swiftly and bloodlessly. She came home late one night and announced that we had gotten married too young, that we were perfectly compatible but weren't soul mates, and that since we hadn't yet had a child, there was no reason we should remain married.

Abigail had a flair for impetuosity as well as, truthfully, a flair for good ideas, and I'm sure that during the half hour it took her to abort our marriage, she thought it was the best idea she'd had since thinking that we should marry in the first place.

In a calmer state of mind I might have agreed. Her prognosis was, in essence, correct. For some time, our relationship had been visited by a creeping unhappiness. I was more interested in my writing than in our marriage, and Abigail's mercurial behavior hinted at a restlessness that neither of us was mature enough to address. Arriving as it did, however, her announcement felt hurtful, criminal, woefully irresponsible. In those first red-eyed moments, as I found myself sucking for breath, an improbable thought entered my head: *My mother would never have done something like this.*

I had not yet learned the depth of my father's depression or the stoicism my mother had employed to prop him up. But I did not need to know all that to know that my mother was incapable of committing such an act as this, and I recognized that no matter how great a distance might ever come between the two of us, she was to be cherished for her relentless decency. That is the conclusion I stumbled upon as Abigail put an end to our marriage, which had lasted four years and five months.

The comforts available to me were slim. I didn't even think about going to God for help—I didn't have that kind of relationship with Him. Nor was I close enough to any brother or sister for a heart-to-heart consultation. It took me three weeks even to tell my mother the news.

On the phone she let out a sad sigh. It was a sigh of selflessness, though, of compassion, and it made me cry. It was a mother's sigh. There was no I-told-you-so to it, which is what I had dreaded.

Five years earlier, when I told her I was getting married, she'd asked if I was sure of myself.

"Of course I'm sure," I said, with the wisdom of a twenty-four-year-old.

She told me then how she and my father had gone to a priest for advice before they were married. "The priest said he didn't believe in long engagements," she recalled, "but that you have to get to know each other very well and learn each other's opinions on everything, from how you want to spend your money to how many baseball games you'll want to listen to on the radio. He gave examples of couples who ran into trouble because they didn't talk things out, and all of a sudden one of them wants children and one of them doesn't want any children for five years. You need to make sure there's nothing to be surprised about."

Now, knowing how fully I had ignored her advice, my mother asked how she could help. I couldn't think of a thing. She said she would pray for me.

I felt like a failure, ashamed and bewildered. My friend Adam Reingold nursed me through it, usually in coffee shops, usually until closing time. I'd sit with the same cup of coffee for three hours while Adam ate both our plates of eggs, home fries, toast. At one point Adam suggested we make a list of all the seemingly inevitable things that Abigail and I hadn't done: bought an apartment, had a child, become Jews. Somehow, this helped. We got to laughing and Adam convinced me that my world hadn't ended.

At that moment, because of the way Abigail left me, I could

not see how far she had brought me. Nor could I appreciate the improbability of it all: that a blue-blooded angel named Abigail Seymour had led me by the hand to an unstoppable Jew named Ivan Kronenfeld, to a reckoning with my ancestry, to the very edge of the promised land. It was as unlikely a connection as Madame Souvorina, as unlikely a route as the minefield my father had stumbled through on his way to salvation.

My father: I still didn't know him. My search was on hold. Especially now, I was in no condition to grapple with him, or with God. I ceased my Bible reading and didn't even think about going to synagogue—or church. I was concerned only with self-preservation, and at the moment that meant writing.

New York magazine was housed in a drab, featureless building on Second Avenue, around the corner from the *Daily News* building. Whenever I walked past the *News*, I thought of my father, his thick black pencils and AP stylebook. I would have liked to work there, to be a newspaperman like him. That, I began to realize, was what I had always wanted. Ever since the *Quaker Street Quacker*, I'd been in love with newspapers: *Impact*, in high school; then the college paper, for which I was a news reporter; then a weekly in Winston-Salem, for which I'd written a music column. Now, every morning, I read *The New York Times* with envy and longing.

But *New York* magazine was my home, quite literally. In the year after my breakup, I rented a series of depressing sublets, but I barely even slept in them. I spent all my time at the magazine, churning out articles about crime and politics, sports and show business. I had become a good journalist by dint of caring about nothing else, and the more attention my articles got, the harder I worked. Often I'd sleep on a spare couch in the office when I couldn't bear to go home. During one stretch, I worked every day for eight months straight, including Christmas. It was a relief, really. Ever since I was ten years old, when my father had ruined

Christmas by dying, I had dreaded the date. By now I pretty much ignored it.

My mother and I still exchanged presents, of course. I would send her picture frames or a vitamin encyclopedia; she'd send me the New Testament on cassette or a book called *Jesus for the Jews*.

My mother had always been a master propagandist, stuffing her every letter with a wad of newspaper clippings. When I was in college, she sent articles about the foods and vitamins thought to increase brainpower. Now her theme was the evolution of Judaism into Christianity. Though I'd been careful to tell her little about my Jewish curiosity, she had obviously picked up on it, in part because I mailed her my magazine articles. The clippings she now sent came from a variety of obscure Catholic pamphlets and newspapers. I once challenged one of these clippings, citing an article I'd read in *The New York Times*.

"Well, just because it was in *The New York Times* doesn't mean it's true," she said, in a voice weighted with zeal and conviction. "That's a very liberal paper, you know, and they have their own agenda, and they're very pro-abortion and anti-Catholic."

Still, because my mother was at heart more mother than zealot, she squealed with pride when, a few weeks later, I told her that *The New York Times* had called me about a job. They were looking for an editor at the Sunday *Magazine*. I went to the *Times* for an interview and then another interview and four or five more over the course of a month. It felt more like joining the CIA than a newspaper.

Finally I met with Joe Lelyveld, the executive editor. He was gentle, focused, dignified. I'd been told that the interview with Lelyveld was a rubber-stamp procedure, but I didn't believe it. My earnestness must have shown. "This isn't a job interview," Lelyveld said as we shook hands. "The job is yours if you want it. I just wanted a chance to sit down and talk for a few minutes."

And I was so relieved that I nearly blurted out: *My father was a newspaperman, you know, at the* Schenectady Gazette *and the* Troy Record, *and he used to bring home these fat black pencils that I loved, and then he died, blah blah blah.* But the God of Good Sense was kind enough to visit me, and I held my tongue, if barely.

Afterward I called my mother from a pay phone on the corner of Forty-third Street, in a drenching rain. "Oh, Dad must be so proud of you right now," she said.

And this infuriated me—not that he *would have been* proud but that he *must be* proud. She was always saying this kind of thing. To her, my father was still alive, awaiting her in Heaven. Usually I dismissed such comments, but on this day it set me off. Did she really *believe* that? Hunching against the rain, a finger in my ear to blot out the yammering taxi horns, I was reduced to speechlessness, and I realized: Now I am jealous, jealous that twenty years after my father died, she *still* knows him, while I never really had the chance. On this day that I had been given everything I'd wanted, I looked upon everything I did not have and finally began to grieve.

3

A month after landing at the *Times*, I got an interesting phone call. A literary agent was looking for a journalist to collaborate on a book about Rabbi Schneerson, the Lubavitcher rebbe, who had recently died. Schneerson's demise had been big news, and I'd followed it closely. As the ninety-two-year-old rabbi lay in the hospital, legions of his followers held a vigil outside his room, a sea of feverish chants and nervous chatter. In my world, especially among the secular Jews who saw the Hasidim as superstitious dupes, there was endless snickering: *If Schneerson is really the Messiah, can't he even save himself?*

I hated this talk. I still carried within me a small piece of heartache for Jesus as he dangled on the cross, spikes through his hands and his mouth bone-dry, the Roman soldiers mocking him: *Come on now, if you're really the son of God, climb down off the cross!*

To me, that was the moment in the Bible when Jesus seemed real. Because just when you expect him to pull a superhero trick, shattering his bonds and swooping down to smite the Romans, he realizes he's beaten and shouts up to God with the shocked dismay of someone who thought the fix was in and found out otherwise. He hangs there helpless, Superman shrouded in Kryptonite, a magician who has run out of tricks.

With this rabbi, though, Schneerson, there was no such eleventh-hour drama. At the age of ninety, he suffered a debilitating stroke, then spent his final months in a hospital bed. Things took an ugly turn one morning when a vanful of young Hasidim, returning home from visiting the Rebbe, was shot up by a Lebanese Muslim named Rashid Baz. One teenager was killed, another gravely wounded. Baz was apparently retaliating for the recent masscre of more than two dozen Muslims in Israel by Baruch Goldstein, a Jewish zealot from Brooklyn. The Baz shooting cast such a pall over the Rebbe's final days that even the devout secularists were no longer in the mood for mockery when he died. The *Times* ran a sober editorial praising Schneerson's dynamic leadership, and he was posthumously awarded the Congressional Gold Medal, with President Clinton praising him as "an extraordinary force for good."

Now this literary agent was trying to find someone to work on a book about him. It wasn't a biography, he explained, but a collection of the Rebbe's teachings, adapted by a younger Lubavitcher rabbi who would need an editor to rewrite and polish his prose.

"Who's the rabbi?" I asked.

"Simon Jacobson," the agent said.

What a small, strange world. It was the same "oral scribe" I'd interviewed for *New York* magazine a few years back. If I was interested, the agent said, I would need to collaborate with Simon on a sample chapter, to win the publisher's approval.

I took the subway out to Crown Heights to meet with Simon. He had an office in Lubavitcher headquarters, which was just around the corner from where my mother had grown up. Now the neighborhood was half black, half Hasidic. The Jewish area was still in shock over the Rebbe's death; placards were propped in every store window: MOSHIACH IS COMING! The first tang of winter hung in the air.

Simon's office was shabby but neat, the walls lined with hundreds of tall, leather-bound Hebrew books, compilations of the Rebbe's teachings. Simon was about forty, with a full beard and yarmulke, a nice suit with a monogrammed shirt, and stylish wire-rim glasses. His eyes practically burned: With learning? With fanaticism? With grief?

He had grown up in Brooklyn, but like most cradle Hasidim, Simon spoke breakneck English with a discernible Yiddish accent. He knew I'd published several articles about Jewish issues, he said, but he was more interested in my writing than my Jewish credentials. He obviously took me to be a Jew. I thought it wise, at that moment, not to volunteer my Catholic upbringing.

"Did you ever meet the Rebbe?" Simon asked.

For years the Rebbe had welcomed visitors to his home every Sunday, often thousands, giving each of them a dollar bill, to be donated to charity, and a *brucha,* a blessing. Politicians kept the lucky dollars in their wallets during a campaign; movie moguls had them framed for their walls. I had always meant to visit one Sunday, but as I now told Simon, I never had.

Simon spoke of the Rebbe passionately, but more as a sage or father figure than a Messiah. I had been leery of coming out here, leery of the cultish aura surrounding the Hasidim. But I trusted Simon instantly, the way I'd trusted Ivan instantly. Yes, he would have his motives, his inconsistencies, his *mishegoss,* but he wore his heart on his face, and it was clearly pure. He was talking now about what a brilliant teacher the Rebbe had been and how this book would spread his teachings to a mainstream audience, Jewish and Gentile. "This whole *Moshiach* issue has been very distracting," he said. "The intention of this book, and I believe the intention of Torah, is not to create an attachment to an individual but to create an attachment to God."

Simon gave me a rough draft of the sample chapter he'd written, "Body and Soul." I read it on the subway back to Manhattan. It dealt with the inherent friction between our material and spiritual instincts and how they can be united only when they are serving the same, Godly purpose.

That night I rewrote the chapter, faxed it back to Simon.

"There's no awe in it," he said. "It needs to be God-filled."

We went back and forth a few more times, then submitted the chapter to the publisher. I got the job. At no point did I stop to ask myself if I actually wanted to work on this project; the opportunity had fluttered into my lap, and it would have seemed churlish to question it. We had four months to finish the book.

I called to tell my mother the news. Before I could, she wished me a happy St. Stephen's Day—I'd had no idea—and said she had prayed for me in church that morning. I thanked her, then brought up Schneerson, whom she knew about; a few years earlier I'd forced upon her an article about him from the *Times Magazine*. "I've been asked to help out on a book of his teachings," I said, "and in light of the fact that you and Dad were both Jewish, I thought it'd be pretty interesting."

I heard a sharp intake of breath. "Are you going to be able to do this book, with your new job and all?"

"Oh, yeah. I'll write before and after work. And it's rewriting more than writing. This rabbi gives me a rough draft, maybe fifty pages, that I rewrite into ten."

"Well, you have to be very careful," she said. "You really have to watch out for those guys. They can be very physical."

"Who can be very physical?"

"Not the Hasidim, but the ones who hate them."

"Who are you talking about?" I wondered if she'd read about the Rashid Baz shooting. "The Palestinians? Hamas?"

"Yes, you know, anyone who hates the Jews."

From her mouth, the words sounded so odd: "hates the Jews." As if the Jews were someone else, not she or I.

"Well, to tell you the truth, I've been operating out in the open for a few years now," I said, because I knew it would sting. "Everyone takes me for Jewish anyhow."

"What do you mean?"

"Because of the way I look. Because of the way I am." She emitted a sort of cluck, one of puzzlement or perhaps denial. I'd already gone too far. The line buzzed with silence. And then, because neither of us wanted to go further, we started talking about the latest tornado that had touched down in Florida.

SIMON and I fell into a grueling routine: writing, rewriting, arguing, capitulating. We exchanged chapters by computer modem, so for most of the winter he rarely left Crown Heights and I rarely left midtown Manhattan, since my apartment was within walking distance of the *Times*.

As I'd known well from the outside, the *Times* was the so-called Paper of Record and, as such, had a say in every political, social, and artistic debate of the day. One slanted headline, one hyperbolic adjective could produce droves of dissent. (My mother had written any number of letters to the editor over the years.) Within the building, everyone felt this external pressure and compounded it by creating every variety of internal pressure imaginable. It was not for nothing that the *Times* had often been compared with the Kremlin. As an editor at the *Magazine* I would have to master the arts of hand-holding and institutional diplomacy, neither of which had been my concern at *New York* magazine. Against such a backdrop, the actual task of editing didn't seem all that difficult. One of my first assignments was to oversee a special issue of the *Magazine*, called "What's New York the Capital of Now?" I started making a list of answers to that question. My first thought: Jews.

I cautiously told my bosses, Jack Rosenthal and Adam Moss, about the Rebbe book. No problem, they said, as long as it didn't interfere with my work. Adam's brow did arch a bit—a book on the *Rebbe?*—but he was too decent to disparage me.

My new girlfriend was less reserved in her judgment. Her name was Ilene Rosenzweig; she was an editor at the *Forward*, an English-language Jewish weekly that was a descendant of the *Forverts,* the Yiddish daily. I loved telling people her name and where she worked. She was my first Jewish girlfriend and, for me, a sort of trophy girlfriend. But Ilene was as secular as I, deep down, was not. She had recently written her own first book, *The I Hate Madonna Handbook,* so she understood how hard I'd have to work on mine, but she didn't even feign interest in the subject.

Our only free time together was Friday night and Saturday, since Simon didn't work on Shabbos. Every Saturday night, though, as soon as darkness fell, my phone would ring and Simon was back at it, prodding me for the rewrite of the "Death and Grieving" chapter, or "Good and Evil."

My life entered a fugue state: the Rebbe in the dawn hours, the *Times* all day, the Rebbe at night, my weekly anti-Shabbos rendezvous with Ilene. She suspected I would fall into the clutches of the Lubavitchers and told me, only half-jokingly, that she'd leave me the minute I started growing Hasidic side curls. One friend took to calling me "the Rebbe's altar boy," and we laughed at the absurdity of it, a Catholic boy rewriting the *Moshiach.*

The book was hard work. I would get irritated when Simon sent me hundreds of shapeless pages, excerpts of the Rebbe's teachings overflowing with dense Talmudic citations and folksy Hasidic fables. Then, after I had whittled a chapter down to ten too-slick pages, it was Simon's turn to be irritated with me. I was the journalist, the fact shaper; he was the holy man, the truth seeker.

But gradually our instincts began to collide. Even more gradually, the Rebbe's teachings began to penetrate me. I began to do what the book counseled. First came simple things: spending my last waking moments each night considering what I'd done that day, and why; breathing a thank-you to God every morning for the new day; reminding myself, constantly and often to little avail, that I was not the center of the universe. And I tried, though this was most difficult, to listen to what my soul had to say.

Over the years, I had flirted with the standard strands of philosophy and psychology, but I had managed to avoid ever putting my soul under the microscope. I had never isolated its most essential qualities. Now, encountering Schneerson's teachings on the soul, I found them honest, sensible, worthwhile—and blessedly removed from the reward-and-punishment school of religion that I knew. Schneerson believed that when the soul is in torment (when *isn't* it? I thought), it is yearning to be reunited with its divine source. For the soul, as he taught, and as Simon (and I) now wrote, "is the one part of our being that directly reflects our connection to God." Not so much an umbilical cord, I decided, as a modem, a two-way channel coursing with great activity— mental and physical and, what the hell, maybe spiritual activity too.

What a strange and liberating thought: the soul as an active partner in life. I had always considered the soul more of a conscience, an underlayer of being. This, I suppose, was at best a slight sharpening of my childhood thinking—the soul as a sort of report card that can accommodate only so many failing marks before your most precious privileges are revoked.

But what were those privileges? Safe passage to Heaven, which I'd never come to believe in, and the avoidance of Hell, which I had pretty much willed myself also to discount. And once Heaven and Hell were done away with, what was the use of the soul? It couldn't speak to me encouragingly; it could only torment me, prodding me back toward the path I'd abandoned.

Now, though, I began to look upon the soul with new interest. What if it really was some sort of modem? Or, perhaps, a musical instrument—a piano, say, even a hapless old piano that is sitting cold and out of tune in some drafty barn but can be rehabilitated and produce extraordinary music, but only by someone who has mastered an intricate system of melody and rhythm, a system that has been perfected over many years and requires a great deal of discipline and, in the end, a certain desire that only humans possess, a desire to turn silence into music, to turn a void into a celebration, to turn ourselves into more than we were a moment ago.

I sensed that such an instrument, such a soul, lay inside me. It always had. Did it come from my parents? From God? What *was* God anyway? The stern patriarch of my parents' house? A brilliant invention? A fraud? Or perhaps something I hadn't yet considered?

"SO what do you think of this book we're writing?" Simon asked me late one night.

Sometimes, when we both were very, very tired, we would have these conversations. A few weeks into the book I had told him about my parents' conversion, and he'd let out a gasp—the same gasp I was to hear many times in the coming years, from Jews who plainly disapproved of my parents' choice and wondered what kind of bizarre offspring their union had produced. "If you didn't tell me it was true, I would never believe it," Simon had said. Now I pictured him on the other end of the phone: bleary-eyed, white shirttails untucked, twirling a strand of beard with his index finger.

"All I can say is, it's making me think," I answered Simon, though I wanted to say more. I wanted to know what he believed. We had just finished a chapter called "God," which had spun my head around. Instead of dismissing the scientific revolution, as I would have expected, Schneerson had taught at length that science and faith are utterly compatible. At the same time, he stated that God cannot be defined or even imagined. So I wanted to know how such a God could be so real to Simon. And I wanted to know if this God had anything to do with me.

Early one morning, as I trolled through a batch of notes that Simon had sent by modem the night before, my eyes flickered to a halt: "As Maimonides writes to Rabbi Ovadiah ha-Ger, the lineage of a born Jew goes back to the Patriarchs, while the lineage of a *ger*, a convert, goes directly to God."

I felt a surge of delight. Though the informal rabbinic court that Ivan put together had ruled that I was a Jew according to Jewish law, I certainly considered myself more of a convert, if anything. Now I wanted to know what else Maimonides had to say about God. That night, after work, I picked up a copy of *A Guide for the Perplexed,* whose very title made me grin. Maimonides, I was pleased to discover, was a physician and a rationalist. He'd written this book for "thinkers whose studies have brought them into collision with religion." Again I grinned: a collision, indeed. As I began reading Maimonides, I thought of something Ivan often said: God has a habit of placing in your path exactly the foothold you need at that moment.

Maimonides asserted that by "using logic and natural philosophy," he found it far more difficult to disprove the existence of God than to prove it. But he also railed against the shallow thinking that led man to think of God as just another man, however grand, pulling strings from the heavens. What, then, is God? Almighty, to be sure, and our creator, who essentially gave us the means and the will to improve ourselves and our society. Finally, Maimonides assured me: "Do not imagine that these most difficult problems can be thoroughly understood by any one of us."

Within a week, another foothold appeared in my path. Harvey Shapiro, a poet and a fellow editor at the *Times,* loaned me a book called *The Way of Man,* a slim interpretation of Hasidic teachings by Martin Buber. One essay told of a rabbi, imprisoned in Russia, whose jailer baited him with a question: If your God is all-knowing, why, then, in the Bible does he ask Adam, "Where art thou?"

I remembered why, from catechism: because Adam was hiding in the bushes, scared of the whipping he'd get for eating from the Tree of Knowledge.

The rabbi in Buber's tale had a different answer: "God calls out to every man: 'Where are you *in your world*? So many years and days of those allotted to you have passed, and how far have you gotten?' "

How far had *I* gotten? In a way, I felt I had not yet budged from the spot where I was born.

And then Buber warned me that we are not all so fortunate as Adam. "For the Voice," he wrote, "does not come in a thunderstorm which threatens man's very existence; it is a 'still small voice,' and easy to drown. So long as this is done, man's life will not become a *Way*. Whatever success and enjoyment he may achieve, whatever power he may attain and whatever deeds he may do, his life will remain Way-less."

His life—my life—would remain Way-less. Unfettered, surely, but just as surely unordered, and unfulfilled.

BY late winter, Simon and I were down to our last chapter, "Redemption." He had already sent me his rough draft by modem. It was an early Sunday afternoon, and I'd promised to finish by Monday morning.

I decided to run some errands before settling in to work. I put on the same coat I always wore, locked the door as I always did, whistled to myself while waiting for the elevator, as was my habit.

But once I hit the sidewalk, everything seemed acutely different. Shuttling between the dry cleaner and the greengrocer and the newsstand, I was wrapped by what could only be called a cloak of fearlessness.

What was it that I was no longer afraid of? The usual Manhattan things: being mowed down by a delivery bicycle, casting the wrong glance at the wrong stranger. But this fearlessness went far deeper than that. Suddenly I was not afraid of who I was.

For as long as I could recall, I had felt like a trespasser on the earth. After all, I had been born imperfect. No measure of righteousness could remove that blemish. The best I could attempt was to stanch my sins, which hadn't come easily. And so the magnitude of my existence had been steadily eroding. The weight of my parents' Heaven and the horror of their Hell, no matter how I tried to shrug them off, had entrapped me. Every day I lived was another step in the wrong direction.

On this day, though, I felt that trap spring open. My soul had been handed back to me. Hustling back to my apartment, I felt aflame with goodness. I felt that questions were more important than answers. I felt that God knew me and that I could know Him.

I sat down to read over Simon's rough draft of the last chapter. Within ninety minutes the rewrite had bolted from my fingers. I read it through and could barely remember having typed the words. "What do we need redemption from?" it asked. "From being trapped in the darkness of the material world. . . . From a listless and aimless life. From our doubts and fears."

I modemed the chapter to Simon, who called within fifteen minutes. "I just read 'Redemption,' " he said.

"And?"

"It's the best chapter yet. Very, very good. I wish we weren't finished already."

"I didn't really write it," I admitted. "It was kind of spooky. It just sort of *exited* me."

I heard Simon draw in his breath. "The same thing happened to me a few weeks ago!" he said. "I didn't tell you—I thought it would frighten you. The 'God' chapter. I'd been having terrible trouble, and then it just came out of me, like I was in a trance. It felt like the hand of God was on my back."

"Yes!" I said. "That's exactly what it felt like. The hand of God at my back."

We both chuckled, then sat in a sort of luxurious silence. It hung in the air, resonating, like the final chord of a triumphant symphony.

"Well," I finally said, "the book is done. How do we celebrate?"

And Simon said, "I think we just did it."

4

A new idea of God had lodged itself inside me, and I was grateful.

I had never wanted not to believe. Etched somewhere upon my soul was an intuition that a belief in God is primary and healthful. Perhaps this "intuition" was merely learned behavior, a by-product of my parents' zeal. But my own siblings, some of them at least, had certainly weaned themselves. While Marthe, Ann, and Beth all were practicing Catholics, Mona rarely went to church and hadn't even baptized her daughters, and my three brothers had pretty much done away with religion. Catholicism was something they had survived, and surpassed.

At this moment I suppose I might easily have returned to the Church. Surely the Catholic tradition comprised enough sages and soul-probers to engage my curiosities about God. Its theology held countless mysteries I had never bothered to investigate.

But I did not consider this route for a moment. It wasn't theology I needed; it was a Way, and it was the way of Judaism that had called out to me. The "new Christians" of South America, Christians who discovered that their ancestors were converted Jews, had a phrase for it: *la sangre llama,* "the blood is calling." Now my blood was calling, and the only option was to answer with a whole heart.

That wouldn't make my mother happy, of course. I had once asked her if, when she began exploring Catholicism, she considered looking into the Judaism that she'd never really known.

"Oh, yeah," she said. "See, the roots of Catholicism are founded in Judaism. So it's important to know about that."

And that was all she had to say on that subject. For her, Catholicism was Truth, and beyond that was mere history.

I had by now come to judge Catholicism harshly, at least my parents' brand of it. In a world fraught with complication, the religion of my childhood felt like resignation. What was our farmhouse if not some kind of ascetic retreat, a make-believe Eden where my parents could protect their children from the real world? Having recognized the inevitability of earthly suffering, they had chosen a hardscrabble life as a fitting prelude for the hereafter. There was no earthly tragedy, they assured us, for which the glories of Heaven would fail to compensate.

This idea plainly wasn't working for me. I had more faith in life itself. Perhaps it was merely a function of youth, but I was less consumed with beating back the darkness of death than with finding a schematic for the here and now. Judaism, from what I knew so far, seemed to provide that. I took great comfort in a line written by Abraham Joshua Heschel: "The faith of the Jew is not a way out of this world, but a way of being within and above this world; not to reject but to surpass civilization." To surpass civilization!

When the Rabbi Schneerson book was published, I mailed my mother a copy. She sent me back a note, which I deciphered with care, for it was classic Mom:

Great work! [first, praise, often with an exclamation point]
And I can see why you're attracted to Judaism. [A seeming
tolerance of a position counter to her own, quickly followed
by . . .] For me, Catholicism is the blossoming or fruition or
completion of Judaism. [A confident rebuttal of that position]
                            Lots of love,
                            Mom [The cheery sign-off]

I spent several hours composing many drafts of a smart-ass
reply and never mailed any of them.

A few weeks later, my mother came north for the summer, and
the family got together at Mona's lakeside camp in the Adiron-
dacks. One afternoon, my mother and I wound up alone on the
screened-in porch. Everyone else was off swimming or fishing. I
asked if we could talk about her conversion some more. Sure, she
said. I ran inside, grabbed my tape recorder, and settled in.

"What was it about Catholicism that convinced you it was the
truth?" I asked.

She seemed taken aback by the abruptness of the question,
which had been my intention. "Well," she said, almost wearily,
"everything rang true, as I say. It was so logical; I could understand everything."

"But didn't you have any trouble at first, believing the Virgin
Birth and the Resurrection? Did you accept them in a literal
sense?"

"Yeah, I did, I did."

"But for someone who didn't grow up with those beliefs, how
were you able to accept them, as a rational-thinking adult?"

"First of all, it's told in Scripture."

"But what made you accept that Scripture was the truth?"

"Because for one thing, you know that Scripture was divinely
inspired. It's not a fairy tale that's made up, it's divinely—"

"Yeah, but that's what I'm asking. What convinced you of
that?"

Now her voice grew firm. "It's the gift of faith, and faith is a gift."

Ah, her gift-of-faith defense. It reminded me of a faulty syllogism I'd once read: All cats are mortal. Socrates was mortal. Therefore, Socrates was a cat.

I considered sharing with her the reading I had been doing about her Scriptures: The fact that some Christian scholars consider Jesus' bodily resurrection nothing but a metaphor, a myth. The fact that it wasn't until the Gospels were set down in writing, some eighty years after Jesus' birth, that anyone thought to assert that his mother was a virgin. The fact that Jesus may have been married to Mary Magdalene, but since that fact ran counter to his image as the pure son of God, the men who were championing his cause played loose with Mary Magdalene too in the rewrite stage.

These and other hurtful words were just aching to fly off my tongue, but she was my mother, after all, and I couldn't bring myself to go nearly that far.

"What do you make of people who may believe in God but don't believe in Christ?" I asked.

"Well, I'm sure they're well-meaning and sincere and so on, and I feel that they may have a little piece of the Truth but not the whole Truth. I know Dad used to say—we had a lot of Protestants living in Duanesburg—and he said oftentimes, 'Some of these people may be much better than some of the Catholics who go to Mass every Sunday.' "

"What do you think Dad would say about my interest in Judaism?"

"I don't know what he would think. I can't speak for another person—how can you do that?"

"But, I mean, you knew his mind as far as Judaism and Catholicism—"

"Well, I know what *I* think. I think it's the loss of a great opportunity if you were to revert to Judaism. I don't want—" She stopped herself, began again. "You have to be true to your own conscience, and you have to do what you think is right, but the way that I see it, it's so *definite* that Jesus is the Messiah that it's just a flow from there."

A door slammed, and my niece ran in, dripping, wanting to tell Grandma about her swim. "Lauren!" my mother called out, her voice suddenly full of warmth. "Hello! How was the swimmies? Wet!"

I was ashamed of myself when I listened to the tape. Never mind that I was baiting her; I was also forcing her to prove her beliefs when my own were hardly so believable. *The soul is a modem!* Ugh. And where did the early Christians get the idea of bodily resurrection in the first place? From Judaism!

Still, I knew now where we stood. I knew that my mother would find a way to forgive me if I became a drug addict, or a homosexual, probably even a murderer. To become a Jew, though, was an entirely different matter.

So I kept it to myself. I did not tell her when, later that summer, I began studying Hebrew and enrolled in a course called *Derekh Torah,* "the Way of Torah." I did not tell her when I began going to synagogue and studying Talmud with Mychal and Jonathan, a couple I'd met through Ilene (Jonathan was a writer, Mychal a Conservative rabbi). Nor did I tell my mother how dazzled I had become by the tribe I was joining—Rashi and Buber, Gershwin and Salk, Koufax and Rabin—trying to discern the essence of what could possibly knit them all together and what could possibly have allowed them to survive over the centuries despite such ridiculous odds. I certainly didn't tell my mother that every now and then, as I stayed up late studying Jewish texts, I wondered if I should become a rabbi.

That thought, of course, was wildly premature. I was still sounding out Hebrew words letter by letter. The stirrings of a soul, however, are unbound by logic. One summer weekend, Ilene and I made plans to get away to the mountains. As we were leaving New York, the car full of groceries that she'd spent two hours buying, I announced that I would be fasting for Tisha b'Av, the day commemorating the destruction of the Temple in Jerusalem. Ilene promptly and vigorously disabused me of this plan.

Within my ardor, I recognized my parents. It was the way of any convert, the giddy rush to gather up the promises of a new and better life and hold them so tightly to your breast that they might pass through to your heart. Even that, though, was not enough. It was also necessary to demolish the tradition you were abandoning, for the more fully you did so, the more perfect your new tradition would seem.

A few weeks before Rosh ha-Shanah, the Jewish New Year, I decided it was time that I own a yarmulke and a tallis, a prayer shawl. At lunchtime I walked from the *Times* to a Judaica shop on West Thirtieth Street. As I reached the top of the stairs, a man with short red hair and eyeglasses, about thirty-five, grabbed my arm. "Come on, we need you," he said. It was time for afternoon prayers, and they had only nine men, one short of a minyan.

"I can't—I have to get back to my office," I lied.

"Come on," he said. "A couple of minutes."

I sputtered again: can't . . . can't . . . can't. Finally: "I don't know how."

From behind the counter came a woman's voice: "Leave him alone already. You'll get someone else."

I slunk off to buy my things, and a tenth man came up the stairs. As I picked through the prayer shawls—I hadn't known there would be so many variations—the men's prayers, fluid and foreign, seemed to taunt me. At home that night, I stood in front of a mirror, put on the yarmulke, and started to wrap myself in the prayer shawl as I'd seen Ivan do, first kissing the embroidered crown. With a struggle, I got the shawl around my shoulders, but then the yarmulke fell off my head. I put it back on, then my forearms got tangled in the shawl, like a mummy. The yarmulke fell off again. As I grabbed for it, I heard the shawl rip.

For about two seconds, I laughed. Then I grew sad, and angry—that I didn't even know how to put on a prayer shawl. That, at the age of thirty-two, I still had to sound out my Hebrew like a first grader. That, even if I wanted to, I didn't know how to be the tenth man.

My father should have taught me these things. On what grounds had he so grossly obliterated my birthright? What kind of Jew would do that to a son? What kind of Jew would yank his family's roots from the ground where they had grown for generations?

I could not answer these questions, for I still knew nothing about my father as a Jew. My mother hadn't the information—or the inclination—to help. Aunt Bess and Uncle Sam had told me what they could. It was Aunt Dottie, they said, who could really shed some light.

I had had Dottie's phone number for a year. I scolded myself now for not having called her. He was not a ghost, my father; he would not haunt me simply for asking questions about him. But how would Dottie receive me? I had been told that she and Nat had never shut out my father as the others had. Still, I felt like a bastard son, skulking around the family property, begging for handouts.

I finally phoned Dottie at the nursing home where she lived, about forty miles north of Manhattan. No answer. My heart shuddered with relief. A few days later I tried again. Still no answer. I grew bolder, calling every night after work, but I couldn't reach her. I decided to call her son, Mickey, who Bess and Sam told me lived nearby.

Harriet, Mickey's wife, answered the phone. "We hear you've been out to see Bess and Sam," she said. I couldn't tell whether she approved or not. "How's your mom doing?"

"Really well, thanks," I said, which was an assumption, since I was speaking to my mother less and less these days.

Harriet and I chatted for a few minutes, and then I asked about Aunt Dottie.

"Well, Aunt Dottie's had an accident," she said, and I knew instantly that Dottie was dead and that if I hadn't been so stupid and scared, I would have called a year ago and that now I would never learn anything about my father.

"She fractured her hip two weeks ago," Harriet went on. "She's still in the hospital, and her nursing home is only for the ambulatory, so we're worried about getting her back in there."

Aunt Dottie was alive!

When could I see her? As soon as she was settled, Harriet told me, maybe in a month or two.

I said I'd call back, and I wished Harriet *shana tovah,* a happy new year.

WHAT had been awakened in me was not, I assured myself, merely a son's insistence on reclaiming his dead father. True, I felt the tug of his family and of the secular Jewish culture he'd abandoned. But hadn't I also felt the tug of the Covenant itself? If so, was its binding nature so strong that it could reach across a generation to pull me back?

On Erev Rosh ha-Shanah, I went to synagogue with my friend Adam Reingold. Adam's Jewish education had ended with his bar mitzvah, and mine was barely under way. But after two or three *niggunim,* the wordless melodies sung by the rabbi, we both were singing along for all our worth. My brain seemed familiar with the melodies, and they fitted my vocal cords perfectly. When I got home, I sat down at the piano. My fingers, quite on their own, re-created those same *niggunim.* The melodies tumbled forth from my tongue, fully intact. I was euphoric. Where had this come from? I had once asked Simon how he and the other "oral scribes" could remember the Rebbe's speeches well enough to write them down hours after the fact. It was a combination of concentration and inspiration, he'd told me.

Now I understood what he meant. I understood Judaism itself to be equal parts concentration and inspiration, an amalgam of finite law and ineffable faith, of history and timelessness, as earthbound as a loaf of bread and as mysterious as a melody that had lain dormant in my genes.

The next morning I met Ivan for services, at an old Orthodox synagogue on the Lower East Side. "How ya doin', kid?" he said. "*Gut yontef.*"

Even though the Rosh ha-Shanah service would be totally in Hebrew, and many hours long, I felt armed to the teeth. I had bought a prayer book with English transliterations. I had been studying the liturgy, reveling in the opportunity it provided to confess your sins and rejuvenate your soul. And I was wearing my brand-new tallis and yarmulke. No doubt about it, I thought: Today I am a Jew.

Ivan and I sat in the second row. In front of us were a tall, straight-backed man and a teenager who I gathered was his son. They both wore eyeglasses and dark blue suits, and as the service began, the two of them moved like a dancer and his shadow: standing-bowing-sitting-standing-singing, all with effortless passion. The boy was called up to chant from the Torah, and his voice was sweet and clear.

For the first hour or so, I felt as if I belonged. But soon I kept losing my way in the prayer book. The tallis felt scratchy on my neck. Watching the boy and his father, I hated them. I had come here to pray, to account for my jealousies and nasty thoughts of the past year, and here I was, jealous of this boy and having all kinds of new nasty thoughts. At the first break, I told Ivan I'd had enough, folded up my tallis, and went home.

I am a fraud, I told myself. If I were meant to be a Jew, my father would not have deserted me as he did.

I decided I wouldn't go back to synagogue the next week for Yom Kippur. At the *Times*, I was editing a pair of long political articles, relieved to be wrapped up in something that was about neither God nor me.

And then, on a Wednesday night, another foothold revealed itself.

I had decided that since I wouldn't be observing Yom Kippur, the most solemn day of the Jewish year, I wanted to do *something*. I stared at my bookshelves for a while, pulled down and put back three or four books, then spotted a copy of *Pirkei Avot*, "Ethics of the Fathers," which Ivan had introduced me to a few years earlier. It was the section of the Talmud containing ethical maxims, teachings on arrogance and humility, laziness and free will, and of our obligations to God.

What the hell, I thought. What could it hurt?

It wasn't long before I came across the tractate's most famous section: "If I am not for myself, who will be for me? But if I am only for myself, what am I? And if not now, when?"

The words encouraged me enough to read on. The sages went back and forth in their singsong way. At last my eyes settled on this sentence: "You are not required to complete the task, yet you are not free to withdraw from it."

You did not have to—*I* did not have to—complete the task. At least not this week. And I did not have to be perfect to be a good Jew.

On Yom Kippur, I returned to Ivan's synagogue. The straight-backed man and his son held down the front pew again, singing flawlessly. My mind, awash in concentration and inspiration, behaved itself. Even the Hebrew letters, as gnarled and ancient as olive trees, began to make some sense.

The rabbi, a soft-spoken, sad-eyed old man, stepped forward

to give a sermon. After several hours of nothing but Hebrew, his English was jarring.

"During these days of reflection," he said, "I have been asking myself what it is that makes us keep on being Jews when it has been such a struggle. Wouldn't it be natural for us to simply stop? Judaism places such an enormous burden on us. Yet we persist. Why? I asked myself. Why?" The rabbi paused. "And I found the answer in six words. Six words in a Talmud commentary, written by Rashi: 'He will not let us go.'"

It isn't a matter of our choosing whether or not to quit God, the old rabbi explained; it is God who chooses not to quit us.

No, God had not quit me. But if that were true, God had presumably not quit my father either. What happened then? And what was it that made me so desperately want to be a Jew when he so desperately wanted not to be?

5

MY father, I decided, must have been some kind of a golem. But unlike the golems of Jewish legend, he was not fashioned from clay; it was Jewish flesh, rendered inanimate somehow until the Name had been whispered into his ear. Only then did he spurt to life and turn into something new.

But I did not know who had whispered in his ear, nor could I fathom why, *why,* he had been so eager to hear.

I embarked on a mad campaign to find out. I could no longer afford to feel that I was intruding. It was my duty to learn his secrets. I was his son; his life was mine.

A few years earlier, my sister Mona had become a partner in my family project. She was living near Albany, where she worked as an aide in the state senate. In the Albany phone book she noticed a Kevin Dubner, who turned out to be our first cousin. He was the son of Martin, our father's youngest brother, who had died in 1975. When it happened that Kevin's mother, Irene, and our mother were planning a visit to Albany at the same time, Mona arranged a dinner for the four of them.

At this point Mona and I still did not know the name of our grandfather, Shepsel, or how thoroughly he had cut off our father. So at dinner, Mona asked Irene why our grandfather had never come to visit when Mona and Joe and Marthe were young.

Irene seemed about to answer, Mona later told me, but then glanced at my mother, who wore an uneasy look. And then Irene answered by saying that Shepsel hadn't been well enough to travel, even to Long Island.

Now I called Aunt Irene, who lived in Florida. She was, as Mona had said, full of pep, brimming with warmth. At the same time, I could tell she was holding back. After fifteen minutes of small talk, however, she dropped her reserve.

"I have to be very truthful," she said. "When I heard you might call, I thought, I don't know how to handle this situation. It's not that I don't feel comfortable talking to you, but I thought your mother might not be too happy about it." She held up for a moment. "But since Uncle Sam says he already talked to you about everything . . ."

Aunt Irene then told me what she could. She had known the Dubner family since she was a little girl. "I was very close with your dad," she said, "and I loved him very, very much. We all loved him."

She told me, as Bess and Sam had told me, that Solly was extremely close to his mother. "She was very good and caring," Irene said, "very subservient to her husband."

I asked what my father was like as a young man, before the war.

"I really think he wasn't on solid ground, so to speak. He was always—oh, he was wonderful, warm, easy to get to know. But in a way I think he was lost."

I asked Aunt Irene what she knew about his conversion. "Look," she said, "people take different directions in life. Not that it's *wrong*—whatever you feel comfortable with, wherever life leads you, as long as you're not harming anybody."

Just after the war, Irene said, she and Martin were about to be married. Shepsel was very involved in the plans; he had even hired Leibele Waldman, a famous cantor whom Irene had admired since she was a little girl. "And when Marty asked your father to be his best man, he said no, he couldn't. It was very disturbing. We couldn't figure out why he refused, and he just wouldn't say."

It was soon after the wedding, Irene said, that Shepsel discovered the rosary beads in the pocket of Solly's khakis. "If a knife had been plunged into him, I don't think he would have bled. The news went right through the family. I thought Shepsel was going to take his own life. It was like somebody leaving an open letter for you to find. I think, in a way, your dad was hoping it would come to that. Not that he was looking forward to the confrontation, but he knew it had to happen."

Only then, Irene said, did she understand why Sol wouldn't be their best man: He wasn't a Jew anymore and, at a religious wedding he would have felt like a hypocrite.

Was it true, I asked, that Shepsel never again spoke Solly's name, that he never inquired about his grandchildren?

"How can you go see your grandchildren when you've already admitted to God that this child is no longer a part of your family?"

Beyond that, Aunt Irene didn't have much to offer. I'd been expecting more, desperate for some melodramatic tale: Solly raging against God when his mother died, perhaps, or ripping his tallis to shreds in front of his father. I wanted to believe that the Jewishness had been wrung out of him, not that it had simply evaporated.

By the time we hung up, I felt as if I'd been mugged. My gut churned with the pain that my father had put Shepsel through; my head throbbed with anger over whatever Shepsel had done to push Solly away in the first place. And I was annoyed with myself—for having grown so addicted to their plight, and for thinking I could do something about it.

I asked my mother if she had saved the letters my father had written her from overseas. She had, and they were stowed in a trunk in Mona's attic. Could I read them? Of course, she said.

Mona dug them out and sent them to me, eighteen V-mails from Hawaii. There were also a few courting letters he wrote upon his return, including one on letterhead from P. J. Kenedy and Sons, the Catholic publishing house where he'd worked briefly as a clerk. And there were dozens of birthday and Mothers Day cards and Valentine's poems, one of each for every year from the time they married until he died. There wasn't much more written evidence of his life: some of his newspaper articles, a few weathered notebooks in which he'd jotted inspirational sayings, and another notebook from something called Recovery, Inc.—a program, my mother now told me, that he'd enrolled in because of his "lingering melancholy."

This was the first I had ever heard of his melancholy. "It started to come out in the Army," my mother said when I asked. "Even back then he was feeling extremely down."

"How bad was it?" I asked.

"Well, it eased up after the war, but he never shook it." By the time I was a child, she explained, it had grown debilitating. In the saddest tone I had ever heard my mother speak, she described the numbing parade of antidepressants, psychiatric counseling, and electroshock therapy. The blackness only lifted, she said, when he received the Holy Spirit through the Charismatic Christian Renewal meetings. He was healed almost instantly, she said, but within two years he was dead.

Because I remembered those Charismatic meetings so vividly, and hated them so much, and blamed them, ultimately, for my father's death, I did not want to hear about how they had saved him. Nor, truth be told, did I want to hear about the depression they had saved him from.

Instead I gathered up the fragments of writing my father had left behind and studied them as if they were sacred scrolls unearthed in some Babylonian cave. I also began tracking down people who had known him long ago. In Florida there were three first cousins, about my father's age, whose mother, Peshe, was Gittel Dubner's sister. (There were also a half-dozen relatives who, the moment I identified myself on the telephone, ended the conversation, obviously still bitter about my father's apostasy.) I found a few of my father's boyhood pals from Brownsville, who described their teenage hangout, the Do Drop Inn, and asked me, as if asking Satan's courtier, if what they'd heard long ago could possibly be true: Did Solly Dubner really become a Catholic? (Their next question, inevitably, was: So what are *you*?) I also began interviewing friends of my parents from the early days, Peggy Wink and Gertrude Smith, John Dessauer and Father Victor Donovan, as well as retired priests from the Church of the Blessed Sacrament in Manhattan, where my parents had met.

Apart from the half-dozen hostile relatives, they all had their stories to tell, stories my mother didn't know or, for some reason, hadn't told me. They were, to a person, staggeringly gracious and helpful. But there was a sharp discrepancy that none of them could resolve. Those who knew my father before the war described an affable Jewish dreamer who became increasingly forlorn, broken by his mother's death and then smothered by his father's piety. His postwar friends, meanwhile, portrayed a remarkably zealous Catholic, a man who'd been given a second chance at life, and as if the first life had in the end contained nothing but disappointment, he'd vowed never to revisit it.

But how had he passed from that first life to the second? I pictured my father standing on one edge of a deep ravine, a rotting footbridge the only means of crossing. Then, deciding he'd rather die than stay where he was, he broke into a tightrope sprint toward the far side, falling to his knees on solid ground and thanking God with his every molecule.

My father, I knew, had committed this act of great daring. But I could find no one who had witnessed it.

My mother told me about a man named Mac Lerner, an Army buddy of my father's. Mac too was a Brooklyn Jew, and he too had run into emotional trouble during the war. When my father became a Catholic, Mac wondered if the same thing might rescue him. Surely my father would have shared with Mac the details of his daredevil sprint.

But Mac's troubles went even deeper than my father's. He wound up in the mental ward of a VA hospital in Long Island—the same hospital, it turned out, where my father started working in 1948. My mother told me that yes, my father had reconnected with Mac there and even brought him to the house for supper one night, but they eventually lost touch. Now, fifty years later, I could find no trace of Mac.

My father's certificate of baptism, issued by the Military Ordinariate, listed a Father Ulrich J. Proeller as the chaplain who had baptized him in Hawaii. My mother, to my astonishment, was able to help me track him down: He was ninety-three years old, living in a monastery in San Antonio.

I called Father Proeller to see what he could tell me of my father's conversion.

He said he couldn't recall a thing. A wartime conversion, he explained, was often no more than "a momentary transaction." He apologized for his failing memory. Then, suddenly, he said, "I remember he was a very alert young fellow, very interested. It was a joy to instruct him."

He spoke kindly, with a thick German accent. "There were not many Jewish converts," he said. "He took confidence in me somehow. And I was grateful—I wanted to create better feelings between the Christians and the Jews since I had the experience of the Jews in Germany."

Father Proeller paused for a moment. "Wartime is good for converts," he said. "The Jews felt kind of lonely, you know, because they were so few, so they picked out what they thought was the best, as far as services were concerned, and they stuck with that."

I was glad I hadn't visited Proeller in person. Despite his age, I might have felt inclined to deck him. *A momentary transaction.* Please. And if he wanted to create better feelings between the Christians and the Jews, he could have come up with a better solution than turning the rare Jew he met into a Christian.

Regardless, Father Proeller was only the priest who baptized my father as a Catholic in Hawaii. It was a year earlier, my mother had told me, on Christmas Island, that he truly underwent his conversion. Now I tried to crawl inside my father's mind there. What was it he had craved? I tried to imagine how he must have felt, a lonely Brownsville Jew on a barren rock in the South Pacific, dipping in and out of black periods. It must have seemed that the war would go on forever. And if not, he'd return home to a father he couldn't bear.

I began reading the New Testament through my father's eyes. My mother had told me many times that my father was learned in Torah. He could read it in Hebrew, she said, and was excited to discover that the New Testament fulfilled its prophecies. Now I found countless instances in which he must have felt that Jesus was speaking directly to him: "I was sent only to the lost sheep of the House of Israel. . . . I have come to set a man against his father. . . . And everyone who has left houses, brothers, sisters, father, mother, children or land for the sake of my name will be repaid a hundred times over, and also inherit eternal life."

My mother had also told me that my father had a great appreciation for St. Paul, which is why he took that name. Reading Paul's Epistles, I could see that my father was exactly the kind of Jew that Paul had been looking for two thousand years earlier:

fed up with all the old-fashioned rigamarole of Judaism, all the arcane rules and bickering between rabbis.

Yet the Catholicism that my father adopted contained a certain warmth, a fiercely emotional human touch that I did not find in either the Gospels or the Epistles. Someone, or something, must have grabbed his heart.

One summer Friday night, I came home from synagogue, lit my Shabbos candles, said the blessings over the wine and the bread. I ate my supper. Then I sat down with a shoebox of my father's things. I fingered his dogtags, his timeworn rosary beads, his tattered brown scapular, with its image of the Virgin Mary peeking out from behind a square of cracked plastic. On the back was an inscription: "Whosoever dies wearing this scapular shall not suffer eternal fire."

I couldn't recall ever having seen my father without this scapular around his neck. As a child, I thought it was mandatory menswear. I was shocked when, at a church picnic, the other fathers stripped off their shirts to play football and they weren't wearing scapulars.

My father's love for the Virgin Mary, I knew, was profound—a deeper love, even, than his love for St. Paul, perhaps even for Jesus. There was no greater evidence of this love than the twenty-fifth anniversary card he gave my mother. "God made two perfect women," he wrote. "Our Blessed Mother and Veronica Dubner."

My mother had recently sent me a book called *Rebuilding a Lost Faith,* by John L. Stoddard. I had barely glanced at it. I was accustomed to receiving such gifts, and I quickly put them aside. But now, late on this Friday evening, I opened the Stoddard book and sat down to read at the kitchen table, in the light of my Shabbos candles. A pink note slipped from the pages. "This is the book that Dad read," my mother had written, "and it led to his conversion to the Catholic Church."

The copy she had sent was a recent edition, not the actual book he'd read. I saw that it was first published in 1921 by P. J. Kenedy and Sons of New York—the same publishing house where my father had worked after the war! Had he been so moved by this book that he sought employment at its source?

The author had been a student in the Anglican seminary when he lost his faith in God. He spent the next forty years as an ardent rationalist. But in the dark heart of World War I, he explained, he renewed his search for God and became a Catholic.

He chose Catholicism primarily on the grounds that it was founded by Christ's contemporaries and that ever since, its teachings were scrupulously upheld by an extraordinarily disparate band of followers—"in chapel, in cathedral, in hamlet, in metropolis, in Europe, Asia, Africa, America and on the islands of all seas."

These last words caught my eye. I imagined my lonely father, reading this book on an Army bunk in the South Pacific.

I was overcome suddenly by the urge to pray. This was still a novel act for me. Though I'd been going to synagogue often, I would get so wrapped up in the mechanics that I rarely found the space to pray. In any event, prayer came hard. As a child, I knew prayer only as a rote recitation of some holy words. By the time I was a teenager, I had abandoned the habit. Recently, however, I had read that prayer was originally intended as a means for an individual to speak with God, spontaneously and personally. But, because most people were intimidated by such a prospect, the rabbis began writing standard prayers. I much preferred the idea of spontaneous and personal communication, especially after my friend Jonathan told me a midrash, a sort of exegesis, that made God seem utterly accessible.

The midrash asks a question: Does God pray? Yes, it responds. What, then, does God pray for? He prays that His mercy will be greater than His anger.

I liked this idea, of a God who struggles with His own anger.

So now I put down my book and buried my head in my hands and prayed to Him: *Father in Heaven, guide me well in this act of exhuming my father.*

For the first time in months my mind became perfectly peaceful. By the time I opened my eyes, many minutes later, one of the Shabbos candles was flickering out.

I returned to the Stoddard book. It was slow going, and not much to my liking, but I kept on. It was nearing dawn by the time I reached the last chapter, "Some Catholic Privileges and Compensations." This was directed at converts. It noted that the Catholic Church was especially rich because of its consistency. "If Mass is being said, or Vespers sung, or the Benediction is given, the ceremony is the same, the Latin words identical."

True enough, I thought, but couldn't the same be said for Judaism and Hebrew?

Stoddard then described the wealth of Catholic art that had been produced over the centuries, particularly the glorious paintings of the Virgin Mary, "which brings us to another source of consolation, happiness and spiritual aid, peculiar to the Catholic Church: *the love and homage paid to the Virgin Mother,* as well as her responsive love and care for us.

"All hearts," Stoddard continued, "are not alike. Some unimpassioned souls prefer to pray to God alone. . . . Others are moved to hold communion with their Saviour only. . . . And there are others still, lone, orphaned hearts, who crave a mother's love and care, and find the greatest surcease of their pain by coming to the Mother of their crucified Redeemer, and begging her to comfort and to plead for them."

I wished I had my father's copy of the book. Would those sentences be underlined? Tear-stained?

"There are in every life some moments when a mother's tenderness outweighs the world, and prayer to Mary often meets this want, especially when one's earthly mother is forever gone."

The moment I read this passage, I felt that I owned my father's secret. His mother was the repository of all the love in his house. She died when he was fifteen, knocking his feet out from under him. His father cast an ever-blacker shadow over Solly's world. For years he lived in a void. Then, in short order, he fell in love with the Virgin Mary and with Florence Greenglass, two women cut from the same holy cloth. The Virgin Mary had handed him a lamp; my mother showed him where to shine it.

So it was love, not fear, that had inspired my father's daredevil sprint across the chasm. This changed everything.

Outside, on Seventh Avenue, the garbage trucks were already grinding away on their morning rounds. I crawled into bed and recited the Shema: *Hear, O Israel, the Lord is God, the Lord is one*. I waited for sleep, but it wouldn't come.

Was it love that had inspired my return to Judaism? No, I told myself, not love. It was something smaller than love, less desperate. It was instinct. My noisy soul had demanded that I follow the flow of my blood.

But that flow, of course, had now led to my father. I had never been brave enough to consider what his death had truly done to me. Perhaps it had damaged me as much as his mother's death had damaged him. If so, was my embrace of Judaism nothing more than an embrace of my dead father, a glorified nostalgia trip?

These past months, trying to bring him back to life, had been unsettling. Whenever I uncovered a new scrap of evidence, I would turn it over in my mind. I knew I was judging him, but I couldn't help myself. Some of the facts clearly weighed in his favor: his "sterling character," as my mother called it; the fact that you couldn't help smiling when Solly walked into the room, as his cousins told me.

But I had been forced to square that young man with the man who became my father, the one who spent his years on a forced march through depression, who endured electroshock treatment and countless black nights, sleeping alone in his office chair, his neck crooked, his mind seething with desperation.

Lying in bed, on the cusp of sleep, I felt as though I were watching a movie about my father. I knew the ending, and it was sad. But now I could freeze the picture where it suited me. Solly, young and in love: This was an image I could handle. *This* was the man who was my father. Solly, not Paul. Eager, not desperate. A Jew, not a Catholic. And as I finally drifted into sleep, I told myself that the farther back I could trace him, the more of him I could own.

6

HAVING determined, as best as I could, the moment my father ceased being a Jew, I was now intent on gathering whatever shards of him that might exist from before that moment. I was behaving like a member of those Orthodox ambulance crews in Israel who arrive after a terrorist bombing, scraping every piece of Jewish flesh from the pavement so as to bury the entire body and make it fit for resurrection. Paul Dubner had been buried properly, according to his faith, but Sol Dubner hadn't.

I still knew very little about his family's background. I had been told that his parents, Shepsel and Gittel, probably came from Pułtusk, a small city some sixty kilometers north of Warsaw. Shepsel emigrated first, in 1906, and sent for Gittel and their two children five years later. My father was born in Brooklyn in 1916, the fifth of six children, not counting at least two who died young. Gittel's parents, David and Shayna Dubner, moved to New York in the late 1920s but didn't like it and returned to Poland, where they died of old age. Gittel was their eldest of four daughters who came to America; another daughter, Liba, and their only son, who was also named Shepsel, stayed in Poland, married, had children.

This much I had pieced together from my father's relatives and from census and immigration documents. I shared every new piece of information with my mother. Judging from her reaction, I gathered she simply wasn't interested; after a time I realized she was hurt that I wasn't researching her family as well. So I went back to the census and immigration reports to track down the Greenglasses. Finally I drew up the family tree I'd set out to make in the beginning, with both Greenglass and Dubner branches.

But because my father was dead, and my mother was not, it was the Dubners who kept tugging at me. I wanted to get a feel for the land that had given birth to Shepsel and Gittel, the land they had fled. I wanted to visit the graves of my great-grandparents and find out what had become of Liba and Shepsel, their youngest children. My cousin Sarah, in Florida, said they were never heard from after the war. When I told my mother this news, she let out a groan of despair; she hadn't known that my father had still had relatives in Europe.

So I planned a trip to Poland, with my girlfriend, Ilene. Her father's family also came from Poland, and still lived there when the war began. Many were killed; others fled to Siberia. Because of this, and because Ilene had spent her life as a Jew, we arrived in Poland with vastly different connections to the Holocaust.

At the Warsaw airport, we were met by Jankel Syzc, whom we had hired as a guide and translator. Jankel was thirty-one, a punky misfit who, like thousands of Poles, had only recently learned that he was a Jew.

His interest in Judaism, though, was primarily directed at the career opportunity it provided in shepherding American Jews around Poland. Jankel was openly scornful of religion. "I have no use for Jew or Catholic," he said as we got into his car. "I am a citizen of the universe."

Still, Jankel reeled off countless stories about the Polish church's long-standing anti-Semitism. To him, the Catholic Church was a bad idea that got worse. "All that money, sitting under their asses," he'd say whenever we passed a particularly large church, which was often. As we drove from Warsaw to Auschwitz, we passed Czestochowa, home of the famed Black Madonna icon. "She is supposed to be the mother of all Poland," Jankel said. "So all Poles are Jewish, yes?"

Auschwitz did not affect me as I'd anticipated. Perhaps I staved off the emotion by taking notes, page after page, writing down what the guide told us about the volume of Zyklon B used in the gas chambers, about the fact that Jews lived an average of two weeks upon arrival while Catholic priests usually survived a month. I gawked at the heaps of eyeglasses, the mounds of prosthetic limbs (one leg, near the bottom of the pile, was bright pink). On the way in, Jankel, Ilene, and I had scoffed at a Japanese tour bus, as if by dint of our blood, our mission were a thousand times more legitimate. But wasn't I just another tourist? Only once as we toured Auschwitz did I think of myself as a Jew: In front of a mountain of suitcases, Jewish surnames scrawled across each one, I found myself hunting for "Dubner," wanting badly to find it—a perverse instinct, I knew—as if my connection to the Jews would be strengthened and could never be taken from me.

We spent the next few days searching for traces of Ilene's family. In Radom we found the building where her grandmother had run a dress shop. In Krasnystaw we walked the old Jewish quarter, sagging houses with tar paper roofs; we spotted the clock tower that Ilene's great-aunt had remembered, afternoon sunlight glinting off its bronze face, just as she'd said.

But mostly we found cold stares and closed doors. The town clerk in Krasnystaw, a beefy woman with shiny black hair, refused to let us inspect the archives. They were stacked right behind her, leather-bound books on a metal shelf.

She couldn't give them to us, she told Jankel in Polish, because she was the only one on duty, and she might have to attend to other business. What other business? We were the only people in the office.

We wouldn't be able to read them anyway, she said, because they are in Russian. But I can read Russian, Jankel told her.

The woman was unmoved. Jankel shifted from foot to foot. Ilene couldn't believe what was happening. She had traveled seven thousand miles only to be told that she couldn't see even the paper scraps of her ancestors' lives. She pleaded with Jankel to plead with the clerk. No good. Ilene glared at the woman, then at me: If I were half a man, half a Jew, I would wrestle the clerk to the floor and seize the records. Finally we left. Jankel spat on the ground. "You see?" he said. "They still hate the Jews. They think you're coming here to take back their land."

After a few days in Poland, it was safe to say that, had every acre of the country been offered to me free of charge, I would have run in the opposite direction. Even in the countryside, the skies were gray with pollution. The cities felt like horny teenagers, drunk with the first sips of capitalism; the forests seemed, even now, just as Isaac Bashevis Singer had written of them, teeming with goblins and marauders who could imagine no greater pleasure than tearing a Jew limb from limb.

I knew that Jewish tradition and learning had flourished here for centuries. But to have been a Jew in Poland? An absurdly constant stream of plagues: murderous Cossacks, blood-libel charges, government pogroms, and finally the Nazis. I had come to Poland wondering why my grandparents had left; now I wondered how the three-plus million Jews who had stayed until the war could have done so.

When we arrived in Pułtusk, however, even though it was dark, we could see that it was shockingly pleasant. Our hotel, a converted castle, stood on a hill overlooking a picturesque town square. Behind the hotel a plush lawn sloped down to the Narew River, wide and peaceful and, under a fall moon, glistening like knives. "You see," Jankel said, "Poland is not everywhere horrible."

The next morning, I had an appointment with Anna Henrykowska, the curator of the regional museum. Jankel explained that Anna was known in Pułtusk as "the Jew," even though she wasn't. She was, however, the keeper of the town's history, with an inclination to help Jews like me.

Anna was a wiry blond woman in her late forties. She proved to be remarkably blunt and kind at once, as if the ugly history I had come to learn could be dispensed in no other combination. When I told her that my great-grandparents had died here before the war, she immediately informed me that the Nazis had leveled the Jewish cemetery in Pułtusk, as they had in most towns. I asked if the site was worth seeing.

"No," she said. "It was paved over for a factory." But the factory, she added with a conspiratorial smile, was going bankrupt.

"Did any headstones survive?" I asked.

"Follow me."

She led me into the basement of her museum. Stacked at the base of a damp wall were two dozen stone fragments bearing traces of Hebrew lettering. None of them said Dubner. I asked if there were any more.

"No, no more," she said. "Even these were not easy to get." Anna explained: she had dug up the stones from the courtyard of the hotel where we were staying. The hotel, she said, had once been the Catholic bishop's castle. But when the Nazis came, they commandeered it for their regional headquarters.

We were staying in the old Nazi headquarters? I decided we would sleep elsewhere tonight—then just as quickly decided that it wouldn't do any good.

Before killing the Jews, Anna was now saying, the Nazis forced them to haul their ancestors' headstones from the cemetery to lay a new courtyard outside the castle.

Pułtusk, Anna said, was forty percent Jewish before the war. It was a market town of about twenty thousand people, more prosperous than some, and the Jews were generally tolerated. But the Jews of this region were among the first Nazi victims. By the end of 1939, all but five hundred of them had been killed or driven out. The rest were herded into a ghetto and later sent to Auschwitz or Treblinka.

Thinking of Liba and Shepsel, my father's aunt and uncle, I asked Anna if there were any records listing which Jews were killed and which might have survived. The only account she knew of was the Pułtusk Yizkor book, a kind of scrapbook that surviving Jews from all over Europe compiled to commemorate prewar life in their towns. Anna said I could probably find a copy of the book in Israel, or New York.

By the time we climbed out of the museum basement, the sun was shining for the first time in a week. The market square was just waking up, Russian and Romanian vendors laying out used car parts, cheap socks, repackaged batteries.

Anna gave me a tour of the old Jewish quarter. She showed me the *bes midrash*, the study house, and the mikveh, the ritual bathhouse, both boarded up. The synagogue had been burned to the ground. I took notes, snapped pictures. The rest of Pułtusk had been faithfully rebuilt after the war and shimmered in the crisp morning sun. Only the Jewish quarter lay abandoned. I checked the doorframes for mezuzahs. All I found were the faded outlines they had left in the wood and occasionally a sharp scar from the knife someone had used to pry up the mezuzah. Who had used the knife, I wondered: a Nazi, or a plundering Pole, or the Jew himself, stuffing the sacred marker in his pocket on his way to the death camp? The buildings themselves seemed heartbroken. The sagging doors looked like mouths in mourning, the crumbling lintels like weepy eyes. Their emptiness was so pronounced only because their fullness, at least the way I imagined it, was so substantial. Standing on this crumbling sidewalk in northern Poland,

I felt just as I had as a child in upstate New York when our big old farmhouse would empty out after Thanksgiving, the siblings I loved and admired retreating to a distant place, leaving me as sole witness to a future that grew sadder by the minute.

I must have been looking particularly forlorn. Anna suddenly grabbed my arm and said, "Come, now, let's see if we can find something about your family, yes?"

She marched me into the regional archive building. Three unsmiling women, the clerks, sat with their morning coffee. Anna asked to see the family tree I'd brought. With a red pen she circled several dates: Gittel's birth date, the year she married Shepsel, the birth date of their first child, my Uncle Nat, my father's eldest brother. Anna waved the paper in front of the clerks' faces, demanding twenty-five years' worth of records.

The women just sat there. Anna snapped at them in Polish, sending all three of them upright as if their chairs had caught fire. Anna smiled; I didn't ask what she'd told them.

Each book contained birth, marriage, and death records for a given year. Until 1919 they were written in Russian. Anna showed me how "Dubner" was spelled in Russian, and we began going through the books. Just then, a Jewish family from Philadelphia arrived on a similar mission. The clerks didn't even bother to stonewall this time.

Within five minutes, the Philadelphia family was yelping with delight. Anna and I, meanwhile, were striking out. I kept sneaking jealous glances at these Philadelphia Jews. Where were the Dubners? If my parents hadn't converted, I said to myself, my family's past wouldn't be such a goddamn mystery.

Anna and I had searched every book. The Philadelphians were long gone. The three clerks wore smirks of triumph.

"Is there another last name we could look for maybe?" Anna asked me.

No, I told her. Everyone was named Dubner. I shouldn't have come here, I thought. Maybe my father's relatives had remembered wrong about Pułtusk. Maybe the family had a different name here. I should have done more research; I should have stayed in New York, where I belonged.

"What about your grandmother's sisters?" Anna asked. "Did they marry?"

We pulled out the family tree again. Peshe Dubner had married a man named Avram Kalb in 1918. The next year they had a son, Leibl. Did any of this happen in Pułtusk?

Anna, taking no chances, went over to the shelves herself and pulled down the records for 1918 and 1919. Sure enough, there they were: Avram Kalb, a tailor from Pinsk, had married Peshe Dubner of Pułtusk, daughter of David Dubner and Shayna Frayda Rosenowicz, my great-grandparents. A year later, Peshe gave birth to Leibl Kalb, my great-uncle Lou, now living in West Palm Beach, the same Uncle Lou I had interviewed just weeks earlier, the same Uncle Lou who, when he and my father were kids, sliced open his arm on a wrought-iron schoolyard fence, trying to get away from the principal, and still has the scar to prove it. ("Your father got off scot-free," Lou told me, and I replayed the scene in my head again and again: swift, crafty Solly making his bold escape.)

The rest of the day, as I walked around town, Pułtusk looked different. My father's family had lived here. Some of them might have died here. Those details would have to come later. Where was David and Shayna's house? Where did Gittel go to school? What became of Liba and Shepsel?

Anna was sorry that we hadn't found more records. Perhaps my family didn't register with the civil authorities, she said. Many Jews didn't, and the records the Jews themselves kept had been torched by the Nazis.

As we parted, Anna's smile was wide as the moon. "So this is your hometown after all," she said. "You were worried, yes? Hah! For what? I knew when I first saw you—we are landsmen, you and I. Good luck to you."

That night was our last in Poland. I was exhausted, but couldn't sleep. Auschwitz hadn't done it to me, but now, lying in bed in the very building from which the Nazis had operated, I tasted my first mouthful of Jewish rage. It was shocking to realize what I had become a part of. My mind was taking great leaps back and forth in time, huge conclusions brought about by the tiny details of the day. The vanished headstones, the nasty clerks, the subhuman Nazis: They were all assaulting me. *You wanted to be a Jew?* they taunted me. *This is what you get for being a Jew.* My parents' conversion had shielded me from this rage. Should I praise them or curse them? Suddenly I had a strange thought: if my parents had not become such fervent Catholics, I probably would not have been born—after all, how many Jewish families of my parents' time had eight children?

And this thought led me to something Ivan had said not long ago. We had just finished studying a piece of Torah. I was complaining about what a fledgling Jew I was, and wishing my parents hadn't converted.

"Not so fast," he said. "They were following their *ruach hakodesh,* the holy spirit. You're following yours, they followed theirs. The world is drenched in Jewish blood, and they take eight children out of the fold. Who's going to evaluate that? Not you and me, honey. Let God figure that one out."

7

CHRISTMAS was coming and, with it, my father's *yahrzeit*, the anniversary of his death. I decided I would visit his grave in Delanson to recite Kaddish. I thought about rounding up nine other Jews so I'd have a minyan. I pictured myself standing over his grave site with Ivan and Adam, Simon and Jonathan, our tallises snapping in that shrill upstate winter wind, our words carried off to the brown hills. But my plan began to feel like grandstanding, too reminiscent of the Charismatic Renewal crowd my mother had assembled when she buried him, so I decided to go alone.

On the way, I would finally meet with Aunt Dottie. She was back in her nursing home. We had talked briefly on the phone. "What's this I hear about you becoming Jewish again?" she asked. I told her it was true, noting the "again" in her question. "Oh, that's good," she said, "that's good."

What I had wanted most from the Poland trip was a copy of

Uncle Nat's birth certificate to bring to Dottie, his widow. Instead I brought a potted plant and my sister Mona.

Mona remembered Dottie from our father's funeral and from one long-ago visit, when my father took three of my sisters to visit Nat and Dottie in Far Rockaway. I had never even seen a picture of Dottie. She had by now assumed a mythic stature in my mind. At close to ninety years old, she was the family sage. If Dottie couldn't deepen my understanding of my father's conversion, no one could.

The nursing home where she lived was fairly attractive, laid out long and low, like an elementary school. Mona and I walked down the wide hallway. A mezuzah was posted on every doorframe. Why did this sight give me such pleasure? I envisioned visiting my mother in a Catholic nursing home someday, a crucifix on every door. The image made me shudder. The crucifix, in which my mother saw salvation, to me represented a gory threat; the mezuzah, in which I saw righteous tradition, to her represented nothing but antiquity. It was hard to imagine we'd ever resolve that discord.

Aunt Dottie had to use a walker to get to her door, but the hugs she gave us were strong. Her room was small and neat, the walls decorated with reproductions of Marc Chagall's stained-glass windows from Hadassah Hospital in Jerusalem. Dottie's smile was small, sincere, constant. Jabbing the air with a long, bent finger as she talked, she reminded me of Anna Henrykowska: blunt but kind, and eager to help.

"So what do you want to know?" she asked.

"The big topic for me is Sol's conversion," I said. By now, when talking to family, I was accustomed to calling him Sol, as if slipping into a second language.

"Well, I was the only one he was close to," Dottie said. "And when I asked him, he said, 'Someday I'll tell you.' And he never got around to it. Later he was too involved with your mother, and maybe he felt he shouldn't say anything. I used to ask him,

'They're so close, Jewish and Catholic, so why do you want to change?' And he'd just say, 'Someday I'll tell you.' I guess we'll never know. But there is one God, that we all believe."

"Maybe he just didn't know how to express it," Mona said.

"He couldn't get himself to tell me," Dottie said. "We were the only ones that stuck by him, really. Much as I didn't like what he did, I couldn't stop seeing him or talking to him. The others, they just followed what Shepsel said. They didn't know Solly like we did. They didn't know his likes, dislikes, his ambitions. I used to yell at them, fight with them. I'd say, 'You don't even *know* him, how *dare* you talk against him?' And I couldn't care less how they felt. Truthfully, I'm a mean son of a gun. I said, 'He didn't commit a crime. What he did, he did for himself.' "

"Did Shepsel make the whole family sit shiva when he converted?" I asked.

"Well, I don't know about the others," Dottie answered, but from the way she said it, I gathered she did know and didn't want to point fingers. "All I know is how Nat felt. I said to him, 'What are you going to do if your father tells you to sit shiva?' So Nat says, 'He can do what he wants, and I'll do what I want. Solly's still my brother.' "

A great deal of what I would come to know about my father was given to me by Dottie on this day and on subsequent visits. She recalled in detail the workings of the family she had married into some seventy years earlier. She went on at length about Gittel, the small acts of kindness she carried out every day and how deeply Sol was affected by her death. She told us about the many nights that Sol fled to her and Nat's apartment when he couldn't stand to be under Shepsel's roof and how he kept visiting even after he was married, when the rest of his family was off-limits. It was clear that Dottie had known Sol Dubner as intimately as anyone could have, and within the confines of her small, sunlit room, he finally began to come alive for me.

Midway through our visit, Dottie's son, Mickey, arrived. Mona and I exchanged a wide-eyed glance: He bore an uncanny resemblance to our father, and we told him so.

"Yeah, and when I went in the Army, in '52, I was in the medics too, like Uncle Solly," he said. "And see, because I looked like your father and did things like your father, the family thought I was going to convert too."

Whereas Dottie was Solly's confidante and protector, Mickey was his kid nephew, his greatest admirer. "I certainly idolized your father," he told us. "He was just that type of guy, always sincere, always wanting to take me places—ball games, the rodeo. He was a very good-looking man, well dressed, talked nicely, always polite, always a nice smile on his face even when things weren't going his way. And believe me, that was most of the time. He put up a tremendous front."

"Did you sense his downslide when it began?" I asked.

"He was the type that wouldn't complain," Mickey said. "You couldn't outwardly see depression or anything else setting in. Of course, I remember when he was first with your mother, his face just lit up. Whether it was that he found her or that he found the religion, I don't know—it could have been the combination. And as they started to have children, he was like a pig in shit. So whether you all had a lot to eat or didn't, or had to work hard, we never heard complaints from him or your mother."

Mickey and Dottie told us about a slew of relatives I'd never heard of. A bialy maker, a cantor, a car dealer. Cousins in Philadelphia and England and Israel. One cousin was an actress, Elana Eden, who, in 1960, starred in *The Story of Ruth*.

"It was a good movie," Dottie said. "I remember her saying, 'Whither thou goest, I'll go.' "

A cousin of mine had played Ruth, the most exalted convert in Judaism! Ruth, from whom King David is descended! A cousin of *mine*.

And then Mickey and Dottie told us about Shepsel's dying days. In the five years after Sol's conversion, they said, Shepsel hadn't once uttered the word "Shloime," the name he called my father. He had stomach cancer, and by the time he entered Kings County Hospital, he had wilted to seventy pounds. He lay in a noisy, sprawling ward with thirty other patients, dazed by morphine, a graying sheet pulled up to cover his bony shoulders. The closer he moved toward death, they said, the more boyish he looked, as the stern creases melted from his forehead. Dottie, Nat, and Mickey visited at least once a week. Mickey was eighteen by now, just about to join the Army. His hair was dark and wavy, just like his uncle Solly's, and he had the same upturned smile. At the end of one visit, Mickey bent down to kiss his grandfather's cheek. The old man's skinny arms fluttered up to hug Mickey. "Shloime, Shloime!" he called out. "Shloime, Shloime!" He kept crying out, like a baby wailing for his mother, even as Mickey finally backed away.

"Did my father ever hear about this?" I asked.

"No," Dottie said. "No."

Dottie, Mickey, and Mona kept talking, but my mind was stuck in that hospital. Mickey certainly looked enough like my father for Shepsel to have been mistaken. There he lay, the cancer and the morphine both working on him. When he cried out, did Shepsel know that he was still on this earth and leave it thinking he'd made peace with Solly? Or did he believe he'd slipped into the World to Come and that he'd finally been reunited with the son he'd declared dead?

I felt a chill. I was trying to direct a pair of ghosts in my own little drama, and I was powerless to affect the outcome.

We went on for hours, mostly about Sol. The way he'd start up conversations with strangers, always asking questions. His need for structure and routine. How badly he wanted to be a musician, then a writer, and how much he loved newspapers. The long walks he took through the city, usually alone, always whistling. But he could be a *dershrockener,* Mickey said, afraid of his own shadow, with an almost irrational fear of authority figures.

He was a walking paradox, a hard-core optimist locked in constant battle with anxiety and self-doubt.

My pleasure in their stories gradually gave way to revelation: *It could have been me they were describing.* Down to the smallest detail. The music, the writing, the newspapers. All this time, I thought I was pursuing my father simply because I wanted to understand him. Had it turned out that I'd understood him all along?

As they kept painting this picture of my father, I suddenly heard his laugh, out of nowhere. I *remembered* his laugh. I had been waiting for something like this to happen. I'd once clipped a quote by the German writer Gustav Meyrink: "When knowledge comes, memory comes too, little by little. Knowledge and memory are one and the same thing."

Hearing my father's laugh now, the room buzzing with conversation about him, I laughed back, as if he and I were sharing a joke.

Dottie gave a start. "Did you see that?" she asked Mickey. "He looked just like Sol now, when he laughed, a certain expression around the mouth."

"Where you been, Ma?" Mickey said. "That's the first thing I noticed when I walked in here."

After we'd worn out Dottie, Mona and I went back to Mickey's house to visit his family: his wife, Harriet, their daughter, Vicki, and their son, Matthew, a year younger than I was, who had his own fascination with Shepsel and would become my partner in further research. We paged through Mickey's photo albums, faces that looked familiar but weren't. It was a shame, we all agreed, that the family had been so fractured. We talked about planning a reunion.

"How's your mother feel about your becoming Jewish again?" Mickey asked me.

Mona and I both laughed. "Well," I said, "that's not something we talk about so much."

Late that night Mona and I drove north to Albany. I would sleep at her house before visiting my father's grave. The Thruway was empty, dark, serene. Mona and I couldn't stop talking about Dottie and Mickey. We both were overwhelmed at the affection we'd stumbled into, and grateful to learn that such affection had existed for our father.

I did feel slightly let down that Dottie hadn't produced some concrete rationale for my father's conversion. But I was naive to have expected otherwise. A conversion could be no more easily explained in words than could the act of falling in love—which, I was convinced, in the case of my father and the Virgin Mary and Florence Greenglass, were one and the same.

Still, Dottie and Mickey had returned my father to me. In a way, I felt even closer to him now than if Dottie *had* offered some tidy answer. Because it was I alone who knew his secret, the depth of the love he fell into—and how disappointed he must have been in himself when even that love could not rescue him from the rest of his life.

THE next morning, before I drove out to my father's grave, Mona showed me the trunk where his letters had been stored. There were all sorts of other relics inside. The guest list from my parents' wedding: not a single Jewish name. My father's postcard collection: Catholic churches from around the world. Literature about Our Lady of Fátima and the Charismatic Christian Renewal. And dozens of leftover prayer cards my mother had printed up when my father died. They carried a quote from the Gospel of John: "I am the Resurrection and the Life; he who believes in me, even if he die, yet shall he live."

All the evidence proved my father to be a Christian. Why couldn't I face that? He had become what he had become.

I hadn't been to the cemetery in many years, and I couldn't find his grave. It was a small country cemetery, with no map and no attendant. There was also a foot of snow on the ground, and I recalled he'd been buried not with a headstone but with a simple footstone, set flush to the ground, that the government provided free of charge to veterans.

The sun was shining brightly. The snowy glare was disorienting. I wandered past Mark Hebert, just a few years older than I was, whose father, Wally, had attended the Charismatic meeting where my father collapsed. I saw Mr. Guyder, the elementary school principal. I hadn't known he was dead. I saw that his wife had died many years before him; no wonder he'd been so crabby.

I finally spotted a small, weather-worn statue of Jesus, Mary, and Joseph and a small rosebush growing next to it. That was my father's grave. Digging through the snow to excavate the marker, I accidentally snapped off a branch of the rosebush. Its sharp, sweet smell filled the air, so out of place in the depth of winter.

That morning I had stuffed a yarmulke in my pocket, and a copy of the mourner's Kaddish. I had been struggling over whether I should recite it. Now, before I had the chance to decide, I started to cry, the first tears I had ever shed over him. He had become real to me, and I missed him. Instead of reciting Kaddish, I spoke to him for a while. I told him I wasn't sure if he could hear me, but I suspected he could. I told him I hoped he approved of the life I was leading. I told him I was ready to stop being angry about his leaving me here without him, his secrets unexplained. I told him I wished I could have gotten to know him better. Before I left, I dug up a small stone and placed it on his grave marker. I didn't regret not having said Kaddish. Would I want some son of mine reciting the Rosary over my grave when I'm lying in a Jewish cemetery?

On the long drive back to New York, I thought about nothing but my father. He was an ordinary man, as he would have been the first to admit. But he was also extraordinary. He was a man who couldn't catch a break, yet he wouldn't give up. He wouldn't stop banging on God's doors, demanding to be let inside. He was Jacob, crouching in the desert darkness, afraid for his life. And the angel of God descended upon him and wrestled with him and tried to break his body, and still my father refused to surrender. He would not surrender until he learned the identity of his adversary, until he received God's blessing. As with Jacob, my father's encounter with God left him both diminished and augmented, bearing forever the scars of his battle while reveling in the blessing it brought him.

8

"WHEN I was a child, I spoke like a child, I thought like a child, I reasoned like a child; when I became a man, I gave up childish ways."

These were among the last words my father spoke, before he collapsed, before he died. When I was told this, a few years ago, by Sister June Szumowski, the nun who had been sitting near him at the prayer meeting, I cared only as a journalist; it was a new piece of evidence. As for the words' intent, I was dismissive. They were New Testament. They were written by St. Paul, whom my parents regarded as a hero and whom I regarded as a somewhat hysterical Jewish apostate. They had nothing to do with me, with what I was learning, with what I had come to believe.

Over time, though, as I contemplated my father's life and his death, I reflected on these words often. I began to appreciate their wisdom. And I began to dismantle the wall I had been building between my parents and me.

My life had assumed a strange bifurcation. I was spending my days at *The New York Times,* a citadel of secular knowledge. It was a highwire jot-and-tittle act, considering each word as a Talmudist might, then rushing an article into print for a few million people to peruse, critique, pick apart (or, worse, ignore). Despite the pressures and the sheer cacophony, it was a dream job. While my mother might have disagreed, I thought the *Times* was the best newspaper going.

My nights and weekends, meanwhile, were often spent in solitary pursuit of a religious certainty. (I had split with Ilene some time before.) While this mainly took the form of Jewish study, I was looking for something broader than that.

I had come to practice Jewish chauvinism as heartily as a lifelong Jew, if not more so. I had decided that Judaism was the superior religion—*Blessed art Thou, O Lord our God, who has chosen and exalted us above all nations, and hast sanctified us with Thy commandments*—and that I was fortunate to have blundered my way into it.

On a certain level, though, the concept of chosenness made me squeamish. Some of my Jewish friends—and most of my friends were Jewish—could be as cunningly anti-Christian as some Christians could be anti-Jewish.

One Friday night, I sat down to Shabbos dinner with about a dozen people, Upper West Side Jews in their thirties and forties. Most of us had just come from synagogue. The table was laden with fish and rice and grilled vegetables. We made kiddush, washed our hands, said the blessing over the bread. Before long, the conversation somehow worked its way into Christianity, and one man, chipper and confident, began talking about "the Resurrection myth." I recoiled, then mumbled something about Moses on Mount Sinai, as if *that* had somehow been proved beyond doubt.

I was being a hypocrite, of course. In a different setting—if I were speaking with my mother, that is—it would have been *me* bringing up "the Resurrection myth." But now, as the sole quasi-Christian at our Shabbos table, I felt the need to offer a defense.

I put down my fork and turned to the chipper man. "A myth is only a myth until someone fully believes in it, at which point it becomes a truth," I said. "Maybe it is only *that person's* truth. But until you can offer some foolproof evidence that your truth is truer than everyone else's—and in the history of philosophy and religion, with far better minds than ours at work, that hasn't happened yet—I certainly don't want to be the one to play judge. I think anyone brave enough to wrestle with God ought to be brave enough to admit that a finite truth lies beyond any of us."

My rant was rather out of character, and no less insufferable for having been delivered in a quiet, shaking voice. No one would meet my eyes. They all looked as if they'd just witnessed a train wreck, and hastily returned to their fish.

These past few years I had worked myself into an unhealthy predicament: The more vigorously I embraced Judaism, the more vigorously I was inclined to assault Catholicism—and my parents. In the beginning, that's exactly what I wanted to do. Judaism good, Catholicism bad. I could not accept my choice with a full heart unless I rejected theirs with just as much gusto. In truth, the tension was seductive. At the same time that I was learning the facts of my parents' estrangement from their families, I was reenacting such an estrangement, or at least the likelihood of one. Esther Greenglass, Shepsel Dubner, Florence and Solly, and now me: I had inserted myself into some Old World melodrama, half *Jazz Singer,* half *Fiddler on the Roof.*

My mother was, to be sure, a willing partner. Her rigid defenses of Catholicism only made me want to push harder. When I began my Jewish learning, I took great delight in comparing Judaism with Catholicism. The Hebrew Bible was clearly a much better piece of writing than the New Testament. But more important, the Hebrew Bible took great pains to chronicle the failings of its principals. Moses, Abraham, Joseph, David: Their deeds were a virtual catalog of human weakness, arrogance and anger, spine-lessness and lust. I identified with these failings and took comfort in a religion that acknowledged and sought to overcome them. The New Testament meanwhile, in its rendering of Jesus, could tolerate nothing less than perfection.

As an ideal, perfection struck me as a bad idea. It only mag-nified the inevitable failings that any person—my father, for in-stance—is bound to suffer. St. Paul, thinking that the Second Coming was around the corner, declared that all men in pursuit of spiritual perfection should become celibate. Forget that St. Paul was rescinding the commandment to be fruitful and multiply; he was also laying the cornerstone for the practice of celibacy among the clergy, a practice that has led to more sexual misadventure than any Catholic would care to consider. The trickle-down effect of St. Paul's edict, furthermore, led the Catholic Church practi-cally to ignore the existence of sexuality. Which, I asked myself, was wiser: to pretend that a human urge does not exist and shamefacedly clean up the mess every time it asserts itself or to tackle the urge head-on, as the Talmud does at such length and in such detail that I, with an ingrained Catholic squeamishness about sex, am nearly too bashful to handle it?

As I slogged on, pitting one faith against the other, I wondered why religion was invented in the first place. From what I could tell, it came from a pressing need to reconcile human reality with the unknowable. At a not-so-distant point in our history, the un-knowable became synonymous with the divine.

But what if there is no divine, no God? I had entertained this possibility. Then I would think of a story told by Avigdor Miller, the gnomish Hasidic rabbi Ivan had brought me to hear in Brook-lyn. "Nowadays everyone is talking about computers," Miller had said. "They are miraculous machines, yes? They can operate mil-lions of times faster than the human brain. How did such a thing come to exist? Were all the pieces of the computer simply lying in the desert and a big wind came and blew them all together in exactly the right order? It would be absurd to think so. And yet that is the argument made by people who don't believe in a God who made man—that all the pieces of man were simply blown together by a big wind."

In a way, I told myself, it didn't matter: Once we believe there is a God, He exists. I sometimes thought of God as the world's greatest placebo. Merely believing that God exists leads us to uphold the code of behavior that man originally developed in the service of God. Did I really need to see God's face in order to admit that the Ten Commandments were a pretty good idea?

Within the tradition of Judaism, I was allowed, even encouraged, to question God's existence. What mattered most were my actions. Good intentions are lovely; good deeds are harder, and better.

The Catholicism I knew as a child also valued good deeds. But it led me to believe that God controlled every deed, good and bad. The fact that I had seven healthy, agreeable brothers and sisters was purely a result of God's will. The fact that my father died at fifty-seven, however, must also have been a result of God's will. In my parents' Eden, no word could be spoken, no leaf could fall, no frying pan could burn unless God had wished it so.

But where did that leave me? Why had He bothered to make me at all—only to suffer through an imperfect life in the hopes of being reborn perfect? It made no sense to me. God's paramount gift, as I saw it, was creating man as we know him: with God's breath in his nostrils and with free will in his soul. Without free will, we were sad puppets. I didn't believe, or want to believe, that ours was a God positioned to hoist man's hand away from the hot stove every time he drew near. Without free will, we could claim no triumph as our own; far worse, we must ascribe every murder, every war, every Holocaust to God's desire. If that were the case, the perpetrator was as blameless as the victim. If that were the case, then yes indeed, we would be better off with no God at all.

In Judaism, I had found a God, and a Way, that made sense to me. But by insisting that my Way was the only way, I was becoming as rigid as my mother, as rigid as Shepsel.

My mother and I both had dug in our heels, and as our relationship grew increasingly brittle, the charm of my little Old World melodrama began to wear off. This was real; this was my mother. Did I really want to let religion drive us apart? Did I really need to re-create the bitterness that still haunted my family? Whom did my recalcitrance benefit? Not me, not my mother, and certainly not my father. God, then? Did God really need me to condemn my parents' conversion? Some people thought so— Simon, for one. I had kept in touch with him after we finished the Rabbi Schneerson book. Simon believed that my parents had committed a grave spiritual error and that my return to Judaism was a justified, if freakish, correction of that error.

For a time, I agreed with him. In the end, though, my thinking changed. It was the Torah that moved me to a new understanding. Specifically, it was the Fifth Commandment: "Honor your father and your mother, that you may long endure on the land which the Lord your God is giving you." According to Jewish tradition, the first five commandments were given to Moses on one tablet, the second five on another. The first tablet was said to concern man's obligations to God; the second, the relationship between men. Why, then, was the commandment to honor one's father and mother included on the first tablet? Because, as one Torah commentary answered, "Parents are God's representatives and partners in the rearing of their children, and children who fail to respect this special position are offending against God as well."

These words bypassed my brain, went straight to my heart. I could curse my parents all I wanted to, but I would be cursing God as well. Was there any *truth* to this interpretation? It rang true for me. Just as Jesus rang true for my mother. Maybe we both were fools, hopelessly antiquated mortals clinging to religion out of fear and longing and heartache. Or maybe—and this is what I chose to believe—maybe we both were right.

IT was toward the end of summer, and my sister Beth was throwing a birthday party for our mother. Beth and her family lived near Buffalo. My mother had been staying with them for a few weeks and would soon return to Florida for the winter.

A flock of us descended on Beth's house: Mona from Albany, Marthe and her family from near Syracuse, Peter and his daughter from Connecticut, and I.

My mother had recently developed a heart condition and was finally starting to slow down. She was most definitely incapable now of lifting me up and cracking my ribs. Witnessing her decline was hard for the whole family; in many ways, she was the strongest woman that any of us had ever known.

Peter and I played a long, bluesy "Happy Birthday" on the piano, and everyone sang. When my mother sat down, Beth's two young children, Lauren and Danny, squeezed in close to her. She blew out the birthday candles.

"With all of you here," she said, "I consider myself the luckiest person on the face of the earth."

"Mom, I think you're stealing that line from Lou Gehrig," Peter said.

"Hey, wait a minute," Mona said. "She's seventy-four—maybe he stole it from her."

It was a good, long weekend. We all had lots of catching up to do, with our mother and one another. We played Monopoly and poker into the wee hours, Peter and I slipping out for a smoke every now and again.

My brothers and sisters were by now well aware of what I had been up to: the Rabbi Schneerson book, the family research, and the fact that I'd begun writing an article for the *Times Magazine* about our parents' conversion and my own return trip to Judaism. I had been interviewing them one by one for their recollections. Now they had questions for me: Do you go to synagogue? What do you think of Jesus now? How much have you told Mom? On the drive to the farmer's market to buy some corn for supper, Marthe asked me to explain the fundamental differences between Judaism and Catholicism. She was also curious about Julius and Ethel Rosenberg, asking if Mom had ever opened up about them. Not yet, I said.

Beth and I, still the babies of the family, had a long talk about our childhood as we dried the dishes. "I remember, in the third grade, learning that anyone who isn't Catholic is going to Hell," she said. "And I remember thinking, That can't be right—why would a just God do that? So even though we still go to Catholic church and everything, I consider myself more a Christian than a Catholic."

Late Saturday night, Peter and I were having a cigarette in the backyard. I still admired him as much as I had twenty years earlier: He was substantial in every way, but also funny, good-hearted, and sly. The previous year, he had invited me to spend Christmas with his family. As it happened, Christmas Eve was also the last night of Hanukkah. The night before, I had gotten sick after eating potato latkes. They had been especially greasy, and that may have caused the illness, or it may have simply been an overdose, for as a new Jew, I was on many Hanukkah invitation lists and had eaten latkes for seven nights straight. Now I was looking forward to a reprieve. Peter picked me up at the train station, and as I walked into their kitchen, I saw that they had made me a treat: potato latkes. They also had a menorah, which we lit, and then I gobbled down the latkes for the eighth, and best, time.

Now, in the darkness of Beth's backyard in Buffalo, Peter wanted to know about Shepsel's cutting off our father. "I had no idea it was that bad," he said when I told him. Peter and I then got to talking about music. Though he was a financial analyst for General Electric and had been leading an executive life for nearly twenty years, Peter was still the best and most avid musician in the family. Lately, he told me, he'd started listening to some klezmer, old Jewish music from Eastern Europe. "What really surprises me," he said, "is that even though I'd never heard it before, the minor keys and the modulations are just like the music I've always played." I told Peter about the night I sat down at the piano after synagogue and played those *niggunim* as if I'd been raised on them. "Strange stuff," Peter said. "Very strange stuff."

On Sunday morning, Beth, Marthe, and my mother went to church. When they got home, my mother said she had a late birthday present for me. With everyone watching, I unwrapped it: a coffee-table book called *The Living Gospels of Jesus Christ*. I was embarrassed, and quietly furious.

"It's got beautiful paintings," my mother said. "I thought you'd like it."

Later that afternoon, I got her alone in the kitchen. I asked if we could have a talk. "I don't see why not," she said. Just as we sat down, the oven timer buzzed. Beth rushed in to turn it off. "Okay, Dan," she called into the den, "it's time to give the statue to Lauren now." Beth's children had been fighting over a statue of the Virgin Mary.

"Mom," I said, "I need to tell you something, but I want you to know that I mean no disrespect by it. The thing is, I've been increasingly drawn to Judaism, and I've decided that what I'm going to be is a Jew."

"Well, if you don't have the Jewish roots, it's hard to be a good Catholic," she said.

"Yeah, but I don't want to be a Catholic, I want to be a Jew."

"Well, you've just got to follow your conscience on that."

"I know. I have. But I've got to tell you, I'm feeling guilty about it because I know how much Catholicism means to you."

"Oh, I understand that you're a great pleaser by nature. But I wouldn't want you to do something just to please me. I find that the more reading you can do about the connections between Judaism and Catholicism, the more you'll see that Catholicism is a necessary development because the old Jewish things don't apply."

"I've done quite a bit of reading. But I really don't want—" I took a breath. "Like this book you gave me today. I know you mean well, but I would really prefer it if you could stop foisting things like that on me."

"Well, you see, the Jewish teachings were fulfilled when Jesus came as the Messiah. The problem is, many Jews don't recognize that. It's not their fault, but it's a gift as far as I'm concerned, you have to have this gift of faith."

We went on a bit longer, neither of us budging. She knew she was right. I knew I was right. We had run up against the paradox of religion itself: When a set of spiritual beliefs, subjective by nature, are fully taken to heart, they eventually accumulate the weight of objectivity, of unassailable Truth. On the flight back to New York that night, I was morose. I came to the conclusion that my mother, an admirable and stoic and tenacious woman, was incapable of just one thing: accepting even an inch of apostasy.

But when she got back to Florida a few weeks later, we started talking on the phone again. And my mother began to share herself with me, pieces of history she'd hidden so completely—perhaps even from herself—that I had come to believe they didn't exist: her family's Seders, and how every year she wanted to ask the Four Questions but her cousin Irving got to. Her childhood run-ins with anti-Semitism. She even started talking about the family story that pained her the most: the atom spies, David Greenglass and Ethel and Julius Rosenberg.

"I didn't tell anybody about it," she said quietly. "I thought it was just terrible, the whole trial and everything."

"What did Dad think about it?"

"We didn't really discuss it. I just felt so sorry and so bad when they were killed, I couldn't believe it."

The most tangible sign of our budding détente came through the mail a few weeks later. She sent a Christmas card, offering me a novena. And, in a separate envelope, a Hanukkah card. "I don't remember my letters enough to translate this," she wrote beneath the Hebrew greeting, "but I'm sure it's a good wish."

By now I was well along on the article I was writing for the *Times* about our family. My mother kept insisting that her story wasn't so interesting. But she tirelessly answered my questions, constantly plucking new details from the far edge of her memory. In my more cynical moments, I challenged her change of heart. My mother is spinning me, I thought. She knows I'll write the article one way or another, and she wants to come off well. And I thought, What a smart lady. She hooked me up with dozens of people from her past. She sent me old photos, her high-school yearbook, her first daily missal. And she continued, for the time being, to hold her tongue about my becoming a Jew.

9

THE calendar in 1996 conspired to situate Passover and Easter right next to each other. My article was published in the *Times Magazine* a week earlier, on Palm Sunday. I had arranged to be out of town, scouting a theater festival in Louisville for the *Times*. I didn't want to be in New York when the piece landed, didn't want to be wondering what people thought of it. But on the flight home, a man one row ahead of me began reading the article. He seemed intent. He studied my parents' wedding photo, then the picture of Shepsel. He turned the page, read some more. I shut my eyes. I couldn't bear the idea of his abandoning my family halfway. I counted to one thousand. I looked again: He'd made it to the last page. When he finished, he closed the magazine and looked at the picture of my mother and me on the cover. I was seized by a fear, obviously irrational, that he would turn around and recognize me. I thought about what I would say. It came to me quickly: "How do you think my mother will take it?"

I was unprepared for the reaction to the article. Within a few days, I'd received a few hundred phone calls, letters, and E-mails. People had their own stories to tell, conversions and cover-ups and breakthroughs. Jewish families invited me to their Seders, Hasidic rabbis invited me to daven with them. I heard from high-school friends, astounded that the most Catholic family they knew had started out Jewish. Dozens of people praised my mother's spiritual fortitude, and several cursed me to Hell. Some thought my entire family was worthless. "Your mother was a ditsy disturbed woman married to a very unsettled and unhappy man and you are obviously the issue of a classically dysfunctional family," one man informed me, adding that "you are of a very unsettled mind."

I smiled at his choice of insult: "unsettled." You don't know the half of it, mister.

There were priests who lauded my return to Judaism and Jewish atheists who said I was crazy, like a parolee breaking back into jail. I heard from retirees who, as children, had eaten in Shepsel's restaurant. I received letters from aged Pułtusk Jews who had survived the Nazis' slaughter. And I was contacted by nearly a dozen new relatives, whom I would spend the coming year getting to know.

It was my mother's reaction, of course, that concerned me most. "Well, I think it's absolutely fantastic," she said when I called her. "And I congratulate you and the *Times* for running it. What I really liked is that it gave your point of view, because you never really discussed it with me."

"Yeah, but how did *you* feel about the article, Mom? You're a pretty major part of it, after all."

"Well, you and I have very different perspectives."

"But do you think I rendered your perspective fairly?"

"Well, we just have very different perspectives. And you're the writer—it's natural that you would give your point of view."

As it turned out, I had hurt her in several ways. She thought it

was unfair to have theorized that my father fell in love with the
Virgin Mary as a sort of mother figure. She said the article
sounded as if I were bitter about growing up in the country. "You
have to remember," she said, "you could have been raised in a
tenement in the city, but we thought the country would be better
for the kids. The other big thing is, you wrote that I was more
concerned about eternity. But I always felt that Catholicism gave
me a way of life here and now, a pattern of living, a way to raise
the children."

Above all, my mother was hurt that a child of hers had so
publicly rejected the religious truth that she and my father had
fought so hard to gain. I found out later that she was getting her
own share of mail. Her friends commiserated about my return to
an outmoded faith. One friend assured her that my search wasn't
spiritual at all, that it was just a roots-seeking expedition, and
that someday I'd distinguish between the two and come back to
the Church.

Late in the day on Good Friday, two friends from the *Times*
told me they'd just come from Mass at St. Patrick's Cathedral.
John Cardinal O'Connor, they said, had read from my article
during his sermon, citing my mother's recollection of the moment
she felt her heart go out to Jesus.

I called her, excitedly. She was a great admirer of the Cardinal,
especially for his staunch pro-life advocacy. Still, the news didn't
cheer her. "Well," she said, "if someone hears what the Cardinal
said and that helps them become a better Catholic, I guess it's all
right." Then she told me that if I wanted to interview her anymore
for the book I was planning, I'd better hurry up, because she
wasn't feeling so well and might not be around much longer.

A few weeks later I visited my mother in Florida. The trip had
been long planned, but the timing turned out to be dreadful. The
article had destroyed whatever tentative peace we had achieved.

I arrived late at night. The clutter of her apartment closed in on me as never before. My mother was visibly less energetic than even a few months ago. She held on to the back of a chair when she stood. "I can no longer go picket at abortion clinics," she said plaintively as we sat down at the kitchen table. "I no longer have the stamina for that." She told me that in the morning she had to meet with her lawyer to revise her living will; she didn't want Beth or Mona wondering whether to resuscitate her if she had a heart attack while she was visiting. I pictured her lying on the tile floor of Mona's kitchen, one of the dogs licking her face, trying to revive her.

I slept until nearly noon, then went out for the papers. My mother was napping when I came back, so I read by the pool for a few hours. At about five we drove in to West Palm Beach for an early dinner with Charles, a close friend of hers. As they crossed themselves and said grace, I kept my hands in my lap. Charles was a good man, a devout Catholic and a Canadian, nearly ninety years old but still hale, a former firefighter. My mother had contemplated marrying him, and a few others who asked, but, after praying about it, decided that my father was an impossible act to follow.

In the newspaper, I had seen that PBS was showing a documentary that night called "Shtetl," and when we got home, I asked my mother if she wanted to watch. She said okay. We settled in, a bowl of grapes between us.

The filmmaker, Marian Marzynski, was a Polish-born Jew who, as a child during the war, was sheltered by Christians. Nearly all of his family was killed. Many years later he returned to Poland, acting as guide for an American-born Jew who wanted to investigate his own family's shtetl, Bransk. Marzynski, meanwhile, was interested in the idea of complicity, the degree to which the Polish Catholic peasants in Bransk had participated in the killing of the Jews during the war. Now Marzynski was grilling one Polish farmer about his actions at the time. The farmer was old, with a leathery face. "But his hair is still dark, you notice?" my mother said. "From eating yogurt probably. You want some grapes?"

It was getting late, and I watched my mother's eyelids repeatedly lower, then jerk up. The movie was making me anxious. I was thinking of everything I'd learned in Auschwitz and Pułtusk and Krasnystaw, succumbing to a mixture of Jewish pride and anger. My mother's occasional questions riled me: "But most of the Catholics were good, weren't they?" I didn't answer.

A Jewish woman from another Polish shtetl recalled how her mother was shot to death by her neighbors. The film then shifted to a religious ceremony in Israel commemorating the fiftieth anniversary of the Nazis' liquidation of the Bransk ghetto. I looked over at my mother and saw she had fallen asleep. I wanted her to see this part. I wanted her to see that not all the Jews are dead. I wanted her to see that there is still such a thing as the Jewish religion, that there are still some people that even the Holocaust could not wrench it from.

I faked a few loud sneezes, an old high-school trick. My mother jolted awake.

The film moved back to Poland. It was becoming obvious that some of the Poles around Bransk had been terrifically anti-Semitic, and some still were. My mother asked me how it was that people could hate each other so much.

Before I opened my mouth, I knew that something impudent would come out. "I hate to say it, but a lot of it has to do with organized religion."

"No, it's not religion that causes anybody to do anything bad, certainly not the Catholic Church, but maybe *individuals* who aren't following the true teachings of the Church."

I told her that in Poland, the Catholic Church itself had a long history of encouraging anti-Semitism.

"Religion doesn't make bad things happen," she said.

I couldn't believe what she was saying. How about the Crusades, the Spanish Inquisition? "How about the war right now in Bosnia?" I said. "That's between Muslims and Orthodox Christians."

"Well, Catholicism and Judaism certainly don't teach people to hate. But there are other religions—who was the guy who took the American hostages, in Iran?"

"Ayatollah Khomeini," I said.

"Yes, yes, that's right."

"What about Yigal Amir, the guy who assassinated Yitzhak Rabin? He was a religious Jew. What about John Salvi, the Catholic who shot up those people at the abortion clinic? They both murdered on the basis of interpreting their religious teachings."

"Well, that's the problem with interpreting. With the Pope, there's no need for that, while in Judaism, you've got all these different factions."

I shouldn't have been surprised that she'd find a way to drive one last nail into Judaism. But I was, surprised and exasperated.

"Mom," I said, "I really can't have this fight with you. We're talking different languages here."

It was the first real argument we'd ever had, about anything. We both sat quavering, staring at the TV even though the film had been over for ten minutes.

HOW odd that the Holocaust became the wedge that would divide us—my mother, who admitted to knowing little about it and to have been affected even less, and I, who had come to it so late and with such naïveté. But in one regard it made perfect sense.

For years I had been keeping a timeline of my parents' lives. It chronicled all the significant events I'd learned in my research. But when I returned from Poland, I began tracking down distant relatives who had survived the war there; I began chronicling their stories, and the stories of those who hadn't survived, within the same timeline. Now it had become a network of messy overlaps, like a zipper whose teeth won't close.

In June 1939, my mother graduated from high school. Three months later, the Jews of Pułtusk were set upon, and my great-grandparents' headstones were turned into a Nazi courtyard.

In February 1942, my father entered the Army; on Christmas Eve of that year, my mother was baptized. Sometime in between, my father's aunt and uncle in Pułtusk, Liba Dubner and the other Shepsel Dubner, were killed by the Nazis. I had learned about them from two sources. The first was the Pułtusk Yizkor book, which I'd found at the YIVO library in New York. Even in Yiddish, the name Dubner jumped out at me on the list of Pułtusk dead. The book also contained a pen-and-ink drawing of the Nazis herding the Pułtusk Jews to their death, the massacre staged on the gently sloping lawn behind the very hotel where I had stayed. The other source was Moishe Silberman, an elderly cousin now living in Montreal. Moishe himself had been sent to Auschwitz, Buchenwald, and Teresienstadt. Of ten children, he was the only one who survived. Now he recalled that Shepsel Dubner of Pułtusk was a tailor who made ladies' clothing. Shepsel was forty-two when he was killed, along with his wife and their five children, three boys and two girls. The oldest, a son, was eleven, which means he was born just as his Aunt Gittel, my father's mother, was dying in Brooklyn.

On December 8, 1945, my parents were engaged to be married. Around that same time, another Polish cousin, Martin Dubner, was returning to his shtetl near Pułtusk to see if anyone in his family had survived the war. They hadn't. Martin eventually made it to Philadelphia. He didn't want to talk about the war with me, but he did, between choking sobs. He was in the resistance, he said, and he couldn't even begin to explain how he'd survived. He described his fruitless trip home after the war. His train, he said, was stopped en route and boarded by local thugs. "One girl on the train said to me, 'They're looking for Jews, hide yourself!' I don't know how she knows I'm a Jew, though, maybe my nose. They took out another Jew sitting right in front of me, and they shot him and three others, I could see through the window. Young people. I myself had a gun, I could have shot them, I could shoot these murderers. But the girl stopped me. She was Polish. I don't know what happened—it was like God. So I asked her later. I said, 'Why?' She said, 'Because it's enough, we have enough blood.' So I said to her, 'Can I help you?' She said, 'No, I don't want anything. God bless you, just go.' "

There were more stories, from Martin and other relatives. I felt guilty about dragging them through it again. There was nothing therapeutic about it. They did it for me, some distant, quizzical cousin who seemed to think that sticking his fingers in their wounds would somehow bring him closer to his own Jewishness.

My family tree, which began with ten Catholics, had grown to include more than six hundred Jews, living and dead, over five generations. I met quite a few of the living ones. I spent the first night of Passover with Aunt Dottie and Mickey's extended family, the second night in Philadelphia with another big group of Dubners. ("Gee, you know the Seder pretty good for a Catholic," one of them said.) The Philadelphia cousins put me in touch with more relatives: a family named Rubin in Cobleskill, New York, a farming town just ten miles from Duanesburg (to think that there were other Jews there all along, and that we were related!) and a huge clan of cousins in Buenos Aires named Dibner. (This family included a Solomon Dibner, the same name as my father's more or less; his daughter Nora, the principal of a Hebrew day school, sent me her grandmother's Shabbos candelabra to welcome me to the family.) I met with a cousin on the Greenglass side, a lifelong leftist who'd lived for years in Greenwich Village;

we swapped stories about the Rosenbergs. It turned out that another cousin, a Manhattan psychoanalyst in her fifties, had studied Torah with the same teacher I'd once studied with, and we
quickly became close friends.

There were more Dubner cousins in Israel, and I took a trip
there with my friend Adam Reingold. Until recently, Israel hadn't
meant a thing to me. But from the moment I landed, eager to try
out my Hebrew and to taste Jewish life in a Jewish state, the trip
felt oddly like a homecoming. Adam and I started out in Jerusalem, where, at the end of each day, we found ourselves gravitating
to the Western Wall. We traveled to the desert, to the Galilee,
then to Tel Aviv to spend a few days with my newfound cousins.

The patriarch of this family was Moti Cooper, a retired sea
captain. He was the brother of Elana Eden, the actress who had
starred in *The Story of Ruth*. Moti was a robust man, a sabra,
and his family was Israeli to the bone. On our last night in Israel,
they threw us a party, their apartment windows open to the gusty
Mediterranean breeze, a torrent of food and wine and storytelling.
Odi, a cousin slightly older than I was, recalled having her third
child just as the Gulf War began and having to decide whether
to wear her gas mask or nurse her baby, since it was impossible
to do both at once. (She nursed.)

This sprawling new family of mine, scattered among the con-
tinents, included Jews of every stripe: neo-Hasidim and proud
atheists, nostalgists and moderns, paragons of righteousness and
at least a few rogues. (Alas, there were no other Catholics.) On
the surface they had little in common—with one another or with
me. But once I sat in a room with them, whether the room was
in Tel Aviv or Greenwich Village or Philadelphia, a connection
would reveal itself, as ethereal as moonlight and just as haunting.
It was the long arm of Jewish tradition that bound us one to the
other. Our shared past may or may not have included religion,
but it did include Abraham. It may or may not have included

even a whiff of piety, but it did include the Ten Commandments. And it may or may not have included a pogrom, but it certainly included the Holocaust, for to be a Jew was to live forever with the knowledge that the Holocaust had scarred your people as irrevocably as Jacob had been scarred by his encounter with the angel. So when I met with them, I could not help pressing them about the Holocaust, for their stories of unanswered letters and vanished siblings and, occasionally, a miraculous escape.

But in my mind, the Holocaust had also emerged as a flash point in the story of my own family. Those years, 1939 to 1945, demarcated my parents' lives: They had entered as Jews and emerged as Catholics. Even if it were true, as my mother insisted, that the war had not influenced their conversions, I could no longer disassociate the two events. The schizophrenic timeline I had constructed would not allow that. It was not possible to disentangle a pair of converted Jews from the calamity that had visited all those who had died simply because they were Jewish. Had my parents been living in Europe, even as converts, they too surely would have been killed. And I was incensed that my mother refused to acknowledge that her adopted home, the Catholic Church, had been even remotely hostile to the religion that she and my father had abandoned.

I sent my mother an article from the *Times* about the Pope and the Holocaust. "Pope John Paul has called the Holocaust a 'monstrous abyss,' " it said, "but has not so far produced a promised definitive text on the Church's relationship toward it. An early draft two years ago spoke of an 'anti-Jewish theological tradition of the Church that was an important component of the Holocaust.' It said centuries of Catholic hostility toward Jews 'prepared the way for modern anti-Semitism.' "

I attached a note: "Here's an article that gets into what we were talking about in Florida—the Catholic Church's unfortunate history with the Jews, and why emotions run so high."

At least it was a fight my mother and I could have. As a point of debate, Jesus was useless: She believed, I didn't. The Holocaust was a far sturdier fulcrum. It could weigh her denial against my insistence, ignorance against arrogance. If we could somehow balance those forces, then perhaps a broader peace was possible.

10

BACK in New York, the article I'd written had turned me into a sort of Jewish poster boy. I had created a public display from a well of private sentiment, and it made me uncomfortable. Won't you come spend Shabbos in Borough Park? Won't you come speak at our synagogue? Wouldn't you like to fly to Israel, all expenses paid, to be bar-mitzvahed at the Western Wall?

I did accept a few invitations. Simon Jacobson asked me to speak at his son's bar mitzvah. It was held in a cavernous auditorium in Crown Heights that the Lubavitchers used for public events. A few beggars worked the room, straight out of a Sholom Aleichem story, circling the guests for dollars and sidling up to the head table for shots of whiskey. I was introduced to Joseph Malovany, the renowned cantor from the Fifth Avenue Synagogue. I recalled reading that he also had roots in Pułtusk. "You are from Pułtusk!" he said. "Which street did your family live on?" I told him: Ulica Warszawa. "The same street where my parents lived!" He threw an arm around his new landsman, setting flashbulbs popping left and right. Then I met Simon's son, Menachem Mendel Jacobson, a sweet and earnest young man named in honor of Rabbi Schneerson. I asked him what was the most important thing he had learned in preparing to be bar mitzvah. "How lucky I am," he said, "to be a part of this tradition." Simon had requested that I speak from "a non-Hasidic, non-traditional Jewish perspective." Standing at a podium bordering the men's and women's section, I explained my family's background and the degree to which the Rebbe's book had influenced my return to Judaism. (Indeed, I had come to consider myself more a returnee than a convert, as a return bore a certain weight of inevitability.) I repeated what Simon's son had told me, how lucky he felt to be a part of this tradition, and that I could understand why. The few hundred guests, all but a few of them Lubavitcher Hasidim, applauded when I finished. The men slapped me on the back, filled my glass repeatedly with chilled red wine. Yet as receptive as they were, I left feeling like something of an exotic pet.

I also agreed to speak at the Orthodox synagogue on the Lower East Side where I'd gone to services with Ivan. A close friend, Barry Singer, called to say that his father had seen the lecture advertised in the *Jewish Week*.

"It's the first night of Hanukkah," Barry said. "You'll be their guest of honor, you know. I'm sure they'll have you light the menorah."

"No way."

"Do you know the *brucha*s? You want to learn them just in case?"

Barry, whose father was a retired cantor, sang the Hanukkah blessings over the phone. They were lovely, and rather long. When the day arrived, I studied the blessings again, futilely, as I rode the subway downtown.

The street was just darkening when I arrived. About a hundred people were clustered in front of the synagogue. Inside the gated courtyard stood a twelve-foot-high menorah, with a wingspan of ten feet. I was directed to join the rabbi in the courtyard: *Go in the synagogue, down those stairs, then left, through the basement, left again, up through the wooden door—not the steel one, that's the fire escape—then a hard left into the courtyard.*

I took a variety of wrong turns. By the time I finally found the courtyard, my heart was thrumming, from exertion and nerves. The rabbi shook my hand, gave me a lit candle and a glass globe, motioned me toward the huge menorah.

"Tell me what you'd like me to do," I said.

"Well, climb up on the ladder," he said. "You'll light the first candle with the *shamash*." The *shamash*, I gathered, was the lit candle he had given me. "Then you'll lead us in the *brucha*s—a nice, loud voice. We're outside here, so you've got to make it carry."

"Um," I said, "I think it'd be better if you helped me out."

The rabbi understood perfectly. I climbed the ladder, a hundred faces glowing beneath me in the throw of the streetlamps. The opposite side of the street was lined with Indian restaurants, and a dozen waiters watched from the sidewalk, greatly attentive. As I reached the top rung, my friend Barry turned the corner, flanked by his father and uncle, grinning broadly at the spectacle he'd predicted.

With shaking hand, I lit the first candle. I placed the *shamash* in its holder, but it wouldn't stand straight. I finally placed the glass globe over it, worried that the flame might break the glass. We sang the first *brucha*, which I remembered a little bit, and from there on, I trailed a half note behind the rabbi, as best I could. The congregation sang heartily; the Indian waiters across the street looked delighted. On the final *brucha*, I heard a sharp *ping*: the crooked candle had shattered the glass globe, which fell with a tinkle onto the concrete below.

I was not meant, I concluded, to be a light unto the nations.

It wasn't just that I was still a novice, though that was certainly unnerving. A large piece of me simply defied becoming "a religious person." The thought of spending an entire Shabbos with a Hasidic family was flat-out frightening. Simon and others invited me often, and while I felt guilty for never accepting, I just couldn't do it. In their devotion, as in the devotion of my mother, was a dogmatism that, at the gut level, made me uneasy. Their lives revolved around the belief that every action was in service to God. Deep down, I believed that too, but I was incapable of turning belief into daily life. It would suffocate me. Did that make me a dilettante? Was it true, what my mother's friend had written in her letter: Had I embarked on nothing more than a glorified search for my roots?

Sometimes I wondered. Though I understood that Judaism was a communal religion—indeed, it would not have survived otherwise—I was far more comfortable studying Torah on my own or with a small group of friends. I stopped eating pork and shellfish, but I didn't keep kosher. I lit Shabbos candles, recited the Shema at night, and often put on tefillin in the morning, but there was a pile of Jewish laws that I did not uphold, and countless more I did not even know. I was frustrated by my ambivalence and both leery and envious of the piety that others so easily embraced.

When Adam and I were in Israel, we visited Safed, the Galilean mountain town that was a medieval center of Jewish mysticism and where it is still revered. After touring the local synagogues, we stopped for lunch at an open-air schwarma joint. The counterman was maybe thirty years old and preternaturally surly. I ordered in broken Hebrew, which didn't help. He gave us our food without a word. As we sat down to eat, two teenage Hasidim stepped inside. The counterman swaggered over, whipped off his paper hat, and snatched a yarmulke from the Hasidim. They held out a prayer book and a set of tefillin. He wrapped the leather straps around his forearm with practiced vehemence, the way a junkie might, mumbled the prayers inside of a minute, and slammed the whole works back down on the counter. The Hasidim hurried out, satisfied. The counterman put on his paper hat and returned to the grill.

This transaction haunted me for months—a shakedown, apparently, for doing business in a religious town.

But what did I know? I could not see inside the counterman's heart. I could not know how he treated his wife, his children, his business partners. Even if this enforced prayer—if it even *was* enforced—represented his sole contact with God, I could hardly glean from a sixty-second encounter the nature of this man's relationship with God. Nor was I supposed to.

I was judging him, punishing him. And by doing so, I was judging and punishing myself.

I had created an entire hierarchy of piety. The Hasidim were more pious than I was. I was more pious than the counterman. Shepsel was more pious than my father. My mother was more pious than any of us.

But where was this hierarchy written? By whom?

After all these years, I was still trafficking in the idea of perfection. From my father's life alone, I should have learned by now that perfection is a yoke. I should have learned that most of us were not meant to be saints. Perhaps my mother was an exception. But I was not, and neither was my father. I was, like him, a plain man; the only treasure we possessed was the God-given obligation to become better than we were. It was the sheer fact of my ancestry that first brought me to consider Judaism. Soon after, my soul responded with whispered encouragements. But it was *pirkei avot,* the ethics of the fathers, that clinched the deal. It was Jewish teaching that had begun to shape my life, however gradually, for the better: teachings about doing business and conquering fear, about humility and charity, about not judging others and letting God alone judge me. This was all between God and me. It was not my job to compare myself with a schwarma counterman in Safed any more than it was my mother's job to compare herself with me. *If I am not for myself, who will be for me? But if I am only for myself, what am I? And if not now, when?*

As a Jew, I would never become a saint, a tzaddik. But I could achieve the supreme distinction of becoming a mensch—a man. "You shall be men holy to Me," God commanded the Israelites. A midrash explains further: "Your holiness shall consist of being truly human, not angelic. God has plenty of angels."

Being truly human would be plenty hard enough. But I had found a Way to try. I had found a way to ask God what He wanted of me and to learn what I wanted for myself. This much I knew: I wanted to lead a Jewish life, to marry a Jewish woman and raise a Jewish family and make our lives a celebration of the highest order.

The day I began to demolish my hierarchy of piety was the day I began to feel truly comfortable as a Jew. I continued to seek out teachers, and brilliant teaching continued to land in my lap. In New York, I attended a lecture by Adin Steinsaltz, the Israeli scholar whose translation of the Talmud afforded even Jews like me a chance to study it.

Steinsaltz spoke in a wispy singsong, the voice of an aged imp. "Learning," he declared, "is a pure choice. Belief is a complex and far more psychological thing."

A member of the audience asked Steinsaltz to describe what Judaism had contributed to the world. Inside, I groaned, as if the question were directed at me. How was such an answer possible?

Steinsaltz had no trouble. "Judaism in the First Temple period gave the world monotheism," he said. "It still exists, even in secular forms. In the Second Temple period, Judaism gave the world another idea: the notion of the Messiah, the basic belief that the human story has a happy ending. Also, Judaism became, in secular form, the notion of revolution and the notion of progress. And in Talmud, we were given the gift of sanity. When I say sanity, I don't mean just choosing the middle path, a place between laughing and crying where nothing happens. That's a pitiful form of existence. I see sanity as the ability to be both extremes at one time, jolly and sad, a balance between Heaven and Hell."

That's right, I thought. A balance between Heaven and Hell. The notion of revolution and of progress. But especially the belief in a happy ending—the belief that our lives are not meant to be simply endured but to be exalted, for even an animal can endure, but only we, who were made in the image of God, have the capacity to fling ourselves toward sanity, toward celebration, toward a happy ending.

My mother plainly believed in one version of that happy ending. I believed in another. It seemed a shame we couldn't even agree to disagree. Since my visit to Florida, she and I had settled into a chill. In Israel, I had filled up a bottle with water from the Galilee, but I never sent it to her. Our phone conversations were quick, polite, dutiful.

My cousin Mickey and his wife, Harriet, had followed through with plans to host a reunion. It would be the first gathering of my Catholic and Jewish families. We chose a date just after my mother was due to arrive north for the summer. She said she would try her best, but she couldn't promise she'd be up for it. I was disheartened by the void that had come between us. We had both traveled so far. My mother's path had wound through such unlikely terrain: a nominally Jewish family and a domineering ballet teacher, Peggy Wink and Ethel Rosenberg, St. Paul and Paul Dubner. An equally improbable litany of voices had spoken to me: Bob Dylan and Mimi of Florida, Abigail Seymour and Ivan Kronenfeld, a flock of rabbis and a battalion of Jewish aunts, uncles, cousins.

There was one voice yet to come, a voice that I was reluctant to seek out and whose message my mother would be reluctant to hear. It was the unlikeliest voice yet and, in the end, the most persuasive.

11

AT the *Times*, I came across a press release announcing that John Cardinal O'Connor was giving a lecture at Temple Emanu-El on Catholic-Jewish relations. I had recently written to the archdiocese for a videotape of the Mass during which he quoted my mother. I planned to make it her seventy-fifth birthday present, no matter how unenthused she professed to be.

When I went to the Cardinal's lecture, I knew about him only what I'd read in the papers for years. He was a controversial figure, a consummate politician who was a hero of conservative Catholics like my mother and a scourge of liberals and AIDS activists. The Jewish community, by and large, considered him a friend. His lecture showed why! "May I suggest," he began, "that before we can answer the question about Jewish-Catholic relations, we ask ourselves, 'Where am *I* in terms of being a Jew?' 'Where am *I* in terms of being a Catholic?'" The distinction between Jew and Catholic, he said, was less important than how we choose to live out our faith. "A great, great rabbi, Abraham Joshua Heschel, once wrote, 'What *we are* depends on what *the Sabbath is* to us."

I smiled at the Cardinal's reference. The line he'd cited was from *The Sabbath*, a book I had come to cherish. In it, Heschel argued that we should think of our existence not as space hurtling through time but as time hurtling across space. It is time that is holy—not space, not our possessions—and the Sabbath is the holiest of times. "While Jewish tradition offers us no definition of the concept of eternity," Heschel wrote, "it tells us how to experience the taste of eternity or eternal life within time." He related a legend in which God promises His most precious possession if Israel accepts the Torah. And what, Israel asks, is that precious possession?

"The World to Come," God answers.

"Show us in this world an example of the World to Come," Israel demands.

"The Sabbath is an example of the World to Come."

The next day, I told Ivan about the Cardinal's lecture. "You should write him a letter, set up a meeting," he said.

"What are you talking about?"

"Look, the Cardinal's a pretty bright guy, right? Well, you're a pretty bright guy. The Cardinal's a Catholic, right? Well, your mother's a Catholic, and you used to be. You want to get to the root of this trouble with your mother? The Cardinal knows a little bit about Judeo-Christianity, wouldn't you say? If I were you, I'd ask for a sit-down with him. He'd be a good influence on you."

Ivan loved to dispense advice. He had never stopped pushing me—not to be more of a Jew necessarily, just to be *more*. He was constantly sending me books, setting up meetings, hounding me to run into the eye of whatever storm was brewing, either within my soul or in the world around me. A year or two earlier, when I'd grown particularly bitter about my parents' conversion, he invited me to his house for coffee. "There's a guy I want you to meet," he said, typically cryptic. "I think it'll do you good." The guy was Asher Finkel, an Orthodox rabbi and the chairman of the religion department at Seton Hall, a Catholic university in New Jersey. (It turned out that Finkel's predecessor was a Monsignor Oesterreicher, a Jewish convert to Catholicism whom my parents had known well when he was a young priest.) The three of us sat down in Ivan's living room. Rabbi Finkel wore a black suit and a broad-brimmed black hat; his face was ruddy and intense. Ivan asked me to tell Rabbi Finkel the story of my parents' conversion. I did, then waited for the standard Jewish response to their apostasy. Instead, Rabbi Finkel shook his head in wonder and praised my parents. "They were plainly people of great spirit," he said, "and they passed it on to you. You should be grateful for that. It's not for us to say why the *ruach ha-kodesh*, the Holy Spirit, does one thing to one person and another to someone else. What you must do is surround yourself with people of good influence, like they did, and find God as best as you can."

So now Ivan had decided that Cardinal O'Connor would be a person of good influence. But what was I to the Cardinal? A lapsed altar boy from Duanesburg, a sorry soul who fell off the trail his parents had blazed. A Jew. I had no intention of writing to him, and it was only after a month of Ivan's haranguing that I finally did. I thanked the Cardinal for his lecture and for reading from my article on Good Friday. I explained that my mother and I were still struggling to reach some sort of peace and asked if it might be possible to meet with him one day.

The Cardinal's secretary called to invite me for a cup of coffee. He wouldn't be available for several weeks, she said, but we made a date.

This news excited my mother, but before long we settled back into our standoff. She hadn't yet responded to the newspaper clipping I sent her about the Pope and the Holocaust. Maybe I went too far, I thought. From here on out, maybe we would maintain our wary distance.

A few weeks later, though, I received an astonishing letter from her:

I certainly agree that there were terrible, horrible injustices done to the Jews, and anti-Semitism done by members—bishops and clergy also—of the Catholic Church. No excuse for any of this. I don't know why—only that human beings make dreadful errors in dealing with their fellow humans. They are certainly *not* following the teachings of Jesus, the Messiah. And I am as heartsick and angered as you are by the Holocaust. As Fr. Victor Donovan said, "*No one* did enough" to save the Jews. My friend Charles said that the U.S. turned away boatloads of Jewish refugees and sent them back to Germany. He said Canada could have accommodated all the refugees but didn't. There are many instances of the "Righteous" who individually hid and saved Jews. Also, stories of Catholic prelates (Vatican included) who hid Jews and who got them false passports. There must be books and accounts telling more. If I can find out more, I'll let you know.

Again, going back to the *N.Y. Times* article you sent me—I have many times found slants or colors in news reports. I'm not saying this isn't true, but there may be more to it. I suppose you see it as Vatican politics—and maybe it is. But perhaps there is more. At any rate, I hope we—you and I—can discuss differing viewpoints without any anger or estrangement. That would break my heart, as I love you dearly and would never want to hurt you for anything in the world.

I was stunned in many directions. She had obviously taken it upon herself to research the subject. That alone meant a lot to me. The fact that she ultimately defended the Church didn't surprise me, but her passion did. I reread the letter many times. I had been calling myself a writer for several years now, but her last two sentences were more powerful than anything I would ever write. She had been pushed against the wall by her petulant child, and she responded with love. Where did that love come from? In the end, it came from her faith. Her stubbornness, I knew, also came from her faith. And if I couldn't find it within myself to accept both her stubbornness and her love, then I didn't deserve her.

MY mother made it to the reunion after all. She was the star attraction, the woman who had helped create all this drama fifty years earlier. Any residue of ill will, however, had died with the last generation. She was greeted with an ardor befitting Queen Esther, and resplendent in white, she looked the part, all but for the tiny gold crucifix dangling around her neck.

My cousin Mickey lived in Monsey, New York, about forty-five minutes north of the city. Except for his family, the neighborhood was almost entirely Hasidic. We had chosen a Saturday for the reunion—there were no Jews among us who rigorously kept the Sabbath—and on the drive in, we'd all seen the Hasidim out in force, strolling to and from shul, the men in their fur-trimmed hats even as summer approached.

Our turnout was impressive: fifty-five people, including all my siblings except Dave and Joe, who both lived three thousand miles away. Peter set up a CD player with klezmer music; Mickey and Harriet fed us nonstop; cousins met for the first time; the older folks studied the family tree with great intensity, and then their children and grandchildren got interested, tracing themselves back three or four generations; the Jews pored over the Catholics' photo albums and vice versa, marveling at the genetic resilience of the Dubner eyebrow, the Dubner smile. Aunt Dottie and my cousin Reba, a Philadelphia Dubner whom I met that day, decided I needed a Jewish name, so they dubbed me Shloime, after my father.

I had worked up a trivia quiz—a scavenger hunt, really, whose answers could be gleaned only by interviewing the family's senior members. So Aunt Dottie and Aunt Irene and my mother were swarmed by inquisitors (there were prizes at stake), and within a few hours we were all so thoroughly intermingled that a stranger would never have guessed the bitter history that preceded this event.

There were speeches, songs, a few tear-choked reminiscences. For me, the day floated by as if behind a gauzy scrim, the past and present locked in a lovers' kiss. I felt woozy with excitement, my neurons working too hard.

The day's only calm arrived as we assembled for a family photo. It took a good fifteen minutes to herd us into position. Even the kids quieted down. I was happy to see my siblings dotted throughout the multitude, not in a clump. Across the street, a half dozen Hasidic children lolled on a lawn after their Shabbos lunch, taking in the scene. I wondered what they thought of us; I wondered if my mother noticed them. My nieces and nephews, in their tank tops and Hard Rock Cafe T-shirts, stared back at the Hasidic kids, at their black felt yarmulkes and silky earlocks.

And then the photos were done and the calm was shattered and we mixed it up again for a few more hours, dispersing only when darkness fell, hugs and kisses and promises to do it again soon, just like a family.

My mother rode north with Mona to settle in for a few weeks' stay. The rest of us were driving over to Peter's house in Connecticut to extend the reunion, but my mother needed to rest. I had barely had a chance to speak with her.

At Peter's house, we played some music, waited for the rain to lift, watched a videotape of the reunion. We talked about the family late into the night. Marthe, Peter, and Beth had been pulled into it by now. They wanted to know more about Shepsel, about Poland, about Jews. Were Shepsel and Gittel really first cousins? Mom's parents too? Why had they all come here in the first place? Didn't Dad know how angry Shepsel would get if he converted?

I babbled on, mercilessly. Stories, rumors, suppositions. I recounted my entire trip to Poland, describing what the Sabbath would have felt like in a shtetl, enumerating the pogroms that led so many families like ours to pack up and leave.

"Like at the end of *Fiddler on the Roof*?" Marthe asked.

"Yes!" I said, grateful for the reference.

Peter shook his head. "I can't believe how expendable the Jews were."

It was dawning on them, as it had dawned on me, the distance our parents had put between us and their past. I thought about telling Marthe and Beth that according to Jewish law, their children were Jewish, but decided I'd already said plenty. I had easily expended my quota of zeal for the day.

By the time we all went to bed, I was experiencing a new sensation: relief. As the self-appointed keeper of my parents' story, I had sometimes thought my head would explode. Too many emotions to process, too many layers to peel back. I felt as if I alone had been assigned to guard an irreplaceable treasure. Now, though, we were all sharing the story. Reinforcements had arrived.

These past few years, I had finally become something other than the baby of the family. I had always loved my brothers and sisters but I never really stopped being dazzled by them. They were so solid, so capable and decent. A friend once asked me to describe my siblings. "Well, there are seven of them," I said, laughing. "They're all pretty different. But if I had to say one thing, I'd say this: They are all the kind of people that if you wound up sitting next to them on a transatlantic flight, you'd be happy for their company, and if the plane happened to go down, well, they'd make sure you got out all right."

I realized now that this family mission I had undertaken, this reclamation project, was what made me grow up. In their eyes and mine. Aunt Dottie once wondered aloud to me if Solly might have converted in part because he needed something for himself that no one else in his family could have. Maybe I took after him in that regard too. Did that mean my decision to become a Jew was somehow insincere?

I had given myself many a headache thinking such thoughts. But, I realized, after a time you have to tell yourself to shut up and get on with the business of living. I couldn't reduce my journey to some neat algebraic equation any more easily than I could do the same for my parents'. Even John Henry Newman, the nineteenth-century cardinal my parents admired, had been stymied when he tried to summarize his conversion. "For who can know himself," he wrote, "and the multitude of subtle influences which act upon him?"

A multitude of influences indeed. Our conversions involved every circumstance of our lives: dead parents and overbearing parents, inadequacies and arrogances, the fears of emptiness and the hopes of bounty. A person could go mad considering the possibilities. But then, if you are lucky, you recognize that it is God you are wrestling with, not just your own tired mind, and at a certain point, knowing that is enough.

MY appointment with Cardinal O'Connor had arrived. I didn't know whether to expect a five-minute meeting or something more substantial. Hoping for the latter, I prepared a list of questions and brought my tape recorder.

My mother had also provided me with some questions for the Cardinal. Ivan had prepped me too. "What you have to understand," he said, "is that history spins not on the action of millions but of two men sitting in a room. So you have to ask yourself: What is this meeting all about? You wouldn't be sitting in that room with the Cardinal if your parents hadn't converted. Why that happened, it's not for us to say. But God gave you a mission: to be a Judeo-Christian. You're not supposed to *understand* what that is. You're just supposed to *do* it, and do it with the strength of Hercules."

And so it was that I made my way, with somewhat wobbly knees, to meet the Cardinal. His office was on the twentieth floor of the New York Catholic Center, on First Avenue at Fifty-fifth Street. I was greeted by a Sister Hannah, who ushered me down a short hallway. The Cardinal shook my hand, thanked me for coming. He showed me to a chair, then arranged himself on a green couch facing the windows. His desk was spotless, his in box empty. Behind the desk hung an oil painting depicting the manger scene and a framed drawing of Pope John Paul II. The Cardinal was wearing a black suit and white clerical collar and a small red-rose pin in his lapel, the same pro-life symbol my mother favored.

I asked if it would be all right to record our conversation. "Of course," he said, then nodded at me. The floor was mine.

"I'll start with my mom, because she deserves it. She asked me to say that she admires you tremendously for the example you've set and because you don't back down from positions that she feels are of paramount importance to her as a Catholic." The Cardinal smiled. "She does have a few questions for you, though," I added, and he smiled again.

The Cardinal had recently called for an abstention from eating meat on Fridays, in protest of the pending federal legislation to allow "partial-birth" abortions. But my mother was unclear if he advocated abstention for the entire country or just his diocese, and if for everyone, might he consider issuing a statement to that effect?

"Well, tell her that I'm really touched by that," he said, laughing in wonderment. "I will reflect on the prudence of suggesting it as something good for the entire country."

"Her biggest question for you," I said, "is what can she do, or what can be done in general, to better promote pro-life attitudes. That's really her priority."

"Tell her I think that this thing that we euphemistically call partial-birth abortion, but which is in fact infanticide, if that doesn't in time shock people, I don't think anything will."

As he went on, it dawned on me that he might think my mother was an abortion extremist, a clinic bomber. I thought about interrupting him, but he was well into his rhythm by now. I watched him gesture with his hands, the practiced patting-down motion of a diplomat, or a policeman. He was fairly inscrutable. I found myself glancing at his shoes: sensible black, rubber-soled.

"And I think that in the final analysis," he concluded, "we're going to convert minds and hearts only by way of prayer and fasting."

After a time, we began to talk about Jews and Catholics. The Cardinal spoke solemnly, slowly, in long, well-crafted sentences. He had become very optimistic about the future of Jewish-Catholic relations, he said, since the signing of the diplomatic accord between Israel and the Holy See. "First, I think more and more Catholics are coming to realize that there *has* been, absolutely, categorically *has been* persecution of Jews by people in the Church over the course of centuries. On the other hand, I think that a number of Jews have begun to recognize that some targets that they were prone to attack immediately shouldn't have been attacked, or at least not with vehemence. But I think that we're growing up. I think we're coming more and more to understand the complexities of what has happened in history."

As we had come around to the subject of reconciliation, I asked if I could pose a personal question. He nodded. My mind flashed with the audacity of what I was about to do: ask the Cardinal of the Archdiocese of New York to referee my family dispute. I hesitated for a moment, considering a different question. But I thought of Ivan, and my mother, and I went ahead.

"The greatest conflict between my mother and myself," I said at last, "is that she sees Catholicism as the one true faith and Judaism as a once-valid religion that was necessarily superseded by Christianity. I don't mean to turn this into a shrink session, or a confessional, but how would you suggest that we go about resolving that conflict?"

"I think in two ways," he answered. "First off, I would look at recent declarations of Pope John Paul II about the validity of Judaism. This has radically changed Jewish-Catholic dialogue, *radically*. Until then, every argument, every discussion was couched in this idea that Judaism was intended to preserve monotheism, the concept of monotheism, the Jews were a chosen people but then were replaced. I can send you the particular documentation because it's a very important change. And then secondly, the clearly articulated teaching of the Second Vatican Council about the primacy of an *informed* conscience, a conscience which has been informed by way of thinking, of discussion, of reading, of study, of prayer. Then the deliberate decision that okay, I know Catholicism, or I know this faith or I know that faith. I know what the Church teaches, I have studied it respectfully, I know what the papal encyclicals say, I have prayed over it, and I am convinced in conscience that God wants me to be this or to be that, to be Jewish, to be Lutheran, whatever it is. So I think if you will tell your mother that you have tried to study this, that you have prayed about it, this is not just a revolt or a rejection, this is not a dismissal of what you don't understand—that this is where you think God wants you to be, an informed Jew."

When I left his office, after nearly an hour, I did so with a vague unease. The Cardinal had spoken measuredly; I had been expecting grand proclamations. I felt as if I'd gone to a doctor fearing that I might have cancer and that my fear prevented me from hearing whether his answer was yes or no.

Only that night, as I transcribed the tape, did I fully hear what the Cardinal had said. He *had* played the referee; he'd practically played Solomon. And my mother would have to listen: This wasn't just me talking anymore.

It must be impossible, I thought, for a parent to hear certain things from a child's mouth. *How in the world can he think so differently from me?* I read over the Cardinal's words on the validity of Judaism. This would jolt her, I knew. And what about the informed conscience: Would she accept that? Did *I* accept that? Though I had studied a good bit about Christianity by now, I had hardly read every word of Church doctrine. But where did my allegiance lie? According to Jewish law, I was a Jew. Had my conscience, as a Jew, been informed by thinking, by discussion, by reading, by study, by prayer? Was I convinced in conscience that God wanted me to be a Jew?

I was. I truly was.

I mailed my mother a transcript of the conversation. This is it, I thought. Our time together is not long. If she truly has eyes that see and ears that hear, she can no longer deny me as a Jew. Let her pray for me, let her mourn for me, but let her see me as I am.

12

TOWARD the end of summer, my mother summoned me to visit her at Mona's. This was unusual. Though she encouraged visits at any time, an outright request was rare.

The reason, it turned out, was that she was dying. Or at least thought she was dying. She was having chest pains and shortness of breath, brought on by her heart condition, which was called hypertrophic cardiomyopathy. Surgery was not an option, and though the disease was not immediately fatal, it was certainly degenerative, and her symptoms now convinced her that the end was near.

Driving to Albany, I pondered this mother of mine. She had raised eight children and shepherded a troubled husband to his final rest, all within a belief system she had adopted as an adult. Upholding this system had required great strength. It also required a certain steely vigilance that would brook no dissent, no examination of the past that she had locked away. To my eyes, this stance had always seemed simplistic. But recently, as I had gotten to know my mother better, I came to recognize her as a woman abounding in complication—for a pent-up past is messy enough, but not nearly as messy as being forced to unlock it suddenly and allow your children to rake through it, and to rake through it yourself in the waning light of your final days.

These past few years, in conversations with my brothers and sisters, my mother had expressed remorse over what a tough parent she had been, especially in the early years. She and my brother Dave were still on rocky ground and perhaps always would be. Dave, more than the rest of us, felt that our parents had substituted dogma for love. My mother disagreed, but she had confessed to letting her anger get out of control. Not long ago, when I called her for Mother's Day, she said, "Well, I sure wasn't a perfect mother. I made a lot of mistakes, but that's what being human is all about." She then told me how guilty she felt after my father died. "I had to call Father Victor Donovan," she said. "He was the only one I could voice it to. I said, 'Oh, if I had only been kinder, better, more understanding of his depression.' And he said, 'Veronica, you sound so *human*.' And that just took away the guilt. I did the best I could. You can't do better than your best, even if it's a poor best."

Because I was born at the tail end of the family, the mother I knew had mellowed, and I tasted far less of her anger than my older siblings had. She was a different person then and was yet a different person now. She had been through a lot, lost a lot. And, it seemed fair to say, gained a lot. This was perhaps the most meaningful revelation I was awarded for investigating my parents' lives: Just as children change and grow, so do mothers and fathers.

Not long after sending my mother the transcript of my conversation with Cardinal O'Connor, I received a short reply:

Did I tell you lately how proud I am of you? Your unique qualities remind me more and more of Dad! That's the supreme compliment!

With all my love,
Mama dear

P.S.: I so enjoyed your Cardinal O'Connor transcript. Your questions and his responses really touched me!

That was all she had to say? Naturally, I dissected her note. Why had the O'Connor comment been relegated to the postscript? What did "enjoyed" mean? And "touched"? Was she placating me? Or did she think the *Cardinal* had been placating me? Or—and this was wildly unlikely—perhaps she was experiencing a glimmer of doubt about her own conversion, for if the Cardinal and the Pope could pronounce Judaism to be valid, had she, a born Jew, made an error in abandoning it?

Mona's house was bustling with people and dogs when I arrived. My mother was in a candid mood. "I feel like this old body is falling apart on me," she said as I hugged her, "so I don't mind if it happens soon."

Within a few minutes everyone, even the dogs, had cleared out of the house. I wondered if my mother had arranged for them to do so. She and I sat down at the dining room table, across from each other. A strange intimacy insinuated itself, the intimacy of the confessional booth, candid and clouded at once. My mother seemed about to speak, then hesitated, so I began, even though it was she who had invited me here.

"Tell me this, Mom," I said. "What does your faith teach you about death?"

"Maybe I can answer in short form," she said. "I feel that life is a continuum, that before you're born, when you're in the womb, you are alive, and you're *you*, whoever you are, with all your genes and chromosomes, characteristics." She paused, to catch her breath. "On earth you're still you, developing, leading your life the way you see it. And when you die, you're still you, but the house is empty, the body is empty, and you'll be reunited later with your body, and you'll be in the best shape, at the peak of your physical condition, in Heaven."

Heaven, Heaven, always Heaven. I thought of what Abraham Joshua Heschel had to say on the subject: "We believe in an afterlife. But we have no information about it."

I asked my mother how she envisions Heaven.

"Oh, Heaven is being in the presence of God, which makes you so happy that you *just can't stand it.*"

She answered so joyfully that I giggled in appreciation, and she giggled too.

"Do you have a picture of it in your head?" I asked.

"No, it's not a place, so you can't have a picture. But you must have experienced in your lifetime some tremendous joy. It's like that, but many times over, and it *just won't stop.* Plus, you get reunited with all the people who've gone before. So that will be wonderful, because I really miss Dad. And you meet all these saints and angels you read and think about."

"Who are you looking forward to meeting?"

"Oh, all of them, especially St. Thérèse of Lisieux. Of course Our Lady is the big one—the pictures don't do her justice, she's just so wonderful. And what she went through in her lifetime, when Jesus was born, but especially at the end, when he was crucified. That's a real heartbreaker—I mean, to see something terrible like that happen to your son. You hurt when any of your children are hurt, but that one, oh, boy."

Her answer left me dumbstruck. I was stunned by her excitement, the specificity of her belief. Not only did she revere Mary, but she plainly identified with her. I realized that no matter how long I live, I would probably never again encounter a person of such faith. How fortunate she is, I thought, how preposterously fortunate.

In the sliver of silence afforded by my musing, she took control of the conversation. "What I want to know," she said soberly, "is what you're doing—no, not what you're doing, but what your beliefs are now, like what form of Judaism are you accepting, what are you practicing?"

At last it had come to this. It was only fair. For five years I had been grilling her about every step of her past, every nuance of her faith. I had wondered if she brought me here to discuss the Cardinal O'Connor transcript. Now I knew she had. Though she wouldn't mention his name on this day, it soon became clear that she had studied his words; her goal was to plumb her son's conscience to determine if it had been suitably informed.

So I told her, as best as I could, what I believed. I said that, for whatever reason, the idea of Jesus as the Messiah had never lodged itself inside my heart; I could not believe what I did not believe. I described my somewhat patchwork routine of synagogue and study and prayer, then hurried to clarify that a patchwork routine did not signify any lesser a commitment to being a Jew.

"But basically is it more cultural with you," she asked, "like you like the food and everything?"

"Well, that's a part of it. The food, the music, but mainly the tradition of—"

"Well, I like all that too," she said.

In other words, couldn't you just be a gefilte-fish Catholic?

I talked about the Jewish learning I had done, how it was leading to a stronger relationship with God. I told her how Jewish teaching affected my daily life. Then I told her something that surprised even myself: that it was she and my father who had brought me to this point. For even as I grew farther from the religion of my childhood, I never stopped thinking that my soul was stamped with the fingerprint of God. And for that, I said, I was thankful.

After all these years, I was still trying to please my mother! She saw right through it, though, and kept up her questioning.

She wanted to know if I would raise my children as Jews. She wanted to know how observant Ivan was and why our family reunion had been held on a Shabbos. She wanted to know where Mychal, the rabbi with whom I studied Talmud, had been educated. Then she changed tack, telling me again about my father's familiarity with the Hebrew Bible, and how that had made it easier for him to accept Jesus—one last attempt to sway me.

But that was just a footnote. From this day forth she would never again challenge me in earnest. Nor would we ever speak directly about Cardinal O'Connor's comments, but I knew that they had laid the foundation for this understanding.

Our conversation that day lasted for hours, ending only when the phone rang. It was a friend of mine, a heart surgeon named Mehmet Oz—a Turkish Muslim, as it happens, whom I had met years earlier at Ivan's Seder.

When my mother's heart condition was first diagnosed, Mehmet offered to look over her medical file and had since kept abreast of the situation. A few days ago I had told him about her new symptoms and that she seemed prepared, perhaps even eager, to die. Mehmet immediately ordered up a copy of her latest echocardiogram. Between the two of us—a doctor accustomed to saving lives and a youngest son afraid of losing them—we weren't about to let her slip away. So I had asked Mehmet to call during my visit. Now I answered the phone, walked it over to my mother, then picked up the extension.

"With the problem you have," Mehmet was saying, "you're not going to die of heart failure, at least not anytime soon."

"Is that right?" She sounded disappointed.

"No, you're not there yet, and you're not even very close."

"*I* felt I was close."

"I don't know if you *want* to be there or not, but that's a separate conversation. I wouldn't start planning for the end, I can say that. Reports of your demise are premature."

Mehmet described her condition in exacting detail: The muscle walls of her heart had thickened, thereby shrinking the chambers and limiting her circulation. "The problem is, you've got too much heart."

I smiled to myself. In the previous week's Torah portion, Moses had admonished the Israelites: "Cut away, therefore, the thickening about your hearts. . . ."

"This is part pep talk, part physician talking," Mehmet was saying. "There are a lot of people at seventy-five who would kill for that heart. You'll have to reduce your physical activities, but I'd like to encourage you to do as much as you can as long as you can."

"I guess I am," she said, "but I'm just frustrated I can't do more. The problem is, I've got no physical energy. I'm not used to that." Now her voice softened. "I don't know if Stephen thinks I'm depressed . . ."

"Well, he expressed some concern about how you're feeling."

There was a long pause. They seemed to be waiting for me to jump in. But I didn't. As Mehmet had said, that was a separate conversation.

And we would have that conversation, my mother and I, in fits and starts, over the coming months. Mehmet was essentially right: She wasn't about to die. But her condition did worsen.

The following summer, Peter threw a Fourth of July picnic at his house in Connecticut. Most of my immediate family was there, along with Aunt Dottie and Mickey and Harriet, Uncle Sam and his daughters, Carol and Harriet. The family had taken to coming together again: a few weddings, Aunt Dottie's ninetieth birthday party, and shiva for Aunt Bess, who died at eighty-three, the last of my father's siblings.

The Fourth of July picnic was particularly sweet. Catholics and Jews galore but no religion per se, just family. Sam and Dottie and my mother, the elders, clustered together. It was strange to see my mother as an elder. She was still beautiful, still had that ineffable spark around the eyes. But she would get winded easily and take naps more often. Now she had to wait for the grandkids to swarm her, which they did, instead of chasing them down.

Halfway through lunch, the younger kids started dashing all over the yard, inventing mischief. I watched my mother watching them. She was keeping a keen eye; she still didn't go in for too much recklessness. I called over the ringleader, my six-year-old niece Hannah, and gave her whispered instructions. She obediently marched over to my mother.

"Grandma," Hannah explained with a face of stone, "you get a little food in your belly, and you get *rambunctious*!" My mother grabbed her in a hug.

By October she was back in Florida. We were corresponding regularly now. I never did hand over that bottle of Galilee water, but I sent her another keepsake, a copy of her baptismal record from the Church of the Blessed Sacrament. I had gone there one weekday afternoon. The priest, Father Robert O'Connor, was a wry, easygoing man. After locating my mother's baptismal record, he gave me a tour of the church. It was an eerie sensation, to inspect the marble font where my mother had laid her head more than fifty years earlier.

Late one night in January, I got a phone call from my sister Ann: Mom was having trouble breathing. I was afraid to ask if she was dying. I prayed that night, my heart trembling, the same prayer my mother had prayed when my father was stricken: *Dear God, let Your will be done, whatever that may be.* Marthe flew to Florida immediately. She relayed word: Our mother wasn't dying, but she had weakened to the point where she couldn't live on her own anymore. The next few nights we were all over the phone with one another. It was decided that Mom would move in with Marthe's family, near Syracuse. They had an extra room on the ground floor, a house full of activity, and our mother would be close enough for most of us to visit. Mona flew down to relieve Marthe and to start packing Mom's things. The last shift was mine. I would finish packing, then fly with my mother to Syracuse.

When I arrived, I expected her to be in worse shape. She couldn't stay on her feet more than a few minutes, but she was still herself. Her spirits were strong, her smile quick. She was looking forward to moving in at Marthe's, or at least said she was. We spent all of Saturday sorting through towering heaps of photos and newspaper clippings and Catholic magazines. Her vitamins filled an entire suitcase. We joked about the sheer volume of her holdings. "You'll just have to wait until I'm sleeping and then throw it all away," she said.

Peggy and Bill Wink dropped by to spend their last hours with my mother, and her friend Charles visited too. As he left, Charles shook my hand three or four times, delaying the inevitable. His eyes were wet around the corners. I walked him outside. "You take care of her now," he said. "Your mother's a saint. I repeat: Your mother is a *saint*."

She took a nap while I made dinner. When it was ready, I called her to the table. She made her way down the hallway, taking baby steps. I held out the chair for her, and she eased her way in. We folded our napkins in our laps, looked at each other expectantly.

"Shall we say some grace?" I asked.

"Okay," she said.

My mother made the sign of the cross and then prayed, in rusty Hebrew: "*Baruch atah Adonai, Eloheinu melech ha-olam, ha-motzi lechem min ha-aretz.*" *Blessed are You, Lord our God, King of the universe, who brought forth bread from the earth.*

She crossed herself again.

"Amen," we both said.

Postlude

𝔖𝔖𝔖

> When a man has made peace within himself, he will
>
> be able to make peace in the whole world.
>
> —*Martin Buber*

LAST Christmas Eve, I called to wish my mother a happy anniversary of her baptism. This is the way things are now. She'll call me for Passover or Rosh ha-Shanah (*"Gut yontef,"* she'll say cheerily), and I wish her well on her holidays. If nothing else, it keeps us in constant contact. We've been holding actual conversations again, instead of interrogations. When we talk about my father, it's casual, reminiscent. I'm not searching for him anymore and she's not hiding him.

A few days before Christmas Eve, on the anniversary of his death, I'd gone to synagogue to recite Kaddish. The congregation, B'nai Jeshurun, was holding services in a church on West Eighty-sixth Street while its own building was being renovated. On this Saturday morning, I sat high in the balcony, a tallis around my shoulders, the wintry sun bolting through the windows. As I stood for Kaddish, I was thinking about my father, about his spirit, a spirit that was in some ways as indomitable as my mother's. One

of the nasty letters I received about my magazine article told me:
"You've got a long way to go before you are even half the man
your father was." Perhaps that's true. If I had been chosen to live
my father's life, I might have crumbled into dust. It was his faith,
and my mother, that kept him upright. Would my faith do the
same?

As Kaddish ended, I felt the sun playing on my face. The tallis
felt like a warm embrace, a cloak slipped around my shoulders
by a caring hand. *How precious is Your kindness, O God! The
sons of man take refuge in the shadow of Your wings.* I realized
that my eyes were closed, and I opened them. Everyone else was
already seated. I lowered myself into the pew, and just as I did,
the church bell began to clang, mightily and impatiently. I chuckled at the symmetry of it all.

I decided right then that I would go to Midnight Mass on
Christmas Eve, in honor of my parents. I would go to Blessed
Sacrament, where my mother had been baptized and where my
father had found his way, and found her.

Christmas Eve was a blustery night. I walked to the church in
the face of a biting wind. I wondered how my mother must have
felt, rushing down this same sidewalk fifty-odd years ago with
Madame Souvorina at her elbow. The church's limestone facade
reached high into the milky midnight sky. On either side of the
doors stood four statues of Catholic saints. I studied them, trying
to imagine the flurry of excitement and peace in my mother's
heart that night. Stepping inside, I instinctively dipped my hand
into the holy water and crossed myself. I instantly recoiled. Then
I told myself that it was all right: It was a habit, a courtesy, not
a heresy.

The pews were jammed. I found a seat up front, near the side
aisle. In the hallway I caught a glimpse of Father O'Connor and
the altar boys, mustering up. The lead altar boy, gripping the
processional cross, stood as erect and solemn as a soldier. Behind
him, a tiny boy tried to hold the censer steady, but his hand was

shaking, and I could smell the incense, the thick, dark aroma that I used to think was God's breath. Within the altar-boy corps, Midnight Mass was the performance of the year. One wrong move would haunt them for months. I said a quick prayer for them.

The organ sounded, and Father O'Connor and the altar boys made the long march down the side aisle and up the center. I held a missal in my hands but had no need for it. All the prayers, even the Apostles' Creed, rushed to the front of my memory. What strange turns our lives had taken. In this very church, on this very night, my mother had recited these prayers for the first time as a Catholic. Now here I stood, a Jew who still struggled with the Hebrew prayers, reciting by heart the prayers my mother had struggled to learn in Latin. And then came the Our Father, *Who art in Heaven, hallowed be Thy name. Thy kingdom come, Thy will be done—*

A sudden thought stopped my heart: What if Jesus were to climb inside my soul tonight and demand, as he demanded of my mother and father, that I follow him?

Only a droll God would do such a thing, I told myself.

And yet the God of our fathers is capable of anything, no? The God who created the universe is certainly capable of a little mischief. As it is written, man plans, God laughs. *Let's set this little pisher loose for a few years to torment his mother and unbury his father, and just when he thinks he's got all the answers, we'll show him what's what.*

So I said to God, *Now wait a minute. Why did You make me wander around for so long if this is what You had in mind all along? Why did You make Yourself so available to me as You did?*

I waited. The Our Father was finished. I half expected a sublime clarity to fall upon me, as had befallen my mother in this very church.

But it didn't happen. Not on that night or any other. I was

relieved. In the tips of my fingers, in my mind and my heart, in my past and present and future, I consider myself a Jew. I believe that God feels the same way. I have a relationship with Him, a little one-sided perhaps, but I am doing my best. We speak more and more.

On occasion He blesses me. We had a conversation, a year ago, during which I expressed my readiness—my extreme readiness—to meet the woman I would marry. And though I had often ridiculed cause-and-effect prayer, I may now be forced to reconsider, for soon after that conversation I met a woman more lovely and decent than I thought possible, whose name is Ellen, and who is Jewish, and who will be my wife and, if God allows, the mother of a few Jewish children.

I dearly hope my mother lives long enough to cradle her first Jewish grandchild. Regardless, I am happy, and grateful, that she and I reached a peace. I am also happy to know that she is not afraid of dying. She remains eager to see my father again. She prays to be reunited with all of us someday, even me.

Who's to say? If I am sure of one thing about God, it is that our most brilliant ideas about Him are sheer guesswork. Though I have a hard time imagining the World to Come—I am still deeply puzzled by this world—I would love to see the two of them together again, Veronica and Paul, Florence and Solly, to put my arms around them, to sit knee to knee and hear their stories, to marvel at everything we wrestled through, the three of us, all on account of having been born with such turbulent souls.

Acknowledgments

Above all, I thank my mother for allowing me to tell her story, and for her generous help on every front. My siblings and their families were similarly encouraging, tolerant, and helpful to an extent that cannot be described. And to my newfound extended family—the Dubners and Dibners as well as the Bernsteins, Bestermans, Coopers, Doris, Einbinders, Eismans, Feldmans, Gladstones, Kalbs, Kesslers, Kirsches, Levins, Lippmans, Remers, Rubins, Strausses, and Silbermans—I offer my deepest gratitude. All of the above scoured their memories and photo albums and file drawers, and committed acts of kindness for which I will always be grateful. Thanks especially to Dottie, Mickey, and Harriet Dubner, Irene Dubner, Sam and Bess Einbinder (she of blessed memory), Matthew Dubner (a fellow traveler), Barbara Koltuv (for countless good conversations), and Nimrod Dori (for pure, unadulterated inspiration).

For their friendship and advice, I would like to thank Anne and Ivan Kronenfield, Simon Jacobson, Adam Reingold, Barry Singer, and Mychal Springer and Jonathan Rosen. Ellen Pall read this book before it was a book and helped make it one; I'm also grateful to Eric Pooley and Marshall Sella for their heady insights.

In the beginning, there was Claire Wachtel, my editor, to whom I give loud thanks, as well as to Michael Murphy, Sharyn Rosenblum, Katherine Beitner, and the other good folks at William Morrow. At Avon, Jennifer Hirshey and Hamilton Cain were full of good cheer and suggestions. Suzanne Gluck at ICM was everything an agent ought to be, and then some; thanks, too, to Karen Gerwin.

Among the many people who allowed me to interview them, and/or who offered help of the theological, genealogical, historical, and familial varieties, I would like to thank Judith Anderson, Moses Alter, Mike Applebaum, Clinton Bailey, Gertrude (Smith) Bennett, Leonora Bergman, Father John Bertolucci, Eleanor Cash, Joe Cooley, John Dessauer, Father Victor Donovan, Daniel Dunn, Joe Ettinger, Asher Finkel, Billy Gorta, Samuel Gruber, Rafael Guber, Estelle Guzik, Anna Henrykowska, Arthur Hertzberg, John Jorgenson, Celestine Kelly, James Kenney, Woody Kessler, Father Arthur Klyber, Barry Kosmin, Irving Marx, Dariusz Mularzuk, Father Robert O'Connor, John Cardinal O'Connor, Mary Jo O'Donnell, Marie Pracher, Father Ulrich Proeller, Yale Reisner, Eric Retslaff, Josh Saltzman, Harold Sevener, Fatima Shama, Andrea Sherman, Steven Siegel, Bishop John Shelby Spong, Sister June Szumowski, Jankel Szyc, Mark Weber, Miriam Weiner, Father James Wilders, and Peggy and Bill Wink. Also, Rita Burke, Alfred Kazin, and Bishop Joseph O'Keefe, all of whom have passed away since we spoke. For information on Ethel and Julius Rosenberg, I am especially indebted to Ilene Philipson, author of *Ethel Rosenberg: Beyond the Myths*.

Of the many excellent journalists I've learned from, I would like to thank Kurt Andersen, Peter Blauner, Peter Herbst, Sandy Padwe, and Chris Smith. Thanks also to my *Times* colleagues, for all sorts of aid and motivation, especially Janet Froelich, Gerald Marzorati, Adam Moss, Gustav Niebuhr, Jack Rosenthal, Kathy Ryan (and Scott Thode), Harvey Shapiro, Camille Sweeney, and Michaela Williams.

Finally, my thanks to Ellen Binder, who read the manuscript more times than even love would demand, and who encouraged me to the end.

About the author

About the book

Read on

Insights,
Interviews
& More . . .

Meet Stephen J. Dubner

Ellen Binder

STEPHEN J. DUBNER was born in Schenectady, New York, on August 26, 1963. He grew up on a farm in Duanesburg, New York, "a long way from anything." The youngest of eight children, he "learned early on that it's not easy to stand out in a crowd."

His father was a newspaperman. "During the course of my childhood," Dubner says, "my father worked for all three dailies in the nearby tri-city area: the *Schenectady Gazette,* the *Albany Times-Union,* and the *Troy Record.*" Dubner's mother managed the house, farm, and children. "She was," he says, "a wonder."

Dubner learned to spell on his father's Underwood typewriter and seems to have taken to reading early. "Apparently I learned to read quite young, but I have no recollection of that," he says. "I recently visited with a man from my hometown, a family friend, who knew me when I was three or so. He said every time he came by our house I was sitting outside barefoot reading a book."

The Dubner children sustained their own newspaper, the *Quaker Street Quacker*. "Competition to get on the front page was fierce," Dubner says. "I learned the value of a scoop and the importance of legwork." His first published work, a poem titled "The Possum," appeared in *Highlights*. "I'd written it in fourth grade but it didn't get published until I was in sixth grade. I remember my fourth-grade teacher, Mrs. Petersen, coming to fetch me with the news. It was a jarring moment—why is my teacher from two years ago coming to yank me out of class? What sin could I have committed back then that was so grave as to warrant such drastic punishment? But it worked out all right."

His childhood reading ran toward conventional tastes. "The staples of my youth were the Hardy Boys books," he says. "They were exactly the same length—212 pages, I believe—with the same plot formula, the same surprises. God, I loved them. I read them over and over and over. And then I read *A Tree Grows in Brooklyn,* which, though I couldn't have expressed it then, was my window onto my parents' past that they never discussed."

Dubner's early employment took him from the hay field to the ball field. "I grew up baling hay, mucking barns, that kind of stuff," he recalls, "then I worked as a carpenter, a house painter, and an organist at a minor-league ballpark in Winston-Salem, North Carolina."

Asked about his collegiate experience, Dubner is quick to call it "unusual." "Appalachian State University in Boone, North Carolina—don't ask, it's a long story," he says. "I started a rock band there, the ▶

> " It was a jarring moment—why is my teacher from two years ago coming to yank me out of class? What sin could I have committed back then that was so grave as to warrant such drastic punishment? "

Meet Stephen J. Dubner *(continued)*

Right Profile, and we toured all over the South (instead of going to classes), and were terrible for a long time, then got better, then got a record contract with Arista and moved to New York, but then I quit. Being in a band is like being married to four people at the same time: grueling. Soon after I quit, I went to graduate school for writing." He holds an MFA in writing from Columbia University.

From 1990 to 1994, Dubner was an editor and writer at *New York* magazine. From 1994 to 1999, he was an editor and writer for the *New York Times Magazine,* where he remains a regular contributor. "I had a million great experiences there," he says, "and wouldn't trade them for anything, but after four years, I was ready to move on and write books. One thing that did encourage me to write more was that, as an editor, I saw raw manuscripts from a great many well-regarded writers and oftentimes they were . . . well, not very good. I thought, Hey, if *they* can turn in some not-very-good articles to a place like this, why shouldn't I be able to?"

Dubner is the author of three books. His second book, *Confessions of a Hero-Worshiper,* was published in 2003. *Freakonomics,* a *New York Times* and international bestseller cowritten with Steven D. Levitt, appeared in 2005.

He has also written for *The New Yorker* and other magazines. His journalism has been anthologized in *The Best American Sports Writing* and *The Best American Crime Writing.* He has been a PBS correspondent and a regular contributor to ABC News, appearing monthly on *Good Morning America* and a

66 I had a million great experiences [at the *New York Times Magazine*] and wouldn't trade them for anything. 99

segment on *World News Tonight* called "Freakonomics Friday."

Dubner goes about his writing in an office, across the street from his apartment. "I spend about nine or ten hours a day there when I'm not traveling," he explains. "I write best in the morning easily. I like to read something before I write, something to get the muscles in the right condition. A journal that John Steinbeck kept when he was writing *The Grapes of Wrath*. A Jewish text called Pirkei Avot. Anything to get me moving forward in a pragmatic, focused way."

What stimulates his writing process? "I used to love taking cigarette breaks when I wrote," he says, "but I quit years ago. *Choosing My Religion* was written with the aid of cigarettes; nothing since then has been. I realized back then that my attention span was about twenty-nine minutes, and after twenty-nine minutes I'd go outside and smoke a Camel Light, which I thought then was delicious, and which delivered just enough stimulant to set me off on another twenty-nine lovely minutes of writing. These days I prefer pacing, eating carrots, and drinking strong coffee."

"I love the NFL in its entirety," he says, running through a short list of his passions and interests. "I love language, especially as filtered through the minds and mouths of my young children. I love traveling, though I'm not a good solo traveler. I also love golf, but if it could be played in one and a half hours instead of four, I would love it a thousand percent more."

Dubner is now working on several book projects, including a second *Freakonomics* ▶

Meet Stephen J. Dubner (*continued*)

book with Steven Levitt as well as a book on Jewish ethics. He lives in Manhattan with his wife, the noted documentary photographer Ellen Binder, and their children, Solomon and Anya. 〜

66 I used to love taking cigarette breaks when I wrote. These days I prefer pacing, eating carrots, and drinking strong coffee. 99

Choosing My Religion
An Update

MY SON, SOLOMON, is five years old, the Age of Great Questions. He wants to know why some people believe in God. He wants to know why my father, his namesake, died at fifty-seven. He wants to know why we—Solomon; his sister, Anya; my wife, Ellen; and I—celebrate Hanukkah and Passover while his multitude of cousins celebrate Christmas and Easter.

Like I said, great questions. I can't wait until he is old enough to read this book. He may find some answers; if nothing else, he'll discover that he is descended from a long line of people who ask hard questions.

This book actually began life as a novel. I was in graduate school, thinking I would one day earn my keep by teaching college and writing fiction. I started three or four novels, all of them quite autobiographical, as most early novels are. They were uniformly terrible—overearnest, unfunny, anchored in real life but somehow devoid of it.

Then I began another one, called *Family Plot*. Its narrator was a young man very much like me with parents very much like my own, a pair of Jews who were so enthralled by their discovery of Catholicism that they obliterated their Jewish pasts. But about fifty pages into the novel, I hit a wall. I was trying to write the scene in which these two ex-Jews had met and fallen in love. But I couldn't summon such a scene from my imagination. I simply didn't know enough about my real family to write a compelling story about an imagined one. That's when I felt the urge, finally, to begin ▶

> ❝ I can't wait until [my son] is old enough to read this book. He may find some answers; if nothing else, he'll discover that he is descended from a long line of people who ask hard questions. ❞

interviewing my mother—deposing her, really. As she began to talk, and as I began to seek out other relatives, I put *Family Plot* in a drawer along with my other novels. After some time, I realized that the truth of my own family's story was more compelling than any fiction I could write.

My mother died in 1999, the year after this book was first published. She and I had reached a comfortable peace by then. As deaths go, hers was a good one: six of her eight children were in the room with her, and she slipped away with a calm grace. Then came the wake, the funeral, the burial, all back in Duanesburg, the little town of my youth.

The day following the burial was Thanksgiving, so the eight of us kids stayed together one more day, with wives and husbands and kids and grandkids. By Thanksgiving afternoon, I was ready to get back to Manhattan and sit shiva for the remaining days. I told this to brother Peter, who asked me to explain shiva, which I did: the Jewish ritual of gathering to mourn a loved one's death and, at the same time, to celebrate her life. Peter, who is irreligious enough to call himself a "lapsed agnostic," listened thoughtfully.

A few mornings later, on the final day of shiva, Peter called me. It was his first day back in the office since our mother died— he worked for General Electric in Stamford, Connecticut—and he told me he couldn't get her out of his thoughts. "No matter how you feel about her religious beliefs," he said, "you can't deny that she really lived her life according to the courage of her convictions." Then he asked how I'd feel if he took the train

66 [My brother] Peter asked me to explain shiva, the Jewish ritual of gathering to mourn a loved one's death and, at the same time, celebrate her life. Peter, who is irreligious enough to call himself a 'lapsed agnostic,' listened thoughtfully. 99

into New York that afternoon to sit shiva with me.

It was a most welcome visit. Soon after he arrived, Ellen came home from a doctor's appointment. And on that final day of sitting shiva for my mother, I learned that I would become a father. As it is written: when a door closes, a window will often open.

Nine months later, with Ellen lugging her big tummy all through a sweltering New York summer, I received an e-mail from my sister Ann. Since our mother's death, all of us siblings had leaned inward, inch by inch, each in our own way, to fill the huge space that our mother had left behind. Ann had apparently taken on the evangelist duties. In her e-mail, she wrote that "I have a little message for you from Dad." It wasn't clear whether Ann had gleaned this message from a dream or some other, more mystical mode. "He said he has reconciled with his father, long ago. Wanted me to let you know that it is fine to be Jewish. But he said you must believe in Jesus, His Word and supremacy. Said He is the Messiah! Will explain all when I talk with you."

A few nights later, Ellen had her own dream—a *responsa* dream—in which Ann and my other three sisters came to visit us shortly after the birth of our son. We knew that such a visit actually *would* happen once he was born, because my sisters had already planned it. But in Ellen's dream, when my sisters came to visit, Ann was cradling our new baby son and, when no one was watching, she spirited him over to St. Patrick's Cathedral to have him baptized.

Suffice it to say that, once Solomon actually was born, and once my sisters actually came ▶

> In Ellen's dream, when my sisters came to visit, Ann was cradling our new baby son and, when no one was watching, she spirited him over to St. Patrick's Cathedral to have him baptized.

for their visit, Ellen kept a good eye on Ann whenever she held the baby.

And so it is no understatement to say that the strange, powerful mingling of Jewish and Catholic that has permeated my family history has continued to be—well, strange and powerful. This is the question I am asked most often by people who read the book: *So what about your siblings?* There is no short answer to that question, mainly because there are so many of us. Do the math: eight offspring, each of them with seven siblings, seven relationships, seven unique efforts to comprehend the separate journeys our two parents took, along with the unexpected journey that I traveled in reverse. None of the siblings have followed me into Judaism. But we get along well, all of us do—a tribute, I would argue, to my parents, who tried to teach all of us a form of loving-kindness that transcends religious boundaries.

My own little Jewish family, meanwhile, is finding its way, as all families do. Solomon asks his wise questions; now Anya, four years old, is starting to do the same. My greatest dream is that they discover, as I have had the privilege of discovering, that the answers to these questions are not always complete, or satisfying, or even significant. What counts most is the fierce desire to ask the questions in the first place.

May 2006, New York City

Excerpts from *Freakonomics* and *Confessions of a Hero-Worshiper*

FREAKONOMICS: A ROGUE ECONOMIST EXPLORES THE HIDDEN SIDE OF EVERYTHING
(Steven D. Levitt and Stephen J. Dubner)

In the summer of 2003, the *New York Times Magazine* sent Stephen J. Dubner to write a profile of Steven D. Levitt, a heralded young economist at the University of Chicago. Levitt was not remotely interested in the things that interest most economists. Instead, he studied the riddles of everyday life—from cheating to crime to child rearing—and his conclusions often turned the conventional wisdom on its head. For instance, he argued that one of the main causes of the crime drop of the 1990s was the legalization of abortion twenty years earlier. (Unwanted children have a greater likelihood of becoming criminals; with so many unwanted children being aborted in the 1970s, the pool of potential criminals had significantly shrunk by the 1990s.) The *Times* article yielded an unprecedented response, a deluge of interest from thousands of curious, inspired, and occasionally distraught readers.

Levitt and Dubner went on to collaborate on a book that gives full play to Levitt's most compelling ideas. Through forceful storytelling and pungent insight, *Freakonomics* reminds us all that economics is, at root, the study of incentives—how people get what they want, or need, especially when other people want or need the same thing. Among the questions it answers: ▶

11

**Excerpts from *Freakonomics* and
*Confessions of a Hero-Worshiper*** (continued)

Which is more dangerous, a gun or a
swimming pool? If drug dealers make so
much money, why do they still live with their
mothers? What makes a perfect parent? What
do schoolteachers and sumo wrestlers have
in common? (Answer: they both cheat.)

"[A]n engaging and always interesting work,
rich in insights, full of surprises."
— *Washington Post Book World*

"If Indiana Jones were an economist, he'd be
Steven Levitt. . . . Mr. Levitt is famous not as a
master of dry, technical arcana but as a
maverick treasure hunter who relies for
success on his wit, pluck, and disregard for
conventional wisdom.

"The cherry on top of the sundae is
Mr. Levitt's coauthor, Stephen Dubner, a
journalist who clearly understands what he is
writing about and explains it in prose that has
you chuckling one minute and gasping in
amazement the next. Mr. Dubner is a treasure
of the rarest sort; we are fortunate that
Mr. Levitt managed to find him."
— Steven E. Landsburg,
Wall Street Journal

**An Excerpt from *Freakonomics*—a *New York
Times* and International Bestseller**

THE DATA HAVE BY NOW MADE IT CLEAR that
parents matter a great deal in some regards
(most of which have been long determined by
the time a child is born) and not at all in
others (the ones we obsess about). You can't
blame parents for trying to do something—

anything—to help their child succeed, even if it's something as irrelevant as giving him a "high-end" first name.

But there is also a huge random effect that rains down on even the best parenting efforts. If you are in any way typical, you have known some intelligent and devoted parents whose child went badly off the rails. You may have also known of the opposite instance, where a child succeeds despite his parents' worst intentions and habits.

Recall for a moment the two boys, one white and one black, described earlier in this book. The white boy who grew up outside Chicago had smart, solid, encouraging, loving parents who stressed education and family. The black boy from Daytona Beach was abandoned by his mother, was beaten by his father, and had become a full-fledged gangster by his teens. So what became of the two boys?

The second child, now twenty-seven years old, is Roland G. Fryer Jr., the Harvard economist studying black underachievement.

The white child also made it to Harvard. But soon after, things went badly for him. His name is Ted Kaczynski.

> " A huge random effect rains down on even the best parenting efforts. "

CONFESSIONS OF A HERO-WORSHIPER

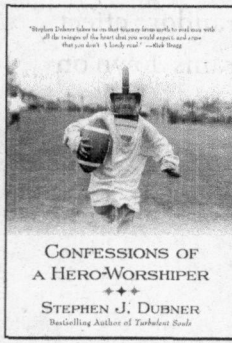

As a boy, Stephen J. Dubner's hero was Franco Harris, the famed and mysterious running back for the Pittsburgh Steelers. When Dubner's father died, he became obsessed— he dreamed of his hero every night; he signed his school papers "Franco Dubner." Though they never met, it was Franco Harris who shepherded Dubner through a fatherless boyhood.

Twenty years later, Dubner, an accomplished writer, sees Harris on a magazine cover. His long-dormant obsession comes roaring back. He journeys to Pittsburgh, certain that Harris will embrace him. And he is . . . well, wrong.

Told with the grit of a journalist and the grace of a memoirist, *Confessions of a Hero-Worshiper* is a breathtaking, heartbreaking, and often hilarious story of astonishing developments. It is also a sparkling meditation on the nature of hero worship—which, like religion and love, tells us as much about ourselves as about the object of our desire.

"Stephen Dubner takes us on that journey from myth to real man with all the twinges of the heart that you would expect, and some that you don't. A lovely read."

—Rick Bragg

"Fascinating." —*USA Today*